KT-502-390

PUBLISHED

Jane Austen: *Emma* DAVID LODGE
Jane Austen: *'Northanger Abbey'* & *'Persuasion'* B.C. SOUTHAM
Jane Austen: *'Sense and Sensibility'*, *'Pride and Prejudice'* & *'Mansfield Park'*
  B.C. SOUTHAM
Beckett: *Waiting for Godot* RUBY COHN
William Blake: *Songs of Innocence and Experience* MARGARET BOTTRALL
Charlotte Brontë: *'Jane Eyre'* & *'Villette'* MIRIAM ALLOTT
Emily Brontë: *Wuthering Heights* MIRIAM ALLOTT
Browning: *'Men and Women'* & *Other Poems* J.R. WATSON
Bunyan: *The Pilgrim's Progress* ROGER SHARROCK
Chaucer: *Canterbury Tales* J.J. ANDERSON
Coleridge: *'The Ancient Mariner'* & *Other Poems* ALUN R. JONES & WILLIAM TYDEMAN
Congreve: *Comedies* PATRICK LYONS
Conrad: *'Heart of Darkness'*, *'Nostromo'* & *'Under Western Eyes'* C.B. COX
Conrad: *The Secret Agent* IAN WATT
Dickens: *Bleak House* A.E. DYSON
Dickens: *'Hard Times'*, *'Great Expectations'* & *'Our Mutual Friend'* NORMAN PAGE
Dickens: *'Dombey and Son'* & *'Little Dorrit'* ALAN SHELSTON
Donne: *Songs and Sonets* JULIAN LOVELOCK
George Eliot: *Middlemarch* PATRICK SWINDEN
George Eliot: *'The Mill on the Floss'* & *'Silas Marner'* R.P. DRAPER
T. S. Eliot: *Four Quartets* BERNARD BERGONZI
T. S. Eliot: *'Prufrock'*, *'Gerontion'*, *'Ash Wednesday'* & *Other Shorter Poems*
  B.C. SOUTHAM
T. S. Eliot: *The Waste Land* C.B. COX & ARNOLD P. HINCHLIFFE
T. S. Eliot: *Plays* ARNOLD P. HINCHLIFFE
Henry Fielding: *Tom Jones* NEIL COMPTON
E. M. Forster: *A Passage to India* MALCOLM BRADBURY
William Golding: *Novels 1954–64* NORMAN PAGE
Hardy: *The Tragic Novels* R.P. DRAPER
Hardy: *Poems* JAMES GIBSON & TREVOR JOHNSON
Hardy: *Three Pastoral Novels* R.P. DRAPER
Gerard Manley Hopkins: *Poems* MARGARET BOTTRALL
Henry James: *'Washington Square'* & *'The Portrait of a Lady'* ALAN SHELSTON
Jonson: *Volpone* JONAS A. BARISH
Jonson: *'Every Man in his Humour'* & *'The Alchemist'* R.V. HOLDSWORTH
James Joyce: *'Dubliners'* & *'A Portrait of the Artist as a Young Man'* MORRIS BEJA
Keats: *Odes* G.S. FRASER
Keats: *Narrative Poems* JOHN SPENCER HILL
D. H. Lawrence: *Sons and Lovers* GAMINI SALGADO
D. H. Lawrence: *'The Rainbow'* & *'Women in Love'* COLIN CLARKE
Lowry: *Under the Volcano* GORDON BOWKER
Marlowe: *Doctor Faustus* JOHN JUMP
Marlowe: *'Tamburlaine the Great'*, *'Edward the Second'* & *'The Jew of Malta'*
  JOHN RUSSELL BROWN
Marvell: *Poems* ARTHUR POLLARD
Milton: *Paradise Lost* A.E. DYSON & JULIAN LOVELOCK
O'Casey: *'Juno and the Paycock'*, *'The Plough and the Stars'* & *'The Shadow of a
  Gunman'* RONALD AYLING
Eugene O'Neill: *Three Plays* NORMAND BERLIN
John Osborne: *Look Back in Anger* JOHN RUSSELL TAYLOR
Pinter: *'The Caretaker'* & *Other Plays* MICHAEL SCOTT

Jane Austen
Emma

A CASEBOOK

EDITED BY

DAVID LODGE

Revised Edition

M
MACMILLAN

First published 1968
11th reprint 1988
Revised edition 1991

Published by
MACMILLAN EDUCATION LTD
Houndmills, Basingstoke, Hampshire RG21 2XS
and London
Companies and representatives
throughout the world

Printed in Hong Kong
Typeset by Footnote Graphics,
Warminster, Wiltshire

British Library Cataloguing in Publication Data
Jane Austen — Emma: a casebook.—Rev. ed.
1. Fiction in English. Austen, Jane, 1775–1817
I. Lodge, David 1935–
823.7
ISBN 0–333–53365–8
ISBN 0–333–53366–6 pbk

CONTENTS

ACKNOWLEDGEMENTS

The editor and publishers wish to thank the following for permission to use copyright material: 'Trollope on *Emma*: an unpublished note', in *Nineteenth-century Fiction*, IV (1949) 145–7 (© The Regents of the University of California, 1949); D. W. Harding, 'Regulated Hatred: an aspect of the work of Jane Austen', in *Scrutiny*, VIII (March 1940) 346–62 (Cambridge University Press); E. N. Hayes, '*Emma*: a dissenting opinion', in *Nineteenth-century Fiction*, IV (1949) 3–7 (© The Regents of the University of California, 1949); Richard Poirier, 'Mark Twain, Jane Austen and the imagination of society', in *Defense of Reading* (E. P. Dutton & Co Inc.) pp. 282–309 (© Reuben A. Brower and Richard Poirier, 1962); Arnold Kettle, 'Jane Austen: *Emma*', from *An Introduction to the English Novel*, I (Hutchinson Publishing Group Ltd) pp. 90–104; Marvin Mudrick, 'Irony as Form: *Emma*', from *Jane Austen: Irony as Defense and Discovery* (University of California Press, 1952) pp. 181–206; Lionel Trilling, '*Emma* and the Legend of Jane Austen', originally published as an introduction to the Riverside Edition of *Emma* (Houghton Mifflin Co., 1957); Wayne Booth, 'Control of Distance in Jane Austen's *Emma*', from *The Rhetoric of Fiction* (University of Chicago Press, 1961) pp. 243–66; 'Jane Austen's *Emma*', in the *Critical Quarterly*, IV (1962) 335–46 (Malcolm Bradbury); 'Narrative and Dialogue in Jane Austen', in the *Critical Quarterly*, XII (1970) 201–29 (Graham Hough); Sandra M. Gilbert and Susan Gubar, 'Jane Austen's Cover Story'; from *The Madwoman in the Attic: the woman writer and the nineteenth-century literary imagination* (Yale University Press, 1979) pp. 154–63; Adena Rosmarin, 'Misreading *Emma*: the powers and perfidies of narrative history', in *English Literary History*, 51 (1984) 315–42 (Johns Hopkins University Press).

Every effort has been made to trace all the copyright holders but if any have been inadvertently overlooked the publishers will be pleased to make the necessary arrangement at the first opportunity.

The editor wishes to thank Farat Ara for her assistance in preparing this revised edition of the Casebook for publication.

GENERAL EDITOR'S PREFACE

The Casebook series, launched in 1968, has become a well-regarded library of critical studies. The central concern of the series remains the 'single-author' volume, but suggestions from the academic community have led to an extension of the original plan, to include occasional volumes on such general themes as literary 'schools' and genres.

Each volume in the central category deals either with one well-known and influential work by an individual author, or with closely related works by one writer. The main section consists of critical readings, mostly modern, collected from books and journals. A selection of reviews and comments by the author's contemporaries is also included, and sometimes comment from the author himself. The Editor's Introduction charts the reputation of the work or works from the first appearance to the present time.

Volumes in the 'general themes' category are variable in structure but follow the basic purpose of the series in presenting an integrated selection of readings, with an Introduction which explores the theme and discusses the literary and critical issues involved.

A single volume can represent no more than a small selection of critical opinions. Some critics are excluded for reasons of space, and it is hoped that readers will pursue the suggestions for further reading in the Select Bibliography. Other contributions are severed from their original context, to which some readers may wish to turn. Indeed, if they take a hint from the critics represented here, they certainly will.

A.E. DYSON

INTRODUCTION

'I am going to take a heroine whom no one but myself will much like,' said Jane Austen, on commencing the composition of *Emma*.[1] Today one is inclined to interpret this remark as the recognition of a problem that was to be successfully overcome, rather than as an accurate prediction. Readers like the author's niece, Fanny Knight, who 'could not bear Emma herself' (see below, p. 33) have been in the minority. Most readers, if they respond to Jane Austen's work at all, have liked Emma Woodhouse and the novel that bears her name. There has been considerable disagreement as to *why* we like her; but that we do, despite all her faults, is one of the most common tributes paid to Jane Austen's skill as a novelist.

Although *Emma* has never been the most widely popular of Jane Austen's novels (that distinction must belong to *Pride and Prejudice*[2]) there has been a growing measure of agreement through the years among her more devoted and discriminating readers that it is her most perfect and fully representative work. It happily combines all the qualities for which she has been most admired: irony, wit, realism, vivid characterisation, moral seriousness and faultless control of tone and narrative method. No other novel presents us so strikingly with the paradox – never inseparable from our reading of Jane Austen – of rich meanings extracted from superficially slight materials. Modern criticism, in particular, has focused attention on *Emma* as the classic example of Jane Austen's art; while its first publication in 1816 marked the peak of the modest fame she attained in her own lifetime.

Jane Austen was born in 1775, at Steventon, Hampshire, where her father was rector, and where she lived until he retired to Bath in

[1] 'She was very fond of Emma but did not reckon on her being a general favourite; for, when commencing that work, she said: "I am going to take..."' James Edward Austen-Leigh, *A Memoir of Jane Austen* (1870).
[2] A check of the British Museum catalogue shows that up to 1953 *Pride and Prejudice* was reprinted approximately twice as many times as *Emma*. Most of the people whose opinions Jane Austen collected (see below, pp. 33–5) seem to have preferred *Pride and Prejudice* or *Mansfield Park* to *Emma*.

1801. After an unsettled period following Mr Austen's death in 1805, she lived with her mother and sister Cassandra at Chawton, also in Hampshire, from 1809 to 1817. In the latter year she became seriously ill and moved, for medical attention, to Winchester, where she died on 18 July. Although she never married, Jane Austen belonged to a large and lively family, and her life was full of human interest and incident. It was not, however, in any sense a public life: her friends and relations took a keen interest in her writings, but she never moved in literary circles, and her novels were published anonymously in her own lifetime.

The six major novels were published in the following order: *Sense and Sensibility* (1811), *Pride and Prejudice* (1813), *Mansfield Park* (1814), *Emma* (1816) and (posthumously) *Persuasion* with *Northanger Abbey* (1818). As regards composition, however, *Northanger Abbey* should be grouped with *Pride and Prejudice* and *Sense and Sensibility*: these three novels were evidently first written in the 1790s, and substantially revised before their eventual publication. The three 'mature' novels were written in order of publication, but probably Jane Austen had not finished working on the manuscript of *Persuasion* when she died. *Emma* is therefore the last novel which she completed to her own satisfaction and personally saw through the press.

Modern scholarship has uncovered a good deal of information about the composition, publication and initial reception of *Emma*.[1] A memorandum in the author's own hand has survived, recording that the novel was begun in January 1814, and completed on 29 March 1815. Jane Austen was therefore no doubt thinking of her own work in progress when she wrote in September 1814 to her niece Anna, an aspirant novelist, that '3 or 4 Families in a Country Village is the very thing to work on'.[2] In May 1814 *Mansfield Park* had been published, and the edition was sold out by November: Jane Austen's reputation was growing. In 1815 she heard indirectly that the Prince Regent (later George IV) was an admirer of her novels, and 'kept a set of them in every one of his residences'.[3] The

[1] See especially Charles Beecher Hogan, 'Jane Austen and her Early Public', in *Review of English Studies*, NS 1 (1950) pp. 44–7, and R. W. Chapman's *Jane Austen: Facts and Problems* (Oxford, 1948) and *Jane Austen: a Critical Bibliography* (Oxford, 1953). The editor is greatly indebted to both these writers.

[2] *Jane Austen's Letters to her sister Cassandra and others*, collected and edited by R. W. Chapman (Oxford, 1932) p. 401.

[3] Chapman, *Facts and Problems*, p. 138.

Prince's librarian, James Stanier Clarke, introduced himself to Jane
Austen when she was in London, and indicated that she might
dedicate her next book to the Prince. Though she had no respect for
his personal character, Jane Austen accepted the compliment to her
literary merit, and *Emma* appeared with a dedication to the Prince.
In the ensuing correspondence Clarke, a well-meaning but somewhat conceited and fatuous man, who might have stepped from the
pages of one of Jane Austen's own novels, provoked one of her most
characteristic letters by suggesting that she try her hand at a
historical romance 'illustrative of the history of the august House of
Cobourg'. Her reply, written (perhaps not fortuitously) on April
Fool's Day, is a masterpiece of politely disguised irony, and also a
serious, perceptive attempt at artistic self-definition (see below,
p. 31).

Emma appeared on 29 December 1815, though the title page is
dated 1816. It was published, in an edition of 2000 copies, by John
Murray, to whom Jane Austen had turned perhaps because her
previous publisher, Egerton, had failed to produce a second edition
of *Mansfield Park*. (Murray published a second edition of this novel
early in 1816.) Henry Austen, who handled his sister's business
affairs, rejected on her behalf Murray's offer of £450 for the
copyrights of *Sense and Sensibility*, *Mansfield Park*, and *Emma*, and
the latter two novels were published on a profit-sharing basis. A note
made by Jane Austen towards the end of her life records a figure of
£39 as 'first profits of *Emma*'.[1]

Whatever its financial advantages, the publication of *Emma* by
Murray indirectly brought its author a considerable gain in reputation. For Murray was the founder of the influential *Quarterly Review*,
and his reader was the editor of that journal, William Gifford.
Gifford was greatly impressed by the new novel – 'Of *Emma* I
have nothing but good to say', he wrote after reading the manuscript[2] – and he suggested that the book deserved a prominent
review in the *Quarterly*. Murray accordingly asked his most distinguished contributor, Sir Walter Scott, if he had 'any fancy to dash
off an article on *Emma*'? Scott's review, a long article of some 5000
words, which also discussed *Pride and Prejudice* and *Sense and
Sensibility*, appeared in March 1816, unsigned, as was the custom.

[1] Chapman, *Facts and Problems*, p. 156.
[2] Hogan, *RES* NS 1 45.

Even without Scott's signature, the extensive and generally
favourable discussion of her work in the *Quarterly* was an important
milestone in Jane Austen's literary career, the first significant
recognition that she was a novelist of unusual distinction. It is not
known whether she was privately told of the identity of her
anonymous reviewer. We know from a letter that she was aware that
Scott was the author of the enormously successful *Waverley* (1814),
although this novel and its successors were published anonymously
and Scott was at this time known to the general public as a poet.[1] In
retrospect, there seems a nice irony in the fact that the first
important tribute to Jane Austen's fiction was made by the arch-
practitioner of the historical romance, a literary form which, she told
James Stanier Clarke, 'I could not sit down seriously to write . . .
under any other motive than to save my life.'

One of the great merits of Scott's review is that he attempts to
place Jane Austen in relation to existing fictional traditions. 'In its
first appearance,' he suggests, 'the novel was the legitimate child of
the romance', and it honoured its parentage by offering the reader
heightened narrative interest and idealised sentiment. But, he
suggests, 'these excitements . . . had lost much of their poignancy by
the repeated and injudicious use of them' and in consequence a
'style of novel has arisen in the last fifteen or twenty years' which
instead exploits 'the art of copying from nature as she really exists in
the common walks of life, and presenting to the reader, instead of the
splendid scenes of an imaginary world, a concrete and striking
representation of that which is daily taking place around him'. Jane
Austen is the prime exemplar of this new kind of novel.

Scott's argument perhaps underestimates the realistic, anti-
romantic quality of much eighteenth-century fiction, especially
Richardson's; and his attempt to see Jane Austen as representing a
current literary trend somewhat obscures the highly individual
character of her work. For Jane Austen's realism does not merely
offer alternative diversions to those of an exhausted romance
tradition: it implicitly discredits the false patterns imposed upon
experience by literary conventions – including those that Scott
himself relied upon. That Scott was half-aware of this challenge is
suggested by the conclusion of his article, where he defends,
somewhat self-indulgently, the code of romantic love. But Scott is

[1] *Letters*, ed. Chapman, p. 404.

both generous and perceptive in his praise of Jane Austen's art, and is fully alive to the difficulties over which it triumphs. His detailed account of *Emma* shows that he had read it with attentive appreciation. Other contemporary reviewers were generally favourable, but only Scott shows any consciousness of dealing with a literary masterpiece.[1]

It was in fact a long time before Jane Austen was generally acknowledged to be a major novelist. In her lifetime, and immediately afterwards, she suffered the penalties of being an anti-romantic writer in an age of romanticism. Coleridge and Southey held her work in high esteem it is true,[2] but no comment is recorded from Byron, Shelley or Keats, and Wordsworth characteristically remarked that 'though he admitted that her novels were an admirable copy of life, he could not be interested in productions of that kind; unless the truth of nature were presented to him clarified, as it were, by the pervading light of the imagination, it had scarce any attractions in his eyes'.[3] It has often been remarked that the Oxford Movement was a child of the Romantic Revival, and it is not surprising to find John Henry Newman in 1837 qualifying his admiration for *Emma* with some regrets for the lack of 'body' and 'romance' in the story (see below, p. 49). Charlotte Brontë, whose own fiction is the antithesis of Jane Austen's, puts the romantic case against her with typical vehemence (see below, p. 50). Anthony Trollope, a novelist who had rather more in common with Jane Austen, responds to the ironic characterisation of Emma, but he sees the novel, rather condescendingly, as essentially a 'period-piece' (see below, p. 51).

Jane Austen always had enthusiastic admirers in the decades following her death – Archbishop Whately, Macaulay and George Lewes, for example, all compared her skill in characterisation to Shakespeare's[4] – but it was not until 1833 that her novels were

---

[1] Scott's respect for Jane Austen was not diminished with the passing of time. In 1826 he noted in his journal: 'That young lady had a talent for describing the involvements, and feelings, and characters of ordinary life which is to me the most wonderful thing I ever met with. The big Bow-wow strain I can do myself like any now going; but the exquisite touch, which renders ordinary commonplace things and characters interesting, from the truth of the description and the sentiment, is denied to me. What a pity such a gifted creature died so early!'

[2] See Chapman, *Bibliography*, p. 25.

[3] Chapman, *Bibliography*, p. 25.

[4] See Chapman, *Bibliography*, pp. 23, 27 and 29. The comparison may surprise the modern reader, but nineteenth-century critics tended to see Shakespeare as above all the master of realistic characterisation.

reprinted; and when her nephew James Edward Austen-Leigh published his *Memoir* in 1871 it was his opinion that 'Seldom has any literary reputation been of such slow growth as that of Jane Austen.' By that date, however, the reputation *was* established, if the wide interest shown in the *Memoir* is any evidence. Among the many long articles it provoked in the periodical press was one of the finest studies of Jane Austen ever written: Richard Simpson's essay in the *North British Review* (see below, p. 53).

Before Simpson's article – and for a long time afterwards – tributes to Jane Austen concentrated monotonously on her skill in conveying an illusion of life. 'Real' and 'natural' were the most common epithets of praise bestowed upon her work, the art of which was seen to consist principally of investing fictitious characters and actions with the kind of interest that we take in people and events within our own actual experience. Such was the response of Jane Austen's own circle, as we see from the 'Opinions' she collected, and it was one she indulged privately by providing sequels to her stories.[1] It is a natural response, and one which we can never entirely suppress – probably we should not try to. But as a way of interpreting and evaluating Jane Austen it has severe limitations. Under its influence, criticism very easily degenerates into gossip, at which level it is incapable of explaining why we should consider Jane Austen an important writer. The most hostile critics of her work – Charlotte Brontë, for example, or E. N. Hayes (see below, p. 74) have acknowledged that she gives a marvellously life-like rendering of the world she knew: their objection has been that she does nothing else, and that the world she knew was too narrow in its scope and too superficial in its values to provide the stuff of great literature.

It is the great virtue of Simpson's essay that he shows how Jane Austen's 'miniatures' of middle-class Regency society mediate a complex and challenging vision of experience, and he does so in terms which remarkably anticipate the conclusions of the most sophisticated modern criticism. That Jane Austen had an essentially critical and ironic vision, defined initially by parodic contrast with literary stereotypes; that her fiction was not thrown off by a kind of effortless knack, but 'worked up by incessant labour into its perfect

[1] According to tradition, she predicted that Mr Woodhouse would live for two years after his daughter's marriage, and that Mrs Frank Churchill would die young. See R. W. Chapman, *Facts and Problems*, pp. 123 and 186.

form'; that her novels, arranged in order of composition, reveal a coherent pattern of development; that she was a subtle and unsentimental moralist, particularly concerned with the processes of self-discovery and the attainment of maturity through personal relations – all these points, made by Simpson, reappear in such modern critics as Dr and Mrs Leavis, Marvin Mudrick and Lionel Trilling.

Criticism in the decades following Simpson's article, however, failed to maintain the standard he had set. The first two full-length studies of Jane Austen, Mrs Charles Malden's *Jane Austen* (1889) and Goldwin Smith's *Life of Jane Austen* (1890) rarely rise above the level of chatty paraphrase. The extract from Walter Herries Pollock's *Jane Austen: an essay in criticism* (1899) given below (see p. 62) concerning an inconsistency in *Emma*, is characteristic of the tendency of 'Janeites'[1] to concern themselves with minutiae. It was evidently the growth of a cosy, undiscriminating cult of Jane Austen at this period that provoked Henry James's outburst against 'the body of publishers, editors, illustrators, producers of the present twaddle of magazines, who have found their "dear", our dear, everybody's dear, Jane so infinitely to their material purpose'.[2] The meagreness of James's recorded comments on Jane Austen – meagre both in quantity and praise – is one of the great puzzles and disappointments of literary history, for of all earlier English novelists she seems closest to him in spirit and in concern for formal artistry – in particular the narrative method of *Emma* has been picked out as anticipating James's experiments with 'point of view'.[3] William Dean Howells, James's compatriot and friend, was more sympathetic, as his sensitive character-sketch of Emma shows (see below, p. 63). American critics are now among the most enthusiastic and perceptive readers of Jane Austen; but as Richard Poirier suggests in his comparison of *Emma* and *Huckleberry Finn* (see below, p. 77), her art concentrates all the qualities that characterise English literary culture and distinguish it from the American. She has always been a peculiarly 'English' classic. Though her novels were translated into French throughout the nineteenth century, no major French novelist

---

[1] This term for devotees of Jane Austen was coined by Rudyard Kipling in a story called 'The Janeites' (1924) and has had a somewhat equivocal currency ever since.

[2] Henry James, 'The Lesson of Balzac', in *The Question of Our Speech* (Boston, 1905) p. 60.

[3] See, for instance, R. W. Chapman, 'Jane Austen's Methods', in *Times Literary Supplement*, 9 Feb 1922, p. 82; and F. R. Leavis, *The Great Tradition* (1948) p. 19 n.

up to and including Proust makes reference to her, and it has been said that 'from the point of view of the European tradition of the novel she might as well never have existed'.[1]

In English criticism of the late nineteenth and early twentieth centuries, *Emma* is more and more frequently cited as the supreme example of Jane Austen's art. Mrs Oliphant, Mrs Malden, Goldwin Smith, A. C. Bradley and George Saintsbury all reach this verdict.[2] For Reginald Farrer, writing in 1917, it was 'the Book of Books'. Farrer's perceptive analysis of *Emma* anticipated much subsequent criticism of the novel in stressing the control of tone and narrative method by which Jane Austen maintains a delicate balance of sympathetic identification and critical detachment in our response to her heroine (see below, p. 65).

The twenties and thirties of this century saw a revolution in English studies, a sudden expansion and intensification of critical activity marked by the development of 'close reading' techniques and the application to literary texts of such disciplines as psychology, sociology and anthropology. But the new criticism concerned itself initially with poetry and poetic drama, and the study of the novel was comparatively late in feeling its effects. As far as Jane Austen is concerned, this period was dominated by the scholarship of R. W. Chapman, who provided definitive editions of the novels (in 1923), the *Letters* (in 1932) and much previously unpublished minor work. By the end of the thirties, most of the extant materials for the study of Jane Austen were generally available, and since then books and articles about her have streamed from the presses in ever-increasing numbers.

In 1939 Mary Lascelles published *Jane Austen and her Art,* which is still in many ways the soundest and most helpful full-length study (though it does not lend itself to representation in extracts). In the 1940s, the highly influential school of critics associated with F. R. Leavis and the journal *Scrutiny* defined Jane Austen as a living classic who answered to the most rigorous demands of modern criticism. Dr Leavis, though he published no extended work on Jane Austen, placed her firmly at the beginning of his 'Great Tradition' of

---

[1] Joseph Cady and Ian Watt, 'Jane Austen's Critics', in *Critical Quarterly*, V (1963) 55. This is the best survey known to the editor.

[2] Margaret Oliphant, *A Literary History of England* (1882) III 206; Goldwin Smith, *Life of Jane Austen* (1890) p. 118; A. C. Bradley, *Essays and Studies*, II (1911) 22; George Saintsbury, *The English Novel* (1913) p. 198.

English novelists (the other members being George Eliot, Henry James, Joseph Conrad and D. H. Lawrence), and characteristically stressed her 'intense moral preoccupation'. 'When we examine the formal perfection of *Emma*,' he said, 'we find that it can be appreciated only in terms of the moral preoccupations that characterise the novelist's peculiar interest in life.'[1] The present writer has suggested that the vexed question of the relationship between formal and moral value might be resolved by inverting Leavis's formulation to read: 'When we examine the moral preoccupations that characterise Jane Austen's peculiar interest in life as manifested in *Emma*, we find that they can be appreciated only in terms of the formal perfection of the novel.' In other words, the kind of interests aroused by *Emma* are fundamentally moral, but their literary value inheres in the formal artistry through which they are communicated.[2]

Two *Scrutiny* articles of particular interest are D. W. Harding's 'Regulated Hatred: an aspect of the work of Jane Austen' and Q. D. Leavis's 'A Critical Theory of Jane Austen's Writings'. Mrs Leavis emphasised Jane Austen's painstaking, dedicated craftsmanship by arguing that the major novels went through several drafts before she was satisfied with them, and suggested that their sources could be detected in the early minor work. According to this theory, *Emma* (where, Mrs Leavis says, 'we see [Jane Austen] at the climax of her art and in completest possible control over her writing') was worked up out of an unfinished story called *The Watsons*, begun probably in 1803, but not published until 1927.[3] Harding's article was a less technical and more radical exercise in reappraisal, and its influence has been profound, though controversial. This was the most forthright attack to date on the 'Janeites'. So far from being a gentle, consoling writer, comfortably confirming the values of her own *milieu*, Jane Austen, Harding argued, was in many ways fiercely hostile to her social environment, and writing was her way of 'finding some mode of existence for her critical attitudes'. Her 'hatred' is 'regulated' so successfully that most readers contrive to overlook it, but to do so is to misunderstand her. *Emma* is interesting precisely for its recognition that 'even a heroine is likely to have

---

[1] Leavis, *The Great Tradition*, p. 17.
[2] David Lodge, 'The Critical Moment, 1964', in *Critical Quarterly*, VI (1964) 268–9.
[3] Q. D. Leavis, 'A Critical Theory of Jane Austen's Writings', in *Scrutiny*, X (1941–2) 75ff. The theory has been seriously challenged by Brian Southam in *Jane Austen's Literary Manuscripts* (Oxford, 1964), pp. 145–8.

assimilated many of the more unpleasant possibilities of the human being in society' (see below, p. 72).

Modern criticism of Jane Austen is concerned less with defending her status as a classic (this is generally taken for granted, and 'dissenting opinions', such as that of E. N. Hayes, are rare) than with defining the precise nature of her achievement and her importance. In this debate *Emma* has occupied a central position, and the essays collected in the second part of this selection have been chosen not only for their intrinsic quality, but as illustrations of the diversity of approach and interpretation this novel continues to provoke. *Emma*, says Edmund Wilson, 'is with Jane Austen what *Hamlet* is with Shakespeare. It is the novel about which her readers are likely to disagree most.'[1] But in all the conflict of opinion we can isolate certain recurrent issues, of which the most important are: the character of Emma and our response to her, the nature of the adjustment she makes to her world, and the relationship of the world of *Emma* to the world of actuality. These are questions of meaning, but they involve at every point questions of form, since it is only by careful attention to the structure and texture of the novel that we can determine what it means.

Most of the contributors agree that Jane Austen gave an important clue to the meaning of *Emma* when she said she was going to take a heroine 'whom no-one but myself will much like', but it was evidently an ambiguous one. To Marvin Mudrick, clearly writing under the influence of D. W. Harding, Emma is indeed in many ways an unlikeable heroine, a latent lesbian, who is essentially incapable of committing herself in normal human relationships, and who finally triumphs only 'because in "her social milieu charm conquers, even as it makes every cruel and thoughtless mistake; because . . . it finds committed to it even the good and the wise, even when it is known and evaluated" '. Emma's 'reformation', and the marriage to Mr Knightley which rewards it are, Mudrick suggests, built on shaky foundations, and the fact that most readers have accepted them at face value is the ultimate irony of a novel steeped in irony: '*Emma* is a novel admired, even consecrated, for qualities which it in fact subverts or ignores.'[2]

---

[1] Edmund Wilson, 'A Long Talk About Jane Austen', in *New Yorker*, 13 Oct. 1945.
[2] Marvin Mudrick, *Jane Austen: Irony as Defense and Discovery* (Princeton, 1952) p. vii.

Mudrick's essay is perhaps more provocative than convincing. Several critics, including Edgar J. Shannon (see Bibliography) and Malcolm Bradbury, have argued effectively that Emma's reformation is genuine and is felt to be so by the reader. By the end of the novel, Bradbury asserts, 'We have been persuaded ... of the importance of true regard for the self and for others, persuaded to see the full human being as fine, morally serious, totally responsible, entirely involved, and to consider every human action as a crucial, committing act of self-definition.'

If, however, we interpret *Emma* as essentially the story of a flawed and self-deceived heroine who finally comes to a state of true self-awareness, it is clear that, in Bradbury's words, 'the artistic problem of the book is .. to make us care for Emma in such a way that we care about her fate, and like her, but that we in no way subdue our moral feelings about her faults'. This is essentially a problem of narrative method, of the 'point of view' from which the story is told; and no one has done fuller justice to this aspect of the novel than Wayne Booth. He shows how Jane Austen ensures our sympathetic identification with the heroine by making her the primary centre of consciousness, through which most of the experience of the novel is mediated, but controls and checks such identification by discreet authorial interventions, ironic deflations of Emma, and well-timed comments from the most morally reliable character in the book, Mr Knightley.

In one respect Booth's analysis was pertinently challenged by W. J. Harvey (see Bibliography). Booth suggested that the ironic distancing of Emma was sacrificed to some extent to the author's desire for mystification, particularly concerning the relationship between Frank Churchill and Jane Fairfax, so that it is only on the second reading of the novel that we fully appreciate the scale of Emma's self-deception. Harvey argues, justly I think, that the 'mystification' is not just an end in itself, but a response 'appropriate to the world of surmise, speculation, misunderstandings and cross-purposes that the novel depicts', without which the ironies would be 'ponderous and schematic'. Even on second reading, 'our attention is so diversified by the thick web of linguistic nuance that we do not concentrate single-mindedly on the ironic results of the mystification'. One might add that we never seem to exhaust the subtle ironies of *Emma*, and this perhaps explains why we can never assume a position of detached superiority towards the heroine.

Becoming aware, at each re-reading, of what we 'missed' in previous readings, we are compelled to acknowledge, like Emma herself, the fallibility of our understanding.

An American critic, R. E. Hughes, has made the interesting suggestion that views of Jane Austen's novels may be divided into the 'microscopic' (which sees them as self-sufficient renderings of a particular, limited milieu) and the 'microcosmic' (which sees them as symbolic structures having analogical relationship to the world at large, and thus conveying a timeless and universal meaning) (see Bibliography). In practice, it would be difficult to maintain either position in an absolute sense, for the kind of fiction Jane Austen writes makes its effects through the illusion of realistic particularity, but just because it is fiction, and not history, our efforts to interpret it inevitably suggest its analogical relation to a larger, more general-ised 'reality'. However, as a distinction of emphasis, it is a useful one. Arnold Kettle, for instance, has difficulty in arguing away his doubts about the major significance of *Emma* because he is a 'microscopic' reader. 'We do not get from *Emma* a condensed and refined sense of a larger entity', he says. 'Neither is it a symbolic work suggesting references far beyond its surface meaning.' *Emma* is about living in Highbury, not about Life, and it is 'as convincing as our own lives'. But, as a critic with strong social – indeed, socialist – interests, Kettle is troubled by the exclusion of so much contempor-ary social reality from the novel. Many readers of Jane Austen have had the same misgivings, but few faced them as honestly as Kettle, or tested them against as sensitive a reading.

Perhaps the boldest solution to the constantly debated question of the relationship between the world of *Emma* and the world of actuality is that of Lionel Trilling, who identifies the novel generically as a combination of comedy and idyll. It is an error to suppose that 'Jane Austen's world really did exist', but a pardonable one, because it is a tribute to the moving and elevating power of her myth, the 'extraordinary promise' and 'rare hope' it holds out to us of 'con-trolling the personal life, of becoming acquainted with ourselves, of creating a community of "intelligent love" '.

Graham Hough's view of Jane Austen is compatible with Trill-ing's, but stated more objectively and astringently. His magisterial essay, 'Narrative and Dialogue in Jane Austen', falls into two parts. The first part is concerned with the formal characteristics of Jane Austen's novels, as exemplified by *Emma*, and usefully complements

Wayne Booth's essay. Taking Plato's distinction between the narrative, dramatic and mixed styles of story-telling as his starting point, Hough points out that in Jane Austen's 'mixture', dialogue predominates, and that the narrative or descriptive passages are frequently 'coloured' by a particular character's point of view, and sometimes completely taken over by that character's linguistic register through the device of 'free indirect speech' (sometimes called 'free indirect style'). Jane Austen was in fact the first English novelist to use this device on any considerable scale, and in *Emma* it is an essential tool for representing the heroine's progress from illusion to reality.

Hough's article, first published in 1970, reflects the growing influence of systematic linguistics and stylistics on interpretative and evaluative criticism. Discriminating between five different types of discourse in *Emma* – the authorial voice, objective narrative, 'coloured' narrative, free indirect style, and direct speech or dialogue, he argues that the second of these is given total authority in the novel, and that characters are evaluated according to how closely their speech approximates to it.

Jane Austen's novels, Hough states flatly in the second half of his article, are 'not ambiguous . . . the action, the characters, the values and the language all work in complete unison'; and what they work to express is the ideology of the English landed gentry as perceived and interpreted by a loyal female member of that class. Jane Austen's novels, Hough asserts, turn away from radical and revolutionary trends in early nineteenth-century culture and society, not because she was ignorant of them, but because she disapproved of them. Her novels incarnate a peculiarly English ideology of social control, compromise and consensus, which has preserved Great Britain from the violent political upheavals of Continental Europe in the last two hundred years, but at the cost of a certain provinciality. That is why Jane Austen is a classic of English literature, but not of world literature.

This is a formidable 'conservative' reading of Jane Austen in general, and of *Emma* in particular. Although a great many books and articles on Jane Austen have been published since, I am not sure that it has been improved upon; but a number of scholars have substantiated its thesis by a more detailed examination of the language of *Emma* and its literary-historical context. Probably the best of these studies is Marilyn Butler's chapter in her *Jane Austen*

and the War of Ideas (see Bibliography), which presents *Emma* as an
'anti-Jacobin novel'. (The 'Jacobins' were the left-wing faction in
the French Revolutionary Assembly, and the name was applied
loosely to all radical thought of a reformist tendency in the early
nineteenth century.) Marilyn Butler regards *Emma* as the greatest
English novel of its time because it translated ideological debate into
the language of interior consciousness, and thus made the reader
experience for herself the dangers of fantasy and subjectivity. In the
last two decades, many new critical approaches have arisen to
challenge the synthesis of traditional historical scholarship and
formalist criticism well exemplified by Hough and Butler: feminist,
deconstructionist, psycho-analytical, and reader-response criticism,
to name but four. All of these approaches have been tried on Jane
Austen, but it is fair to say that they have found her a hard nut to
crack.

Feminist critics are naturally drawn to writers like Charlotte
Brontë or George Eliot, who expressed the longing of their heroines
to escape the restrictions that society placed upon their quest for
personal fulfilment. The plots of Jane Austen's novels, in contrast,
appear to lead their heroines through a phase of skittish rebellion or
egotistical error to meek acquiescence in the values of patriarchal
society by marriage to a paternalistic lover-cum-tutor. Sarah Gilbert
and Susan Gubar face this difficulty squarely in their chapter on
Jane Austen in *The Madwoman in the Attic*, seeing the compromises
of her heroines as an inevitable 'cover-story' for a gifted woman in
her time and place:

Austen's self-division – her fascination with the imagination and her anxiety
that it is unfeminine – is part of her consciousness of the unique dilemma of
all women, who must acquiesce in their status as objects after an adolescence in which they experience themselves as free agents.

Taking their cue from Virginia Woolf's observation that Jane
Austen stimulates the reader 'to supply what is not there', Gilbert
and Gubar invite us to see the submission of the heroines as a kind of
covert victory: 'the heroines *seem* to submit as they get what they
both want and need'.

In comparison, the chapters on *Emma* in LeRoy Smith's *Jane
Austen and the Drama of Woman* (see Bibliography) and Claudia E.
Johnson's *Jane Austen: Women, Politics and the Novel* (see Bibliogra-
phy) seem like special pleading. Smith argues that 'in resisting the

pressure to conform to a feminine stereotype, Emma embraces the masculine stereotype' and 'moves to a center that balances feminine and masculine qualities in a unified whole'. Johnson is more radical, arguing that Emma 'possesses and enjoys power, without bothering to demur about it'. Both these essays entail some tendentious criticism of Knightley's character in order to defend the heroine. Wayne Booth is more subtle and persuasive in his address to the Jane Austen Society of North America, 'Emma, *Emma* and the Question of Feminism' (see Bibliography). He believes it is impossible to deny that Emma submits to the values of patriarchal society, but argues that Jane Austen's witty subversion of fictional stereotypes (by, for instance, refusing to make Mr Knightley's declaration of love the grand emotional climax of Emma's story) signals obliquely to the reader her awareness of the limitations of the plot to which she was bound by social and literary convention.

Like Gilbert and Gubar, Booth puts considerable emphasis on an observation by the narrator towards the end of *Emma*: 'Seldom, very seldom, does complete truth belong to any human disclosure; seldom can it happen that something is not a little disguised or a little mistaken.' For critics influenced by deconstruction, or other varieties of post-structuralist theory, this is probably the most important single sentence in the whole novel. The question is whether what Hough calls the objective narrator in *Emma* is immune from error and evasion. Hough would say: yes. The deconstructionists would say that error, ambiguity, slippage between signifier and signified, is built into the very nature of langage; that all texts necessarily subvert their own claim to a determinate meaning, and teach their readers that lesson.

Perhaps the most persuasive attempt to read *Emma* in this way is Adena Rosmarin's article, 'Misreading *Emma*: the powers and perfidies of interpretative history'. She begins by noting 'Austen's remarkable immunity to the vicissitudes of critical fashion and the remarkable blandness of contemporary Austen studies', which she connects with Jane Austen's realism and the impotence of a criticism in thrall to it. 'Mimesis [realistic imitation] must again and again give us essentially the "same" Austen, the "same" *Emma*.' The way out of this cul-de-sac, she argues, is a recognition of the subversive function of Jane Austen's irony, and of the extent to which the reader is implicated, willy-nilly, in the mistakes, misinterpretations and misjudgments of the characters in the text, leading us 'a hermeneutic dance of bewildering complexity'. Rosmarin makes good use of Stanley Fish's 'affective stylistics', a way of reading texts that demonstrates how they seduce us into making false interpretations which we are later required to revise. We rush to accept Emma's reading of Frank Churchill's letter of apology, for instance (is she not by now a reformed character? must she not now be a reliable judge?) only to find it 'deconstructed' by Knightley's more searching reading.

Another study that deftly brings modern critical theory to bear upon *Emma* is Joseph Litvak's 'Reading Characters: Self, Society, and the Text in *Emma*' (see Bibliography), but the argument puts heavy emphasis on scenes and motifs (games, puzzles, charades, etc.) that are marginal rather than central in most readers' experience of the novel. Indeed, the history of critical commentary on *Emma* in the two decades since the first edition of this Casebook was published seems to illustrate in a particularly sharp form the dilemma of interpretative criticism in general: how to find an alternative to the reiteration of what is already known or the discovery of 'new' interpretations that owe more to the ingenuity and favoured methodology of the critic than they do to the text. But, as Lionel Trilling observed long ago, 'it is possible to say of Jane Austen, as perhaps we can say of no other writer, that the opinions that are held of her work are almost as interesting, and almost as important to think about, as the work itself.'

PART ONE

Earlier Comments, 1815–16

SOME CORRESPONDENCE CONCERNING *EMMA*

To James Stanier Clarke,* from Jane Austen, 11 Dec 1815

Dear Sir

My *Emma* is now so near publication that I feel it right to assure you of my not having forgotten your kind recommendation of an early copy for Carlton House, and that I have Mr. Murray's promise of its being sent to His Royal Highness, under cover to you, three days previous to the work being really out. I must make use of this opportunity to thank you, dear Sir, for the very high praise you bestow on my other novels. I am too vain to wish to convince you that you have praised them beyond their merits. My greatest anxiety at present is that this fourth work should not disgrace what was good in the others. But on this point I will do myself the justice to declare that, whatever may be my wishes for its success, I am strongly haunted with the idea that to those readers who have preferred *Pride and Prejudice* it will appear inferior in wit, and to those who have preferred *Mansfield Park* inferior in good sense. Such as it is, however, I hope you will do me the favour of accepting a copy. Mr. Murray will have directions for sending one. I am quite honoured by your thinking me capable of drawing such a clergyman as you gave the sketch of in your note of Nov. 16th. But I assure you I am *not*. The comic part of the character I might be equal to, but not the good, the enthusiastic, the literary. Such a man's conversation must at times be on subjects of science and philosophy, of which I know nothing; or at least be occasionally abundant in quotations and allusions which a woman who, like me, knows only her own mother tongue, and has read little in that, would be totally without the power of giving. A classical education, or at any rate a very extensive acquaintance with English literature, ancient and modern, appears to me quite indispensable for the person who would do any justice to your clergyman; and I think I may boast myself to be, with all

---

*James Stanier Clarke was Librarian to the Prince Regent, to whom *Emma* was dedicated. See Introduction, p. 13.

possible vanity, the most unlearned and uninformed female who ever dared to be an authoress.

Believe me, dear Sir,

Your obliged and faithful hum^{bl} Ser^t.

Jane Austen

To Jane Austen, from the Countess of Morley, 27 Dec 1815

Madam

I have been most anxiously waiting for an introduction to Emma, & am infinitely obliged to you for your kind recollection of me, which will procure me the pleasure of her acquaintance some days sooner than I sh^d otherwise have had it. – I am already become intimate in the Woodhouse family, & feel that they will not amuse & interest me less than the Bennetts, Bertrams, Norriss & all their admirable predecessors. – I *can* give them no higher praise –

I am

Madam

Y^r much obliged

F. Morley

To the Countess of Morley, from Jane Austen, 31 Dec 1815

Madam

Accept my thanks for the honour of your note, & for your kind disposition in favour of Emma. In my present state of doubt as to her reception in the World, it is particularly gratifying to me to receive so early an assurance of your Ladyship's approbation. – It encourages me to depend on the same share of general good opinion which Emma's predecessors have experienced, & to believe that I have not yet – as almost every Writer of Fancy does sooner or later – overwritten myself. – I am Madam,

Your obliged & faith^l Servt

J. Austen

To Jane Austen, from James Stanier Clarke, 27 March 1816

Dear Miss Austen,

I have to return you the thanks of His Royal Highness, the Prince Regent, for the handsome copy you sent him of your last excellent novel. Pray, dear Madam, soon write again and again. Lord St. Helens and many of the nobility, who have been staying here, paid you the just tribute of their praise.

The Prince Regent has just left us for London; and having been pleased to appoint me Chaplain and Private English Secretary to the Prince of Cobourg, I remain here with His Serene Highness and a select party until the marriage. Perhaps when you again appear in print you may chuse to dedicate your volumes to Prince Leopold: any historical romance, illustrative of the history of the august House of Cobourg, would just now be very interesting.

Believe me at all times,
Dear Miss Austen,
Your obliged friend,
J. S. Clarke.

To James Stanier Clarke, from Jane Austen, 1 April 1816

My dear Sir

I am honoured by the Prince's thanks and very much obliged to yourself for the kind manner in which you mention the work. I have also to acknowledge a former letter forwarded to me from Hans Place. I assure you I felt very grateful for the friendly tenor of it, and hope my silence will have been considered, as it was truly meant, to proceed only from an unwillingness to tax your time with idle thanks. Under every interesting circumstance which your own talents and literary labours have placed you in, or the favour of the Regent bestowed, you have my best wishes. Your recent appointments I hope are a step to something still better. In my opinion, the service of a court can hardly be too well paid, for immense must be the sacrifice of time and feeling required by it.

You are very kind in your hints as to the sort of composition which might recommend me at present, and I am fully sensible that an historical romance, founded on the House of Saxe Cobourg, might be much more to the purpose of profit or popularity than such pictures of domestic life in country villages as I deal in. But I could no more write a romance than an epic poem. I could not sit seriously down to write a serious romance under any other motive than to save my life; and if it were indispensable for me to keep it up and never relax into laughing at myself or at other people, I am sure I should be hung before I had finished the first chapter. No, I must keep to my own style and go on in my own way; and though I may never succeed again in that, I am convinced that I should totally fail in any other.

I remain, my dear Sir,
Your very much obliged, and sincere friend,
J. Austen

To John Murray, from Jane Austen, 1 April 1816

Dear Sir

I return you the *Quarterly Review* with many thanks. The Authoress of *Emma* has no reason, I think, to complain of her treatment in it, except in the total omission of *Mansfield Park*. I cannot but be sorry that so clever a man as the Reviewer of *Emma* should consider it as unworthy of being noticed. You will be pleased to hear that I have received the Prince's thanks for the *handsome* copy I sent him of *Emma*. Whatever he may think of *my* share of the work, yours seems to have been quite right. . .

SOURCE: Extracts from *Jane Austen's Letters to her sister Cassandra and others*, ed. R. W. Chapman (1932).

OPINIONS OF *EMMA*, COLLECTED BY JANE AUSTEN

Captn Austen. – liked it extremely, observing that though there might be more Wit in P & P – & an higher Morality in M P – yet altogether, on account of it's peculiar air of Nature throughout, he preferred it to either.

Mrs. F. A. – liked & admired it very much indeed, but must still prefer P. & P.

Mrs J. Bridges – preferred it to all the others.

Miss Sharp – better than M P. – but not so well as P. & P. – pleased with the Heroine for her Originality, delighted with Mr K – & called Mrs Elton beyond praise. – dissatisfied with Jane Fairfax.

Cassandra – better than P. & P. – but not so well as M. P. –

Fanny K. – not so well as either P. & P. or M P. – could not bear *Emma* herself. – Mr Knightley delightful. – Should like J.F. – if she knew more of her.–

Mr & Mrs. J. A. – did not like it so well as either of the 3 others. Language different from the others; not so easily read.–

Edward – preferred it to M P. – *only*. – Mr K. liked by every body.

Miss Bigg – not equal to either P & P. – or M P. – objected to the sameness of the subject (Match-making) all through.– Too much of Mr Elton & H. Smith. Language superior to the others.–

My Mother – thought it more entertaining than M P. – but not so interesting as P. & P. – No characters in it equal to Ly Catherine & Mr Collins.–

Miss Lloyd – thought it as *clever* as either of the others, but did not receive so much pleasure from it as from P. & P. – & M P.–

Mrs & Miss Craven – liked it very much, but not so much as the others.–

Fanny Cage – liked it very much indeed & classed it between P & P. – & M P.–

Mr Shean – did not think it equal to either M P – (which he liked the best of all) or P. & P. – Displeased with my pictures of Clergymen.–

Miss Bigg – on reading it a second time, liked Miss Bates much
    better than at first, & expressed herself as liking all the people
    of Highbury in general, except Harriet Smith – but cd not help
    still thinking *her* too silly in her Loves.

The family at Upton Gray – all very much amused with it. – Miss
    Bates a great favourite with Mrs Beaufoy.

Mr & Mrs Leigh Perrot – saw many beauties in it, but cd not think
    it equal to P. & P. – Darcy & Elizth had spoilt them for
    anything else. – Mr K. however, an excellent Character; Emma
    better luck than a Matchmaker often has. – Pitied Jane Fairfax
    – thought Frank Churchill better treated than he deserved.–

Countess Craven – admired it very much, but did not think it equal
    to P & P. – which she ranked as the very first of its sort.–

Mrs Guiton – thought it too natural to be interesting.

Mrs Digweed – did not like it so well as the others, in fact if she had
    not known the Author, could hardly have got through it.

Miss Terry – admired it very much, particularly Mrs Elton.

Henry Sanford – very much pleased with it – delighted with Miss
    Bates, but thought Mrs Elton the best-drawn Character in the
    Book. – Mansfield Park however, still his favourite.

Mr Haden – *quite* delighted with it. Admired the Character of Emma.–

Miss Isabella Herries – did not like it – objected to my exposing the
    sex in the character of the Heroine – convinced that I had
    meant Mrs & Miss Bates for some acquaintance of theirs –
    People whom I never heard of before.–

Miss Harriet Moore – admired it very much, but M. P. still her
    favourite of all.–

Countess Morley – delighted with it.–

Mr Cockerell – liked it so little, that Fanny wd not send me his
    opinion.–

Mrs Dickson – did not much like it – thought it *very* inferior to P. & P. –
    Liked it the less, from there being a Mr. & Mrs Dixon in it.–

Mrs Brandreth – thought the 3d vol: superior to anything I had ever
    written – quite beautiful!–

Mr B. Lefroy – thought that if there had been more Incident, it
    would be equal to any of the others. – The Characters quite as
    well drawn & supported as in any, & from being more everyday
    ones, the more entertaining. – Did not like the Heroine so well as
    any of the others. Miss Bates excellent, but rather too much of her.
    Mr & Mrs Elton admirable & John Knightley a sensible Man.–

Mrs B. Lefroy – rank'd *Emma* as a composition with S & S. – not so *Brilliant* as P. & P – nor so *equal* as M P. – Preferred Emma herself to all the heroines. – The Characters like all the others admirably well drawn & supported – perhaps rather less strongly marked than some, but only the more natural for that reason. – Mr Knightley Mrs Elton & Miss Bates her favourites. – Thought one or two of the conversations too long.–

Mrs Lefroy – preferred it to M P – but liked M P. the least of all.

Mr Fowle – read only the first & last Chapters, because he had heard it was not interesting.–

Mrs Lutley Sclater – liked it very much, better than M P – & thought I had 'brought it all about very cleverly in the last volume'.–

Mrs C. Cage wrote thus to Fanny – 'A great many thanks for the loan of *Emma*, which I am delighted with. I like it better than any. Every character is thoroughly kept up. I must enjoy reading it again with Charles. Miss Bates is incomparable, but I was nearly killed with those precious treasures! They are Unique, & really with more fun than I can express. I am at Highbury all day, & I can't help feeling I have just got into a new set of acquaintance. No one writes such good sense. & so very comfortable.'

Mrs Wroughton – did not like it so well as P. & P. – Thought the Authoress wrong, in such times as these, to draw such Clergymen as Mr Collins & Mr Elton.

Sir J. Langham – thought it much inferior to the others.–

Mr Jeffery (of the *Edinburgh Review*) was kept up by it three nights.*

Miss Murden – certainly inferior to all the others.

Capt. C. Austen wrote – 'Emma arrived in time to a moment. I am delighted with her, more so I think than even with my favourite Pride & Prejudice, & have read it three times in the Passage.'

Mrs D. Dundas – thought it very clever, but did not like it so well as either of the others.

SOURCE: Extracts from *Plan of a Novel by Jane Austen* (1926) pp. 20–3.

*This was perhaps the most significant of all the 'Opinions'. Judge Francis Jeffrey (1773–1850), editor of the *Edinburgh Review* at this time, could be a harsh critic.

CONTEMPORARY REVIEWS

Sir Walter Scott   (1816)

There are some vices in civilized society so common that they are
hardly acknowledged as stains upon the moral character, the
propensity to which is nevertheless carefully concealed, even by
those who most frequently give way to them; since no man of
pleasure would willingly assume the gross epithet of a debauchee or
a drunkard. One would almost think that novel-reading fell under
this class of frailties, since among the crowds who read little else, it is
not common to find an individual of hardihood sufficient to avow his
taste for these frivolous studies. A novel, therefore, is frequently
'bread eaten in secret;' and it is not upon Lydia Languish's toilet
alone that *Tom Jones* and *Peregrine Pickle* are to be found ambushed
behind works of a more grave and instructive character. And hence
it has happened, that in no branch of composition, not even in
poetry itself, have so many writers, and of such varied talents,
exerted their powers. It may perhaps be added, that although the
composition of these works admits of being exalted and decorated by
the higher exertions of genius; yet such is the universal charm of
narrative, that the worst novel ever written will find some gentle
reader content to yawn over it, rather than to open the page of the
historian, moralist, or poet. We have heard, indeed, of one work of
fiction so unutterably stupid, that the proprietor, diverted by the
rarity of the incident, offered the book, which consisted of two
volumes in duodecimo, handsomely bound, to any person who
would declare, upon his honour, that he had read the whole from
beginning to end. But although this offer was made to the passengers
on board an Indiaman, during a tedious outward-bound voyage, the
Memoirs of Clegg the Clergyman, (such was the title of this unhappy
composition,) completely baffled the most dull and determined
student on board, and bid fair for an exception to the general rule
above-mentioned, – when the love of glory prevailed with the
boatswain, a man of strong and solid parts, to hazard the attempt,
and he actually conquered and carried off the prize!

The judicious reader will see at once that we have been pleading our own cause while stating the universal practice, and preparing him for a display of more general acquaintance with this fascinating department of literature, than at first sight may seem consistent with the graver studies to which we are compelled by duty: but in truth, when we consider how many hours of languor and anxiety, of deserted age and solitary celibacy, of pain even and poverty, are beguiled by the perusal of these light volumes, we cannot austerely condemn the source from which is drawn the alleviation of such a portion of human misery, or consider the regulation of this department as beneath the sober consideration of the critic.

If such apologies may be admitted in judging the labours of ordinary novelists, it becomes doubly the duty of the critic to treat with kindness as well as candour works which, like this before us, proclaim a knowledge of the human heart, with the power and resolution to bring that knowledge to the service of honour and virtue. The author is already known to the public by the two novels announced in her title-page, and both, the last especially, attracted, with justice, an attention from the public far superior to what is granted to the ephemeral productions which supply the regular demand of watering-places and circulating libraries. They belong to a class of fictions which has arisen almost in our own times, and which draws the characters and incidents introduced more immediately from the current of ordinary life than was permitted by the former rules of the novel.

In its first appearance, the novel was the legitimate child of the romance; and though the manners and general turn of the composition were altered so as to suit modern times, the author remained fettered by many peculiarities derived from the original style of romantic fiction. These may be chiefly traced in the conduct of the narrative, and the tone of sentiment attributed to the fictitious personages. . . .

Here, therefore, we have two essential and important circumstances, in which the earlier novels differed from those now in fashion, and we were more nearly assimilated to the old romances. And there can be no doubt that, by the studied involution and extrication of the story, by the combination of incidents new, striking and wonderful beyond the course of ordinary life, the former authors opened that obvious and strong sense of interest which arises from curiosity; as by the pure, elevated, and romantic cast of

the sentiment, they conciliated those better propensities of our
nature which loves to contemplate the picture of virtue, even when
confessedly unable to imitate its excellences.

But strong and powerful as these sources of emotion and interest
may be, they are, like all others, capable of being exhausted by
habit. . . . And thus in the novel, as in every style of composition
which appeals to the public taste, the more rich and easily worked
mines being exhausted, the adventurous author must, if he is
desirous of success, have recourse to those which were disdained by
his predecessors as unproductive, or avoided as only capable of
being turned to profit by great skill and labour.

Accordingly a style of novel has arisen, within the last fifteen or
twenty years, differing from the former in the points upon which the
interest hinges; neither alarming our credulity nor amusing our
imagination by wild variety of incident, or by those pictures of
romantic affection and sensibility, which were formerly as certain
attributes of fictitious characters as they are of rare occurrence
among those who actually live and die. The substitute for these
excitements, which had lost much of their poignancy by the repeated
and injudicious use of them, was the art of copying from nature as
she really exists in the common walks of life, and presenting to the
reader, instead of the splendid scenes of an imaginary world, a
correct and striking representation of that which is daily taking
place around him.

In adventuring upon this task, the author makes obvious sacrifices, and encounters peculiar difficulty. He who paints from *le beau
idéal*, if his scenes and sentiments are striking and interesting, is in a
great measure exempted from the difficult task of reconciling them
with the ordinary probabilities of life: but he who paints a scene of
common occurrence, places his composition within that extensive
range of criticism which general experience offers to every reader.
The resemblance of a statue of Hercules we must take on the artist's
judgment; but every one can criticize that which is presented as the
portrait of a friend, or neighbour. Something more than a mere
sign-post likeness is also demanded. The portrait must have spirit
and character, as well as resemblance; and being deprived of all
that, according to Bayes, goes 'to elevate and surprise,' it must make
amends by displaying depth of knowledge and dexterity of execution. We, therefore, bestow no mean compliment upon the author of
Emma, when we say that, keeping close to common incidents, and to

such characters as occupy the ordinary walks of life, she has
produced sketches of such spirit and originality, that we never miss
the excitation which depends upon a narrative of uncommon events,
arising from the consideration of minds, manners, and sentiments,
greatly above our own. In this class she stands almost alone; for the
scenes of Miss Edgeworth are laid in higher life, varied by more
romantic incident, and by her remarkable power of embodying and
illustrating national character. But the author of *Emma* confines
herself chiefly to the middling classes of society; her most distinguished characters do not rise greatly above well-bred country
gentlemen and ladies; and those which are sketched with most
originality and precision, belong to a class rather below that
standard. The narrative of all her novels is composed of such
common occurrences as may have fallen under the observation of
most folks; and her dramatis personæ conduct themselves upon the
motives and principles which the readers may recognize as ruling
their own and that of most of their acquaintances. The kind of
moral, also, which these novels inculcate, applies equally to the
paths of common life. . . .

Emma has even less story than either of the preceding novels. Miss
Emma Woodhouse, from whom the book takes its name, is the
daughter of a gentleman of wealth and consequence residing at his
seat in the immediate vicinage of a country village called Highbury.
The father, a good-natured, silly valetudinary, abandons the management of his household to Emma, he himself being only occupied
by his summer and winter walk, his apothecary, his gruel, and his
whist table. The latter is supplied from the neighbouring village of
Highbury with precisely the sort of persons who occupy the vacant
corners of a regular whist table, when a village is in the neighbour-
hood, and better cannot be found within the family. We have the
smiling and courteous vicar, who nourishes the ambitious hope of
obtaining Miss Woodhouse's hand. We have Mrs. Bates, the wife of
a former rector, past every thing but tea and whist; her daughter,
Miss Bates, a good-natured, vulgar, and foolish old maid; Mr.
Weston, a gentleman of a frank disposition and moderate fortune, in
the vicinity, and his wife an amiable and accomplished person, who
had been Emma's governess, and is devotedly attached to her.
Amongst all these personages, Miss Woodhouse walks forth, the
princess paramount, superior to all her companions in wit, beauty,
fortune, and accomplishments, doated upon by her father and the

Westons, admired, and almost worshipped by the more humble
companions of the whist table. The object of most young ladies is, or
at least is usually supposed to be, a desirable connection in
marriage. But Emma Woodhouse, either anticipating the taste of a
later period of life, or, like a good sovereign, preferring the weal of
her subjects of Highbury to her own private interest, sets generously
about making matches for her friends without thinking of matrimony on her own account. We are informed that she had been
eminently successful in the case of Mr. and Mrs. Weston; and when
the novel commences she is exerting her influence in favour of Miss
Harriet Smith, a boarding-school girl without family or fortune, very
good humoured, very pretty, very silly, and, what suited Miss
Woodhouse's purpose best of all, very much disposed to be married.

In these conjugal machinations Emma is frequently interrupted,
not only by the cautions of her father, who had a particular objection
to any body committing the rash act of matrimony, but also by the
sturdy reproof and remonstrances of Mr. Knightley, the elder
brother of her sister's husband, a sensible country gentleman of
thirty-five, who had known Emma from her cradle, and was the only
person who ventured to find fault with her. In spite, however, of this
censure and warning, Emma lays a plan of marrying Harriet Smith
to the vicar; and though she succeeds perfectly in diverting her
simple friend's thoughts from an honest farmer who had made her a
very suitable offer, and in flattering her into a passion for Mr. Elton,
yet, on the other hand, that conceited divine totally mistakes the
nature of the encouragement held out to him, and attributes the
favour which he found in Miss Woodhouse's eyes to a lurking
affection on her own part. This at length encourages him to a
presumptuous declaration of his sentiments; upon receiving a re-
pulse, he looks abroad elsewhere, and enriches the Highbury society
by uniting himself to a dashing young woman with as many
thousands as are usually called ten, and a corresponding quantity of
presumption and ill breeding.

While Emma is thus vainly engaged in forging wedlock-fetters for
others, her friends have views of the same kind upon her, in favour of
a son of Mr. Weston by a former marriage, who bears the name,
lives under the patronage, and is to inherit the fortune of a rich
uncle. Unfortunately Mr. Frank Churchill had already settled his
affections on Miss Jane Fairfax, a young lady of reduced fortune; but
as this was a concealed affair, Emma, when Mr. Churchill first

appears on the stage, has some thoughts of being in love with him herself; speedily, however, recovering from that dangerous propensity, she is disposed to confer him upon her deserted friend Harriet Smith. Harriet has, in the interim, fallen desperately in love with Mr. Knightley, the sturdy, advice-giving bachelor; and, as all the village supposes Frank Churchill and Emma to be attached to each other, there are cross purposes enough (were the novel of a more romantic cast) for cutting half the men's throats and breaking all the women's hearts. But at Highbury Cupid walks decorously, and with good discretion, bearing his torch under a lanthorn, instead of flourishing it around to set the house on fire. All these entanglements bring on only a train of mistakes and embarrassing situations, and dialogues at balls and parties of pleasure, in which the author displays her peculiar powers of humour and knowledge of human life. The plot is extricated with great simplicity. The aunt of Frank Churchill dies; his uncle, no longer under her baneful influence, consents to his marriage with Jane Fairfax. Mr. Knightley and Emma are led, by this unexpected incident, to discover that they had been in love with each other all along. Mr. Woodhouse's objections to the marriage of his daughter are overpowered by the fears of house-breakers, and the comfort which he hopes to derive from having a stout son-in-law resident in the family; and the facile affections of Harriet Smith are transferred, like a bank bill by indorsation, to her former suitor, the honest farmer, who had obtained a favourable opportunity of renewing his addresses. Such is the simple plan of a story which we peruse with pleasure, if not with deep interest, and which perhaps we might more willingly resume than one of those narratives where the attention is strongly riveted, during the first perusal, by the powerful excitement of curiosity.

The author's knowledge of the world, and the peculiar tact with which she presents characters that the reader cannot fail to recognize, reminds us something of the merits of the Flemish school of painting. The subjects are not often elegant, and certainly never grand; but they are finished up to nature, and with a precision which delights the reader. This is a merit which it is very difficult to illustrate by extracts, because it pervades the whole work, and is not to be comprehended from a single passage. ... [In] a dialogue between Mr. Woodhouse, and his elder daughter Isabella, who shares his anxiety about health, and has, like her father, a favourite apothecary. ... [and who] with her husband, a sensible, peremptory sort of person, had come to spend a week with her father. . . . the reader may collect . . . both the merits and faults of the author. The former consists much in the force of a narrative conducted with much neatness and point, and a quiet yet comic dialogue, in which the characters of the speakers evolve themselves with dramatic effect. The faults, on the contrary, arise from the minute detail which the author's plan comprehends. Characters of folly or simplicity, such as those of old Woodhouse and Miss Bates, are ridiculous when first presented, but if too often brought forward or too long dwelt upon, their prosing is apt to become as tiresome in fiction as in real society. Upon the whole, the turn of this author's novel bears the same relation to that of the sentimental and romantic cast, that cornfields and cottages and meadows bear to the highly adorned grounds of a show mansion, or the rugged sublimities of a mountain landscape. It is neither so captivating as the one, nor so grand as the other, but it affords to those who frequent it a pleasure nearly allied with the experience of their own social habits; and what is of some importance, the youthful wanderer may return from his promenade to the ordinary business of life, without any chance of having his head turned by the recollection of the scene through which he has been wandering.

One word, however, we must say in behalf of that once powerful divinity, Cupid, king of gods and men, who in these times of revolution, has been assailed, even in his own kingdom of romance, by the authors who were formerly his devoted priests. We are quite aware that there are few instances of first attachment being brought to a happy conclusion, and that it seldom can be so in a state of society so highly advanced as to render early marriages among the better class, acts, generally speaking, of imprudence. But the youth of this realm need not at present be taught the doctrine of selfishness. It is by no means their error to give the world or the good things of the world all for love; and before the authors of moral fiction couple Cupid indivisibly with calculating prudence, we would have them reflect, that they may sometimes lend their aid to substitute more mean, more sordid, and more selfish motives of conduct, for the romantic feelings which their predecessors perhaps fanned into too powerful a flame. Who is it, that in his youth has felt a virtuous attachment, however romantic or however unfortunate, but can trace back to its influence much that his character may possess of what is honourable, dignified, and disinterested? If he recollects hours wasted in unavailing hope, or saddened by doubt and disappointment; he may also dwell on many which have been snatched from folly or libertinism, and dedicated to studies which might render him worthy of the object of his affection, or pave the way perhaps to that distinction necessary to raise him to an equality with her. Even the habitual indulgence of feelings totally unconnected with ourselves and our own immediate interest, softens, graces, and amends the human mind; and after the pain of disappointment is past, those who survive (and by good fortune those are the greater number) are neither less wise nor less worthy members of society for having felt, for a time, the influence of a passion which has been well qualified as the 'tenderest, noblest and best.'

SOURCE: *Quarterly Review*, XIV (1815) 188–201 (actually appeared March 1816).

British Critic   (1816)

Whoever is fond of an amusing, inoffensive and well principled novel, will be well pleased with the perusal of *Emma*. It rarely happens that in a production of this nature we have so little to find fault with.

In few novels is the unity of place preserved; we know not of one in which the author has sufficient art to give interest to the circle of a small village. The author of *Emma* never goes beyond the boundaries of two private families, but has contrived in a very interesting manner to detail their history, and to form out of so slender materials a very pleasing tale. The characters are well kept up to the end. The valetudinarian fathers, the chattering village belles, are all preserved to the life. . . .

We are not the less inclined to speak well of this tale, because it does not dabble in religion; of fanatical novels and fanatical authoresses we are already sick.

SOURCE: *British Critic*, NS VI (July 1816) 96.

Monthly Review   (1816)

If this novel can scarcely be termed a composition, because it
contains but one ingredient, *that one* is, however, of sterling worth;
being a strain of genuine natural humour, such as is seldom found
conjointly with the complete purity of images and ideas which is
here conspicuous. The character of Mr. Woodhouse, with his 'habits
of gentle selfishness,' is admirably drawn, and the dialogue is easy
and lively. The fair reader may also glean by the way some useful
hints against forming romantic schemes, or indulging a spirit of
patronage in defiance of sober reason; and the work will probably
become a favourite with all those who seek for harmless amusement, rather than deep pathos or appalling horrors, in works of
fiction.

SOURCE: *Monthly Review*, LXXX (July 1816) 320.

Gentleman's Magazine   (1816)

Dulce est desipere in loco; and a good Novel is now and then an
agreeable relaxation from severer studies. Of this description was
Pride and Prejudice; and from the entertainment which those
volumes afforded us, we were desirous to peruse the present work;
nor have our expectations been disappointed. If *Emma* has not the
highly-drawn characters in superior life which are so interesting in
Pride and Prejudice; it delineates with great accuracy the habits and
the manners of a middle class of gentry; and of the inhabitants of a
country village at one degree of rank and gentility beneath them.
Every character throughout the work, from the heroine to the most
subordinate, is a portrait which comes home to the heart and
feelings of the Reader; who becomes familiarly acquainted with each
of them, nor loses sight of a single individual till the completion of
the work. The unities of time and place are well preserved; the

language is chaste and correct; and if *Emma* be not allowed to rank in the very highest class of modern Novels, it certainly may claim at least a distinguished degree of eminence in that species of composition. It is amusing, if not instructive; and has no tendency to deteriorate the heart.

SOURCE: *Gentleman's Magazine*, LXXXVI (September 1816) 248–9.

PART TWO

Some Opinions and Criticism, 1816–1962

Susan Ferrier 'Excellent' (1816)

I have been reading *Emma*, which is excellent; there is no story whatever, and the heroine is no better than other people; but the characters are all so true to life, and the style so piquant, that it does not require the adventitious aids of mystery and adventure.

> SOURCE: From a letter to Miss Clavering, 1816, in *Memoir and Correspondence of Susan Ferrier*, ed. John A. Doyle (1898).

Mary Russell Mitford 'Delightful' (1816)

By-the-way, how delightful is her *Emma*! the best, I think, of all her charming works.

> SOURCE: From a letter to Sir William Elford, 1816, in A. G. L'Estrange, *Life* (1870) I 331.

John Henry Newman 'The Most Interesting of all her Heroines' (1837)

I have been reading *Emma*. Everything Miss Austen writes is clever, but I desiderate something. There is a want of *body* to the story. The action is frittered away in over-little things. There are some beautiful things in it. Emma herself is the most interesting to me of all her

heroines. I feel kind to her whenever I think of her. But Miss Austen
has no romance – none at all. What vile creatures her parsons are!
she has not a dream of the high Catholic $\mathring{\eta}\theta o\varsigma$. That other woman,
Fairfax, is a dolt – but I like Emma.[1]

SOURCE: From a letter to Mrs John Mozley, 1837, in *Letters*, ed.
Anne Mozley (1891) II 223.

NOTE

1. The editor of Newman's letters, Anne Mozley, makes the following
footnote at this point: 'In inserting this critique on Miss Austen's masterpiece the Editor has a sense almost of disloyalty to this delightful writer. But
Miss Austen's novels are a battlefield and the reader has a right to the
opinion here given. The ethos, as Mr Newman calls it, of a book came
always foremost in his critical estimation. He condoned a good deal when
this satisfied him. Miss Austen described parsons as she saw them, and did
not recognise it as in her province to preach to them, except indirectly by
portraying the Mr Collinses and Mr Eltons of the day.' [Ed.]

Charlotte Brontë 'Nothing Profound' (1850)

I have . . . read one of Miss Austen's works – *Emma* – read it with
interest and with just the degree of admiration which Miss Austen
herself would have thought sensible and suitable. Anything like
warmth or enthusiasm – anything energetic, poignant, heart-felt is
utterly out of place in commending these works: all such demonstration the authoress would have met with a well-bred sneer, would
have calmly scorned as outré and extravagant. She does her business
of delineating the surface of the lives of genteel English people
curiously well. There is a Chinese fidelity, a miniature delicacy in
the painting. She ruffles her reader by nothing vehement, disturbs
him by nothing profound. The passions are perfectly unknown to
her; she rejects even a speaking acquaintance with that stormy
sisterhood. Even to the feelings she vouchsafes no more than an

occasional graceful but distant recognition – too frequent converse with them would ruffle the smooth elegance of her progress. Her business is not half so much with the human heart as with the human eyes, mouth, hands, and feet. What sees keenly, speaks aptly, moves flexibly, it suits her to study; but what throbs fast and full, though hidden, what the blood rushes through, what is the unseen seat of life and the sentient target of death – this Miss Austen ignores. She no more, with her mind's eye, beholds the heart of her race than each man, with bodily vision, sees the heart in his heaving breast. Jane Austen was a complete and most sensible lady, but a very incomplete and rather insensible (*not senseless*) woman. If this is heresy, I cannot help it. If I said it to some people (Lewes for instance) they would directly accuse me of advocating exaggerated heroics, but I am not afraid of your falling into any such vulgar error.

SOURCE: From a letter to W. S. Williams, 1850, in Clement K. Shorter, *The Brontës: Life and Letters* (1908) II 127–8.

Anthony Trollope 'Miss Austen's Timidity'[1] (1865)

Emma is undoubtedly very tedious; – thereby shewing rather the patience of readers in the authors day than any incapacity on her part to avoid the fault. The dialogues are too long and some of them are unnecessary.

But the story shews wonderful knowledge of female character, and is severe on the little foibles of women with a severity which no man would dare to use. Emma, the heroine, is treated almost mercilessly. In every passage of the book she is in fault for some folly, some vanity, some ignorance, – or indeed for some meanness. Her conduct to her friend Harriet, – her assumed experience and real ignorance of human nature – are terribly true; but nowadays we dare not make our heroines so little. Her weaknesses are all plain to us, but of her strength we are only told; and even at the last we hardly know why Mr Knightley loves her.

The humour shewn in some of the female characters in *Emma* is very good. Mrs Elton with her loud Bath-begotten vulgarity is excellent; and Miss Bates, longwinded, self-denying, ignorant, and eulogistic has become proverbial. But the men are all weak. There is nothing in *Emma* like Mr Bennet and Mr Collins the immortal heroes of *Pride and Prejudice*. Mr Woodhouse, the malade imaginaire, is absurd, and the Knightleys and Westons are simply sticks. It is as a portrait of female life among ladies in an English village 50 years ago that Emma is to be known and remembered.

We have here, given to us unconsciously, a picture of the clerical life of 1815 which we cannot avoid comparing with the clerical life of 1865. After a modest dinner party, when the gentlemen join the ladies, the parson of the parish, a young man, is noticed as having taken too much wine. And no one else has done so. But allusion is made to this, not because he is a clergyman, nor is he at all a debauched or fast-living clergyman. It simply suits the story that he should be a little flushed & free of speech. The same clergyman, when married, declines to dance because he objects to the partner proposed to him; and special mention is made of card parties at this clergyman's house. How must the mouths of young parsons water in these days as they read these details, if they are now ever allowed to read such books as *Emma*.

I cannot but notice Miss Austens timidity in dealing with the most touching scenes which come in her way, and in avoiding the narration of those details which a bolder artist would most eagerly have seized. In the final scene between Emma and her lover, – when the conversation has become almost pathetic, – she breaks away from the spoken dialogue, and simply tells us of her hero's success. This is a cowardice which robs the reader of much of the charm which he has promised himself–

SOURCE: 'Trollope on *Emma*: an unpublished note', in *Nineteenth-century Fiction*, IV (1949) 145–7.

NOTE

1. Anthony Trollope wrote these comments on the end papers of his copy of *Emma*, in 1865. He was then engaged on his sequence of 'Barsetshire' novels about clerical life – hence his interest in Mr Elton. [Ed.]

Richard Simpson 'The Platonic Idea'[1] (1870)

It is clear that she began, as Shakespeare began, with being an ironical censurer of her contemporaries. After forming her prentice hand by writing nonsense, she began her artistic self-education by writing burlesques. One of her works, *Northanger Abbey*, still retains the traces and the flavour of these early essays. By it we may learn that her parodies were designed not so much to flout at the style as at the unnaturalness, unreality, and fictitious morality, of the romances she imitated. She began by being an ironical critic; she manifested her judgment of them not by direct censure, but by the indirect method of imitating and exaggerating the faults of her models, thus clearing the fountain by first stirring up the mud. This critical spirit lies at the foundation of her artistic faculty. Criticism, humour, irony, the judgment not of one that gives sentence but of the mimic who quizzes while he mocks, are her characteristics. . . .

   The paramount activity of the critical faculty is clearly seen in the didactic purpose and even nomenclature of her novels. *Pride and Prejudice* and *Sense and Sensibility* are both evidently intended to contrast, and by the contrast to teach something about, the qualities or acts named in the titles. In *Persuasion* the risks and advantages of yielding to advice are set forth. *Northanger Abbey* exhibits the unreality of the notions of life which might be picked out of Mrs Radcliffe's novels; and *Mansfield Park* and *Emma*, though too many-sided and varied to be easily defined by a specific name, are in reality just as didactic as the rest. This didactic intention is even interwoven with the very plots and texture of the novel. The true hero, who at last secures the heroine's hand, is often a man sufficiently her elder to have been her guide and mentor in many of the most difficult crises of her youth. Miss Austen seems to be saturated with the Platonic idea that the giving and receiving of knowledge, the active formation of another's character, or the more passive growth under another's guidance, is the truest and strongest foundation of love. *Pride and Prejudice, Emma*, and *Persuasion* all end with the heroes and heroines making comparisons of the intellectual and moral improvement which they have imparted to each other. The author has before her eyes no fear of the old adage, 'Wise lovers are the most absurd.'... [Emma], like Marianne Dashwood and Catharine Morland, is a young lady full of preconceived ideas, which she has not, however, like Marianne and Catharine, borrowed from the traditional romance of poets and novelists, but which are the product of her own reflections upon her own mental powers. Her prejudices are natural, not artificial; she fancies herself cleverer than she is, with an insight into other hearts which she does not possess, and with a talent for management which is only great enough to produce entanglements, but not to unravel them. These ideas of hers govern the plot; and she is cured of them by the logic of events. At the same time, her esteem for the mentor who stands by her and tries to guide her through her difficulties gradually ripens into love; the scholar gratefully marries her master; and the novel ends, as usual, with a retrospect in which both teacher and taught find themselves equal gainers each from the other, even intellectually, and the Platonic ideal is realized, not merely through the heart, but through the intelligence. . . .

There is a decided growth in the general intention of Miss Austen's novels; she goes over the same ground, trying other ways of producing the same effects, and attempting the same ends by means less artificial, and of more innate origin. The same may be said of the details of her works – for instance, of the characters. . . . Her biographer refers to her fools as a class of characters in delineating which she has quite caught the knack of Shakespeare. It is a natural class, better defined than most natural classes are, and less difficult to analyse. It ought therefore to serve very well to test her manner of working. In reality her fools are not more simple than her other characters. Her wisest personages have some dash of folly in them, and her least wise have something to love. And there is a collection of absurd persons in her stultifera navis, quite sufficient to make her fortune as a humourist. She seems to have considered folly to consist in two separate qualities: first, a thorough weakness either of will or intellect, an emptiness or irrelevancy of thought, such as to render it impossible to know what the person would think of any given subject, or how he would act under it; and often, secondly, in addition to this, fixed ideas on a few subjects, giving the whole tone to the person's thoughts so far as he thinks at all, and constituting the ground of the few positive judgments arrived at, even in subject-matter to which the ideas in question are scarcely related. . . . [In]

Emma, where perhaps Miss Austen perfects her processes for painting humorous portraits, the negative fool is ... represented in Miss Bates. Miss Bates has enough of womanly kindness and other qualities to make her a real living person, even a good Christian woman. But intellectually she is a negative fool. She has not mind enough to fall into contradictions. There is a certain logical sequence and association between two contradictories, which it requires mind to discover: Miss Bates's fluent talk only requires memory. She cannot distinguish the relations between things. If she is standing in a particular posture when she hears a piece of news, her posture becomes at once a part of the event which it is her duty to hand down to tradition: 'Where could you possibly hear it? For it is not five minutes since I received Mrs Cole's note – no, it cannot be more than five – or at least ten – for I had got my bonnet and spencer on just ready to come out – I was only gone down to speak to Patty again about the pork – Jane was standing in the passage – were you not, Jane? – for my mother was so afraid that we had not any salting-pan large enough', etc. etc, for it might go on for ever. Any reader can see that here is the same fortuitous concourse of details which makes up Mrs Quickly's description of Falstaff's promising her marriage – the sea-coal fire, and the green wound, and the dish of prawns – in the speech which Coleridge so justly contrasts with Hamlet's equally episodical, but always relevant, narrative of his voyage towards England.

The fool simple is soon exhausted; but when a collection of fixed ideas is grafted upon him he becomes a theme for endless variations. Mrs Bennet, in *Pride and Prejudice*, Miss Austen's earliest work, is one of this kind. . . .

However good [such] characters may be, it cannot be denied that they have in them much of the element of farce. Miss Austen in her later series of novels has given us new and improved versions of them; for example, Mr Woodhouse in *Emma*, a mere white curd of asses' milk, but still a man with humanity enough in him to be loveable in spite of, nay partly because of, his weakness and foolishness. His understanding is mean enough. His invalid's fixed ideas, which divide all that is into two kinds, wholesome and unwholesome, his notion of the superiority of his own house and family to all other houses and families, his own doctor to all other doctors, and his pork to all other pork, and his judgment of all proposals and events by their effect in bringing persons nearer to, or driving them further off from, the centre of happiness which he enjoys, show that the portrait is one of the same kind as that of Mrs Bennet, but improved by the addition of a heart. . . . Miss Austen, in constructing her chief characters, sometimes lets her theory run away with her. For instance, Darcy, in *Pride and Prejudice*, is the proud man; but he is a gentleman by birth and education, and a gentleman in feeling. Would it be possible for such a man, in making a proposal of marriage to a lady whose only fault in his eyes is that some of her connections are vulgar, to do so in the way in which Darcy makes his overtures to Elizabeth? It is true that great pains are taken to explain this wonderful lapse of propriety. But, all the explanations notwithstanding, an impression is left on the reader that either Darcy is not so much of a gentleman as he is represented, or that his conduct is forced a little beyond the line of nature in order the better to illustrate the theory of his biographer. The same criticism is applicable to the most elaborate of the novels, *Emma*. The heroine's suspicions about the relations between Miss Fairfax and Mr Dixon may be natural; but her decision in believing without proof what she suspected, and her open and public reproaches to the lady, are violently opposed to the general notion of feminine grace and good-nature which the character is intended to embody. Here again, theory seems to be pushed a little beyond the line not of possibility but of consistency. . . .

Hints given in Miss Mitford's letters, however strenuously controverted, seem to show that in early days there was something offensive in Miss Austen's manner and conduct. It may be that both Emma and Darcy contain autobiographical elements. There is an air of confession in the conception of each. We find in the novels a theory that, as love is educated by contradiction, so is love the great educator of the mind through sorrow and contradiction. Dante describes philosophy as the amoroso uso de sapienza: wisdom without it talks but does not act wisely. He who acts without love acts at haphazard; love alone shows him how and where to apply his principles, chiefly by the agony it gives him when he wounds it by wrong applications of them. Emma's wisdom nearly ruins her happiness, till she finds that wisdom is nothing unless it is directed by love. Darcy too by his similar love of managing almost ruins the prospects of his friend and himself. With all the importance which Miss Austen attributes to education, she never forgets its double aspect, theoretical and practical. But the practice must be directed by love. Love is however only a tardy teacher; it teaches as the conscience teaches, or as the dæmon of Socrates taught him, by the penalties it exacts for error. Πάθει μάθος, as Æschylus says. If Miss Austen ever was a flirt, as Mrs Mitford reported, it was most likely rather in Emma's style; not with any idea of engaging men's hearts in order to disappoint them, but with a view to show her disengaged manners, and the superiority of which she was conscious. The shade of priggishness with which her earlier novels are tinged is perhaps most easily explicable on this supposition.

But in any case, after all possible deductions, Miss Austen must always have been a woman as charming in mind as she was elegant in person. What defects she had only prevented her being so good as to be good for nothing.

SOURCE: From 'Jane Austen', in *North British Review*, LII (1870) 129–32.

NOTE

1. Richard Simpson (1820–76) was one of the 'Oxford converts' who followed Newman into the Church of Rome. He edited the *Rambler*, and was a Shakespeare scholar of some distinction. [Ed.]

Dublin Review 'Miss Austen's Superiority' (1870)

It is in respect of her portraiture of women that Miss Austen is so superior to almost every other novelist among those who preceded her, to such of her contemporaries as are remembered, and to most subsequent writers of fiction. The heroic type would have been as much out of her line of execution as it was anti-pathetic to her taste; but with all Scott's domestic heroines hers may be compared to her advantage, in those respects in which any comparison is to be instituted. If we pass by the numerous novelists since Scott, and come to the novelists of this age, selecting a few of the representative ones, we shall not find any surpass or equal her in this important regard. Thackeray, Dickens, Mrs Gaskell, and Mr Anthony Trollope suggest themselves at once. Miss Brontë's coarse and repulsive pictures of women, though undeniably clever, serve only to indicate the exact opposites in taste and appreciation. A society composed of Jane Eyres, Shirleys, and Lucy Snowes would be a lamentable spectacle to gods and men; whereas a society in which such women as Emma Woodhouse, Jane Fairfax, Elinor Dashwood, Jane Bennet, and above all Anne Elliot should abound, would present a picture of pure, rational, intellectual, and actual happiness and respectability without room for an 'ism' or toleration for any of those aberrations, whether of passion or conceit, which tend to make men sad and women ridiculous. Miss Austen's Fanny Price is as submissive, as simple-minded, and as jealous as Mr Thackeray's Amelia; she is as little understood and as much snubbed, and she has an antagonist as brilliant, if less base; but she is charming, rational, and ladylike, while Amelia is silly, insipid, and underbred, though Mr Thackeray frequently assures us of her humility and gentility. He *calls* Amelia a lady; Miss Austen *makes* Fanny Price one. Again, Mrs Newcome is a capital picture of purse-proud patronizing vulgarity, but she is not so clever a picture as Mrs Elton, who is indeed unsurpassed, we believe unequalled, and who is indispensable to the story of *Emma*, while Mrs Newcome is not indispensable to that of *The Newcomes*. Calling her 'Virtue', and keeping her dingy gloves perpetually before us, is Mr Thackeray's method of enforcing Mrs Newcome's self-importance and ill-breeding. Mrs Elton is introduced in a few lines of description, never repeated or referred to, but a fresh touch is added to every sentence she speaks, and she is so real as to be positively irritating, but not positively tiresome, as Mrs Newcome is, as Clive Newcome's mother-in-law is, as Mrs Baynes is – (she is indeed a replica of the Old Soldier, as Charlotte Baynes is a copy of Rosy, and Philip a cheap edition of Clive) – as all Mr Thackeray's vulgar people are. Miss Austen was too consummate an artist to produce any such effect. She can make us understand how Mr Woodhouse wearied his clear-headed, decisive, selfish son-in-law, and how the ceaseless stream of Miss Bates's talk was too much for Emma's charity and endurance; but she makes us love Mr Wood-house, and we are sure nobody ever read Miss Bates's monologues once without turning to them again. Mrs Nickleby is Miss Bates in caricature – how inferior to the original will be seen by comparing her absurd remarks to Kate about her early reminiscences, as they are sitting together in the arbour, with Miss Bates's infliction of all the details of Jane Fairfax's letter upon Emma Woodhouse, with her ramblings to pork and roast apples, or her endless eulogium of the delights and splendours of the ball at the Crown. In this branch of her art, we regard Miss Bates as the author's masterpiece. She is highly ridiculous, but most estimable and respectable, and while the reader laughs at her, he feels for her all the friendly regard which she has long enjoyed in her native town of Highbury, and tastes with pleasure the delicate flavour of serious moral interest with which Miss Austen invests the poor, simple old maid's humble, laborious, estimable life. She adjusts this flavour so dexterously, she presents it so adroitly. In Mrs Gaskell's last work, *Wives and Daughters*, unhappily unfinished at the time of her death, there is some resemblance to Miss Austen's men and women. The canvas is larger, the manipulation is bolder, but there are shades and touches like those of the master-hand....

Cranford is worthy of comparison with the miniature portrait of Highbury, Emma's home. Mrs Gaskell's microcosmic performance has more breadth of plan and of feeling; Miss Austen's has more sharpness and superior humour.

SOURCE: From 'Jane Austen and her Novels', in *Dublin Review*, XV (1870) 430–45.

Lord Brabourne 'Too Respectable to be A Hero' (1884)

I frankly confess that I never could endure Mr Knightley. He interfered too much, he judged other people rather too quickly and too harshly, he was too old for Emma, and being the elder brother of her elder sister's husband, there was something incongruous in the match which I could never bring myself to approve. To tell the truth, I always wanted Emma to marry Frank Churchill, and so did Mr and Mrs Weston. Mr Knightley, however, is an eminently respectable hero – too respectable, in fact, to be a hero at all; he does not seem to rise above the standard of respectability into that of heroism; and I should have disputed his claim to the position had he not satisfactorily established it beyond all possible doubt by marrying the heroine. But I have never felt satisfied with the marriage, and feel very sure that Emma was not nearly so happy as she pretended. I am certain that he frequently lectured her, was jealous of every agreeable man that ventured to say a civil word to her, and evinced his intellectual superiority by such a plethora of eminently suitable conversations, as either speedily hurried her to an untimely grave, or induced her to run away with somebody possessed of an inferior intellect, but more endearing qualities.

SOURCE: From *Letters of Jane Austen*, ed. Lord Brabourne (1884) I 89–90.

Mrs Charles Malden 'A Thorough English Gentleman' (1889)

Most readers of Jane Austen will agree in thinking that in *Emma* she reached the summit of her literary powers. She has given us quite as charming individual characters both in earlier and later writings, but it is impossible to name a flaw in *Emma*; there is not a page that could with advantage be omitted, nor could any additions improve it. It has all the brilliancy of *Pride and Prejudice*, without any immaturity of style, and it is as carefully finished as *Mansfield Park*, without the least suspicion of prolixity. In *Emma*, too, as has been already noticed, she worked into perfection some characters which she had attempted earlier with less success, and she gave us two or three, such as Mr Weston, Mrs Elton, and Miss Bates, which we find nowhere else in her writings. Moreover, in *Emma*, above all her other works, she achieved a task in which many a great writer has failed; for she gives us there the portrait of a thorough English gentleman, drawn to the life. Edmund Bertram, indeed, is, in the best sense of the word, a gentleman, but he is a very young one; Mr

Darcy and Henry Tilney at times are on the verge of not being quite thorough-bred; but Mr Knightley is from head to foot a gentleman, and we feel that he never could have said or done a thing unworthy of one. Jane Austen herself classed him with Edmund Bertram in her speech already given, as 'far from being what I know English gentleman often are'. I think she was unjust to both her heroes, but, above all, to Mr Knightley, for it is difficult to see how he could be surpassed.[1] The man, who, in the full vigour of health and strength, was always patient and forbearing towards a fussy, fidgety invalid; who would not propose to the woman he loved because he believed that another younger and more attractive man was on the verge of doing so; then was ready to help and comfort her without any *arrière pensée* of advantage to himself, when she was deserted by her supposed lover; who took with indifference any annoyance or impertinence to himself, but whose righteous indignation was instantly roused by any slight to those whose position made them defenceless; who was refined in thought and language, sincere to friends and foes, and uncompromisingly straightforward in every transaction; surely this is a very real type of English gentleman, and few writers have drawn it so successfully. Emma Woodhouse, too, is very good. Her faults, follies, and mistakes are completely those of a warm-hearted, rather spoilt girl, accustomed to believe in herself, and to be queen of her own circle. She deserves the amount of punishment she gets, but we are glad it is no worse; and, with Mr. Knightley to look after her, she will do very well.

SOURCE: From *Jane Austen* (1889) pp. 128–9.

NOTE

1. Mrs Malden was evidently insensitive to irony. [Ed.]

Walter Herries Pollock 'One Slip in Miss Austen's Accuracy' (1899)

The one slip in Miss Austen's accuracy in observation and description of features in landscape . . . occurs in *Emma*, where, to quote . . . from my father's article in *Fraser*,[1] at almost midsummer

> Strawberries are described as being eaten from the beds at Donwell Abbey, while the orchard is in blossom at the neighbouring Abbey Mill Farm – an anachronism which we have never met with any horticulturist able to explain by bringing together even the earliest and latest varieties of apple and strawberry.

The passage in question runs thus: Emma, when the party are on their way to see the view of Abbey Mill Farm from Donwell, perceives 'Mr Knightley and Harriet distinct from the rest, quietly leading the way'. There had been a time when Harriet Smith and Mr Knightley were not likely to be companions, and when Emma would have been sorry Harriet should see so favourable a view of Abbey Mill Farm. However, a young farmer wishes to marry, and finally does marry, Harriet Smith; but at first this is a most displeasing idea to Emma, who has 'taken up' Harriet, and thinks, foolishly, that she ought to do better. 'Now' Abbey Mill Farm 'might be safely viewed with all its appendages of prosperity and beauty, its rich pastures, spreading flocks, *orchard* in *blossom*, and light column of smoke ascending.' With regard to this I find, on the fly-leaf at the end of the volume in which the article on 'British Novelists' is bound up, the following copy, in my father's handwriting, of a letter written by Miss Caroline Austen, niece to Jane:

Ferog Firle.

My dearest Charlotte, – There is a tradition in the family respecting the apple-blossom as seen from Donwell Abbey on the occasion of the strawberry party, and it runs thus –That the first time my uncle Knight [this was the first Mr Edward Knight of Chawton House] saw his sister after the publication of *Emma* he said, 'Jane, I wish you would tell me where you get those apple-trees of yours that come into bloom in July.' In truth she did make a mistake – there is no denying it – and she was speedily apprised of it by her brother – but I suppose it was not thought of sufficient consequence to call for correction in a later edition.

Mr W. Austen Leigh writes to me that 'the *Charlotte* to whom my aunt wrote must, we think, have been Charlotte Warren – a school friend. She afterwards became Mrs Roberts, and was the mother of the Margaret Roberts who wrote *Mademoiselle Mori*'.

SOURCE: From *Jane Austen, an essay in criticism* (1899) pp. 90–1.

NOTE

1. The reference is to Sir William Frederick Pollock's 'British Novelists – Richardson, Miss Austen, Scott', in *Fraser's*, LXI (1860) 20–38. [Ed.]

William Dean Howells 'Her Most Boldly Imagined Heroine' (1901)

Emma Woodhouse, in the story named after her, is one of the most boldly imagined of Jane Austen's heroines. Perhaps she is the very most so, for it took supreme courage to portray a girl, meant to win and keep the reader's fancy, with the characteristics frankly ascribed to Emma Woodhouse. We are indeed allowed to know that she is pretty; not formally, but casually, from the words of a partial friend: 'Such an eye! – the true hazel eye – and so brilliant! – regular features, open countenance, with a complexion – ah, what a bloom of full health, and such a pretty height and size; such a firm and upright figure.' But, before we are allowed to see her personal beauty we are made to see in her some of the qualities which are the destined source of trouble for herself and her friends. In her wish to be useful she is patronizing and a little presumptuous; her self-sufficiency early appears, and there are hints of her willingness to shape the future of others without having past enough of her own to enable her to do it judiciously. The man who afterwards marries her says of her: 'She will never submit to anything requiring industry and patience, and a subjection of the fancy to the understanding.... Emma is spoiled by being the cleverest of her family. At ten years old she had the misfortune of being able to answer questions which puzzled her sister at seventeen. She was always quick and assured . . . and ever since she was twelve Emma has been mistress of the house and you all.'

An officious and self-confident girl, even if pretty, is not usually one to take the fancy, and yet Emma takes the fancy. She manages the delightful and whimsical old invalid her father, but she is devotedly and unselfishly good to him. She takes the destiny of Harriet Smith unwarrantably into her charge, but she breaks off the girl's love-affair only in the interest of a better match. She decides that Frank Churchill, the stepson of her former governess, will be in love with her, but she never dreams that Mr Elton, whom she means for Harriet Smith, can be so. She is not above a little manœuvring for the advantage of those she wishes to serve, but the tacit insincerity of Churchill is intolerable to her. She is unfeelingly neglectful of Jane Fairfax and cruelly suspicious of her, but she generously does what she can to repair the wrong, and she takes her punishment for it meekly and contritely. She makes thoughtless and heartless fun of poor, babbling Miss Bates, but when Knightley calls her to account for it, she repents her unkindness with bitter tears. She will not be advised against her pragmatical schemes by Knightley, but she is humbly anxious for his good opinion. She is charming in the very degree of her feminine complexity, which is finally an endearing single-heartedness.

Her character is shown in an action so slight that the novel of *Emma* may be said to be hardly more than an exemplification of Emma. In the placid circumstance of English country life where she is the principal social figure the story makes its round with a few events so unexciting as to leave the reader in doubt whether anything at all has happened. . . . Duels and abductions, of course, there are none; for Jane Austen had put from her all the machinery of the great and little novelists of the eighteenth century, and openly mocked at it. This has not prevented its being frequently used since, and she shows herself more modern than all her predecessors and contemporaries and most of her successors, in the rejection of the major means and the employment of the minor means to produce the enduring effects of *Emma*. Among her quiet books it is almost the quietest, and so far as the novel can suggest that repose which is the ideal of art *Emma* suggests it, in an action of unsurpassed unity, consequence, and simplicity.

SOURCE: From *Heroines of Fiction* (1901).

Reginald Farrer 'The Book of Books' (1917)

But now we come to the Book of Books, which is the book of Emma Woodhouse.[1] And justly so named, with Jane Austen's undeviating flair for the exact title. For the whole thing *is* Emma; there is only one short scene in which Emma herself is not on the stage; and that one scene is Knightley's conversation about her with Mrs Weston. Take it all in all, *Emma* is the very climax of Jane Austen's work; and a real appreciation of *Emma* is the final test of citizenship in her kingdom. For this is not an easy book to read; it should never be the beginner's primer, nor be published without a prefatory synopsis. Only when the story has been thoroughly assimilated, can the infinite delights and subtleties of its workmanship begin to be appreciated, as you realise the manifold complexity of the book's web, and find that every sentence, almost every epithet, has its definite reference to equally unemphasised points before and after in the development of the plot. Thus it is that, while twelve readings of *Pride and Prejudice* give you twelve periods of pleasure repeated, as many readings of *Emma* give you that pleasure, not repeated only, but squared and squared again with each perusal, till at every fresh reading you feel anew that you never understood anything like the widening sum of its delights. But, until you know the story, you are apt to find its movement dense and slow and obscure, difficult to follow, and not very obviously worth the following.

For this is *the* novel of character, and of character alone, and of one dominating character in particular. And many a rash reader, and some who are not rash, have been shut out on the threshold of Emma's Comedy by a dislike of Emma herself. Well did Jane Austen know what she was about, when she said, 'I am going to take a heroine whom nobody but myself will much like.' And, in so far as she fails to make people like Emma, so far would her whole attempt have to be judged a failure, were it not that really the failure, like the loss, is theirs who have not taken the trouble to understand what is being attempted. Jane Austen loved tackling problems; her hardest of all, her most deliberate, and her most triumphantly solved, is Emma.

What is that problem? No one who carefully reads the first three opening paragraphs of the book can entertain a doubt, or need any prefatory synopsis; for in these the author gives us quite clear warning of what we are to see. We are to see the gradual humiliation of self-conceit, through a long self-wrought succession of disasters, serious in effect, but keyed in Comedy throughout. Emma herself, in fact, *is never to be taken seriously*. And it is only those who have not realised this who will be 'put off fire' by her absurdities, her snobberies, her misdirected mischievous ingenuities. Emma is simply a figure of fun. To conciliate affection for a character, not because of its charms, but in defiance of its defects, is the loftiest aim of the comic spirit; Shakespeare achieved it with his besotted old rogue of a Falstaff, and Molière with Célimène. It is with these, not with 'sympathetic' heroines, that Emma takes rank, as the culminating figure of English high-comedy. And to attain success in creating a being whom you both love and laugh at, the author must attempt a task of complicated difficulty. He must both run with the hare and hunt with the hounds, treat his creation at once objectively and subjectively, get inside it to inspire it with sympathy, and yet stay outside it to direct laughter on its comic aspects. And this is what Jane Austen does for Emma, with a consistent sublimity so demure that indeed a reader accustomed only to crude work might be pardoned for missing the point of her innumerable hints, and actually taking seriously, for example, the irony with which Emma's attitude about the Coles' dinner-party is treated, or the even more convulsing comedy of Emma's reflexions after it. But only Jane Austen is capable of such oblique glints of humour; and only in *Emma* does she weave them so densely into her kaleidoscope that the reader must be perpetually on his guard lest some specially delicious flash escape his notice, or some touch of dialogue be taken for the author's own intention.

Yet, as Emma really does behave extremely ill by Jane Fairfax, and even worse by Robert Martin, merely to laugh would not be enough, and every disapproval would justly be deepened to dislike. But, when we realise that each machination of Emma's, each imagined piece of penetration, is to be a thread in the snare woven unconsciously by herself for her own enmeshing in disaster, then the balance is rectified again, and disapproval can lighten to laughter once more. For this is another of Jane Austen's triumphs here – the way in which she keeps our sympathies poised about

Emma. Always some charm of hers is brought out, to compensate some specially silly and ambitious naughtiness; and even these are but perfectly natural, in a strong-willed, strong-minded girl of only twenty-one, who has been for some four years unquestioned mistress of Hartfield, unquestioned Queen of Highbury. Accordingly, at every turn we are kept so dancing up and down with alternate rage and delight at Emma that finally, when we see her self-esteem hammered bit by bit into collapse, the nemesis would be too severe, were she to be left in the depths. By the merciful intention of the book, however, she is saved in the very nick of time, by what seems like a happy accident, but is really the outcome of her own un-suspected good qualities, just as much as her disasters had been the outcome of her own most cherished follies.

In fact, Emma is intrinsically honest (it is not for nothing that she is given so unique a frankness of outlook on life); and her brave recognition of her faults, when confronted with their results, con-duces largely to the relief with which we hail the solution of the tangle, and laugh out loud over 'Such a heart, such a Harriet'! The remark is typical, both of Emma and of Emma's author. For this is the ripest and kindliest of all Jane Austen's work. Here alone she can laugh at people, and still like them; elsewhere her amusement is invariably salted with either dislike or contempt. *Emma* contains no fewer than four silly people, more or less prominent in the story; but Jane Austen touches them all with a new mansuetude, and turns them out as candidates for love as well as laughter. Nor is this all that must be said for Miss Bates and Mr Woodhouse. They are actually inspired with sympathy. Specially remarkable is the treat-ment of Miss Bates, whose pathos depends on her lovableness, and her lovableness on her pathos, till she comes so near our hearts that Emma's abrupt brutality to her on Box Hill comes home to us with the actuality of a violent sudden slap in our own face. But then Miss Bates, though a twaddle, is by no means a fool; in her humble, quiet, unassuming happiness, she is shown throughout as an essentially wise woman. For Jane Austen's mood is in no way softened to the second-rate and pretentious, though it is typical of *Emma* that Elton's full horror is only gradually revealed in a succession of tiny touches, many of them designed to swing back sympathy to Emma; even as Emma's own bad behaviour on Box Hill is there to give Jane Fairfax a lift in our sympathy at her critical moment, while Emma's repentance afterwards is just what is wanted to win us back to

Emma's side again, in time for the coming catastrophe. And even Elton's 'broad handsome face,' in which 'every feature works', pales before that of the lady who 'was, in short, so very ready to have him'. 'He called her Augusta; how delightful!'

Jane Austen herself never calls people she is fond of by these fancy names, but reserves them for such female cads or cats as Lydia Bennet, Penelope Clay, Selina Suckling, and 'the charming Augusta Hawkins'. It is characteristic, indeed, of her methods in *Emma*, that, though the Sucklings never actually appear, we come to know them (and miss them) as intimately as if they did. Jane Austen delights in imagining whole vivid sets of people, never on the stage, yet vital in the play; but in *Emma* she indulges herself, and us, unusually lavishly, with the Sucklings at Maple Grove, the Dixons in Ireland, and the Churchills at Enscombe. As for Frank, he is among her men what Mary Crawford is among her women, a being of incomparable brilliance, moving with a dash that only the complicated wonderfulness of the whole book prevents us from lingering to appreciate. In fact, he so dims his cold pale Jane by comparison that one wonders more than ever what he saw in her. The whole Frank–Jane intrigue, indeed, on which the story hinges, is by no means its most valuable or plausible part. But Jane Fairfax is drawn in dim tones by the author's deliberate purpose. She had to be dim. It was essential that nothing should bring the secondary heroine into any competition with Emma. Accordingly Jane Fairfax is held down in a rigid dulness so conscientious that it almost defeats another of her *raisons d'être* by making Frank's affection seem incredible.

But there is very much more in it than that. Emma is to behave so extremely ill in the Dixon matter that she would quite forfeit our sympathy, unless we were a little taught to share her unregenerate feelings for the 'amiable, upright, perfect Jane Fairfax'. Accordingly we are shown Jane Fairfax always from the angle of Emma; and, despite apparently artless words of eulogy, the author is steadily working all the time to give us just that picture of Jane, as a cool, reserved, rather sly creature, which is demanded by the balance of emotion and the perspective of the picture.[2] It is curious, indeed, how often Jane Austen repeats a favourite composition; two sympathetic figures, major and minor, set against an odious one. In practice, this always means that, while the odious is set boldly out in clear lines and brilliant colour, the minor sympathetic one becomes subordinate to the major, almost to the point of dulness. The

respective positions of Emma, Jane, and Mrs Elton shed a flood of
light back on the comparative paleness of Eleanor Tilney, standing
in the same minor relation to Catherine, as against Isabella Thorpe;
and the trouble about *Sense and Sensibility* is that, while Marianne
and Elinor are similarly set against Lucy, Elinor, hypothetically the
minor note to Marianne, is also, by the current and intention of the
tale, raised to an equal if not more prominent position, thus jangling
the required chord, so faultlessly struck in *Northanger Abbey*, and in
Emma only marred by the fact that Jane Fairfax's real part is larger
than her actual sound-value can be permitted to be.

SOURCE: From 'Jane Austen, *ob*. July 18, 1817', in *Quarterly
Review*, CCXXVIII (July 1917) 24–8.

NOTES

1. 'Heavens, let me not suppose that she dares go about Emma-
Woodhouseing me!' – *Emma*, ch. 33 – a typical instance of a remark which,
comic in itself, has a second comic intention, as showing Emma's own
ridiculousness.
2. Remember, also, that Jane Austen did herself personally hate everything that savoured of reserve and disingenuousness, 'trick and littleness'.

D. W. Harding 'Regulated Hatred' (1940)

The impression of Jane Austen which has filtered through to the
reading public, down from the first-hand critics, through histories of
literature, university courses, literary journalism and polite allusion,
deters many who might be her best readers from bothering with her
at all. How can this popular impression be described? In my
experience the first idea to be absorbed from the atmosphere
surrounding her work was that she offered exceptionally favourable
openings to the exponents of urbanity. . . . I was given to understand
that her scope was of course extremely restricted, but that within her
limits she succeeded admirably in expressing the gentler virtues of a

civilised social order. She could do this because she lived at a time
when, as a sensitive person of culture, she could still feel that she had
a place in society and could address the reading public as sympathetic
equals; she might introduce unpleasant people into her stories, but
she could confidently expose them to a public opinion that condemned them. Chiefly, so I gathered, she was a delicate satirist,
revealing with inimitable lightness of touch the comic foibles and
amiable weaknesses of the people whom she lived amongst and
liked.

All this was enough to make me quite certain I didn't want to read
her. And it is, I believe, a seriously misleading impression. Fragments of the truth have been incorporated in it but they are fitted
into a pattern whose total effect is false. And yet the wide currency of
this false impression is an indication of Jane Austen's success in an
essential part of her complex intention as a writer: her books are, as
she meant them to be, read and enjoyed by precisely the sort of
people whom she disliked; she is a literary classic of the society
which attitudes like hers, held widely enough, would undermine.

In order to enjoy her books without disturbance, those who retain
the conventional notion of her work must always have had slightly to
misread what she wrote at a number of scattered points, points
where she took good care (not wittingly perhaps) that the misreading should be the easiest thing in the world. Unexpected astringen-
cies occur which the comfortable reader probably overlooks, or else
passes by as slight imperfections, trifling errors of tone brought
about by a faulty choice of words. ... In *Emma* ... Jane Austen
seems to be on perfectly good terms with the public she is addressing
and to have no reserve in offering the funniness and virtues of Mr
Woodhouse and Miss Bates to be judged by the accepted standards
of the public. She invites her readers to be just their natural
patronising selves. But this public that Jane Austen seems on such
good terms with has some curious things said about it, not criticisms, but small notes of fact that are usually not made. They almost
certainly go unnoticed by many readers, for they involve only the
faintest change of tone from something much more usual and
acceptable.

When she says that Miss Bates 'enjoyed a most uncommon degree
of popularity for a woman neither young, handsome, rich, nor
married', this is fairly conventional satire that any reading public
would cheerfully admit in its satirist and chuckle over. But the next

sentence must have to be mentally rewritten by the greater number of Jane Austen's readers. For them it probably runs, 'Miss Bates stood in the very worst predicament in the world for having much of the public favour; and she had no intellectual superiority to make atonement to herself, or compel an outward respect from those who might despise her.' This, I suggest, is how most readers, lulled and disarmed by the amiable context, will soften what in fact reads, '. . . and she had no intellectual superiority to make atonement to herself, or frighten those who might hate her into outward respect'. Jane Austen was herself at this time 'neither young, handsome, rich, nor married', and the passage perhaps hints at the functions which her unquestioned intellectual superiority may have had for her.

This eruption of fear and hatred into the relationships of everyday social life is something that the urbane admirer of Jane Austen finds distasteful; it is not the satire of one who writes securely for the entertainment of her civilised acquaintances. And it has the effect, for the attentive reader, of changing the flavour of the more ordinary satire amongst which it is embedded.

Emma is especially interesting from this point of view. What is sometimes called its greater 'mellowness' largely consists in saying quietly and undisguisedly things which in the earlier books were put more loudly but in the innocuous form of caricature. Take conversation, for instance. Its importance and its high (though by no means supreme) social value are of course implicit in Jane Austen's writings. But one should beware of supposing that a mind like hers therefore found the ordinary social intercourse of the period congenial and satisfying. In *Pride and Prejudice* she offers an entertaining caricature of card-table conversation at Lady Catherine de Bourgh's house.

Their table was superlatively stupid. Scarcely a syllable was uttered that did not relate to the game, except when Mrs Jenkinson expressed her fears of Miss de Bourgh's being too hot or too cold, or having too much or too little light. A great deal more passed at the other table. Lady Catherine was generally speaking – stating the mistakes of the three others, or relating some anecdote of herself. Mr Collins was employed in agreeing to everything her ladyship said, thanking her for every fish he won, and apologising if he thought he won too many. Sir William did not say much. He was storing his memory with anecdotes and noble names.

This invites the carefree enjoyment of all her readers. They can all feel superior to Lady Catherine and Mr Collins. But in *Emma* the style changes: the talk at the Coles' dinner party, a pleasant dinner party which the heroine enjoyed, is described as '. . . the usual rate of conversation; a few clever things said, a few down-right silly, but by much the larger proportion neither the one nor the other – nothing worse than everyday remarks, dull repetitions, old news, and heavy jokes'. 'Nothing worse'! – that phrase is typical. It is not mere sarcasm by any means. Jane Austen genuinely valued the achievements of the civilisation she lived within and never lost sight of the fact that there might be something vastly worse than the conversation she referred to. 'Nothing worse' is a positive tribute to the decency, the superficial friendliness, the absence of the grosser forms of insolence and self-display at the dinner party. At least Mrs Elton wasn't there. And yet the effect of the comment, if her readers took it seriously, would be that of a disintegrating attack upon the sort of social intercourse they have established for themselves. It is not the comment of one who would have helped to make her society what it was, or ours what it is.

To speak of this aspect of her work as 'satire' is perhaps misleading. She has none of the underlying didactic intention ordinarily attributed to the satirist. Her object is not missionary; it is the more desperate one of merely finding some mode of existence for her critical attitudes. To her the first necessity was to keep on reasonably good terms with the associates of her everyday life; she had a deep need of their affection and a genuine respect for the ordered, decent civilisation that they upheld. And yet she was sensitive to their crudenesses and complacencies and knew that her real existence depended on resisting many of the values they implied. The novels gave her a way out of this dilemma. This, rather than the ambition of entertaining a posterity of urbane gentlemen, was her motive force in writing. . . .

Whether or not Jane Austen realised what she had been doing, at all events the production of *Mansfield Park* enabled her to go on next to the extraordinary achievement of *Emma*, in which a much more complete humility is combined with the earlier unblinking attention to people as they are. The underlying argument has a different trend. She continues to see that the heroine has derived from the people and conditions around her, but she now keeps clearly in mind the objectionable features of those people; and she faces the far bolder conclusion that even a heroine is likely to have assimilated many of the more unpleasant possibilities of the human being in society. And it is not that society has spoilt an originally perfect girl who now has to recover her pristine good sense, as it was with Catherine Morland, but that the heroine has not yet achieved anything like perfection and is actually going to learn a number of serious lessons from some of the people she lives with.

Consider in the first place the treatment here of the two favourite themes of the earlier novels. The Cinderella theme is now relegated to the sub-heroine, Jane Fairfax. Its working out involves the discomfiture of the heroine, who in this respect is put into the position of one of the ugly sisters. Moreover the Cinderella procedure is shown in the light of a social anomaly, rather a nuisance and requiring the excuse of unusual circumstances.

The associated theme of the child brought up in humble circumstances whose inborn nature fits her for better things is frankly parodied and deflated in the story of Harriet Smith, the illegitimate child whom Emma tries to turn into a snob. In the end, with the insignificant girl cheerfully married to a deserving farmer, 'Harriet's parentage became known. She proved to be the daughter of a tradesman, rich enough to afford her the comfortable maintenance which had ever been hers, and decent enough to have always wished for concealment. Such was the blood of gentility which Emma had formerly been so ready to vouch for!'

Thus the structure of the narrative expresses a complete change in Jane Austen's outlook on the heroine in relation to others. And the story no longer progresses towards her vindication or consolation; it consists in her gradual, humbling self-enlightenment. Emma's personality includes some of the tendencies and qualities that Jane Austen most disliked – self-complacency, for instance, malicious enjoyment in prying into embarrassing private affairs, snobbery, and a weakness for meddling in other people's lives. But now, instead of being attributed in exaggerated form to a character distanced into caricature, they occur in the subtle form given them by someone who in many ways has admirably fine standards.

We cannot say that in *Emma* Jane Austen abandons the Cinderella story. She so deliberately inverts it that we ought to regard *Emma* as a bold variant of the theme and a further exploration of its underlying significance for her.

SOURCE: From 'Regulated Hatred: an aspect of the work of Jane Austen', in *Scrutiny*, VIII (March 1940) 346–62.

E. N. Hayes   Emma: A Dissenting Opinion   (1949)

The material which Jane Austen uses in *Emma* is singularly confined. All the fully developed characters of the novel are of the same social and economic group, the upper middle class; the two possible exceptions, Miss Harriet Smith and Miss Bates, really 'belong', for the first aspires to a position in that group, and the second has once been a prosperous member of it. The scene of the novel is Highbury, a large and populous village sixteen miles from London, and most of the incidents of the book occur in the drawing rooms and gardens of the characters, the streets of the town, Ford's clothing establishment, and several rural spots near the village. The rest of the village is quite neglected, although Emma does once journey to the poorer section in order to relieve the distress of the sick and needy. The subject of the novel is courtship culminating in marriage: more specifically, of Miss Harriet Smith and Mr Robert Martin; of Miss Hawkins and Mr Elton; of Mr Frank Churchill and Miss Jane Fairfax; and of Miss Emma Woodhouse and Mr George Knightley.

It is essential to note what is omitted from this sketch of English life in the early years of the nineteenth century, for I take the initial function of a novel to be the description of human nature and values in a particular social setting. The aristocracy does not appear; Mrs Churchill, a woman of mighty descent and mightier selfishness, is talked about but never seen; the reaction of Emma and the Westons to reports of Mrs Churchill's character reveals a class attitude which charges those above them with pride and malice. The lower middle class receives similar treatment from the novelist; Robert Martin, a young farmer, is allowed to make his appearance in only two or three scenes, and Emma's remarks about him are those of a snob – she does not even consider him of sufficiently high social standing to marry a bastard daughter of the gentry. The poor are admitted into the novel only in the scene already mentioned, and then simply to show that Emma is kindhearted. What is of major significance is that Jane Austen again and again hints at a class conflict which is never allowed to develop in the pages of this pleasant romance.

There are frequent suggestions that the middle class is struggling for position in a world until then dominated by the aristocracy, and that the struggle is being won by the bourgeoisie's adopting the social attitudes and habits of the upper classes. For example, although Mr Woodhouse and the Knightleys derive their money directly or indirectly from commerce, the attitude of Emma is that of an aristocrat – trade is degrading; of Mr Hawkins she thinks that 'merchant, of course, he must be called'. The author's unwillingness or inability to develop this theme constitutes one of the major inadequacies of the novel, an inadequacy which could have been avoided only by her enlarging her view of society. She does not completely understand the gentry, because she does not see their essential relationship to the rest of England.

One of the consequences of this emphasis on the social rather than the economic activities of the middle class is that the world described is one of idle pleasure, of vacation play. In this respect the novel bears comparison to *The Sun Also Rises* – as it also does in the use of dramatic scene; and if Hemingway's people are vicious and immoral because unproductive, we must remark the same of Jane Austen's in *Emma*. However, Jane Austen is incapable of arriving at the conclusion that elegance, 'nice' manners, and simpering performances on the piano are stupid and wasteful. Her view is too narrow, her understanding too limited, her ethic too much bound to that of her class to understand the true nature of the lives of these people.

Of the limitations of scene little need be said, for an author has the privilege of restricting the action to whatever background he thinks appropriate, and certainly as much can be said about the world and society in terms of Highbury as in terms of any other place. As Thomas Hardy confined the action of his novels to an area of only a few hundred square miles, and Emily Brontë that of *Wuthering Heights* to even less, we have no grounds for criticizing Jane Austen for limiting the events of *Emma* to a small village.

The limitations of subject, however, are of more importance. We have remarked that the novel is about courtship culminating in marriage, and thus we have every right to expect that the author will speak of love and its effect on the minds and thoughts of the characters. She does devote a great many pages to the manner in which a young lady of 1814 should find and 'seize' a husband, but of the passion of love little is said, I think for the obvious reason that

Jane Austen knew nothing of it firsthand. If her men and women feel the thrill of love, certainly the reader is never aware of the fact.

At this point we run the obvious risk of criticizing not Jane Austen but her characters, of condemning not her attitudes and feelings but those actually apparent in the society in which she lived; for English men and women of the middle class during the early years of the nineteenth century were reticent in matters of sex, and abided by conventions which today we consider foolish. The point is, however, that the novelist should rise above the particularities of her time and show her characters totally and in relation to mankind, and this is precisely what Jane Austen does not do. For example, much of the plot centers on the problem of a secret engagement – a gross sin in the eyes of Mrs Weston and the others, – and the reader is expected to take the matter seriously. Now it is legitimate for the novelist to say that the question of a secret engagement was important to Mrs Weston, but not that it is of the same importance to her. We expect the novelist to deal with more basic problems: of birth, death, love, work, leisure.

Perhaps a comparison will be useful at this point. *Clarissa Harlowe* begins as a tract on the necessity of filial devotion and obedience; had not the heroine disobeyed her father, she would not have been carried to a house of prostitution by the villainous lover. Now similar problems exist in our time, but not in the same terms and not in the same manner, and an entire novel devoted to an eighteenth-century version of the matter would be dull in the extreme except to a historian. However, Richardson soon expands the theme of the fiction to that of the eternal relationship between a man and a woman, and to the manner in which a society helps or hinders that relationship. We read the novel today not for the initial problem, but for the larger, more universal one. Had Jane Austen been similarly able to expand her view of the affair between Jane Fairfax and Frank Churchill, we might now be better able to enjoy the novel.

To return for a moment to the theme of courtship, we note that the same hints of social and economic conflict occur here as well. Harriet cannot marry Elton because she is illegitimate and has no money; Jane is forbidden to Frank because she is not of the proper station in life. Here an ambiguity of the novelist is revealed, for Jane Austen seems not quite sure what she should think on these matters. Although she ends the novel with suitable, conventional marriages for the main characters, and although her spokesman, Emma, is certainly bound to the accepted views of the age in most respects, yet several times, particularly in Emma's conversations with Harriet, there is apparent a certain freedom of opinion which is surprising. And when the true parentage of Harriet is discovered, when Emma learns that her father was a tradesman, she thinks (or is it Jane Austen?): 'Such was the blood of gentility which Emma had formerly been so ready to vouch for! It was likely to be as untainted, perhaps, as the blood of many a gentleman.' However, it is impossible to conclude precisely what were Jane Austen's opinions on these matters.

Summing up these limitations of substance, we can say that the intellectual and psychological understanding is so superficial and the range of characters so small that the novel has little meaning beyond the particularities of bourgeois courtship and marriage in England at the beginning of the nineteenth century. There is revealed in the book no attitude toward the major political, economic, psychological, or philosophical problems with which most novelists of importance since Richardson have more or less been concerned in their books. And if irony is the tone of *Emma*, the voice with which the author addresses her reader, it never carries any conception of the essential nature of man and society, which I take to be the ultimate subject of any good novel.

SOURCE: From '*Emma*: a dissenting opinion', in *Nineteenth-century Fiction*, IV (1949) 3–7.

Richard Poirier   Emma and Huck Finn   (1962)

In part, the objections to Jane Austen by Mark Twain[1] and American writers of roughly similar prejudice can be explained as a blindness to society as she imagines it. Their prejudice gets between even these illustrious readers and what in fact the work of Jane Austen does express about society and artifice. They are apparently unable to see, so alien to them is her positive vision of social experience, that she is fully aware of the dangers *in* society which for them are the dangers *of* it. The capacity to imagine society as including the threat of conformity and artificiality and as offering, nevertheless, beneficial opportunities for self-discovery is never evident in Emerson, only sporadically in James, and in Twain mostly in the works before *Huckleberry Finn* and inferior to it.

The contrast to Jane Austen, so obvious in a general way, can be meaningfully particularized. In *Emma*, for example, Mrs Elton imagines a party at Knightley's which will be held out of doors so that everything may be as 'natural and simple as possible'. ('I shall wear a large bonnet, and bring one of my little baskets hanging on my arm . . . a sort of gipsy party.') Knightley's reply, typically direct and restrained, affirms how much for Jane Austen, as for him, words like 'simple' and 'natural' can be defined very adequately by an uncomplicated observation of unfussy social habits:

'Not quite. My idea of the simple and the natural will be to have the table spread in the dining-room. The nature and simplicity of gentlemen and ladies, with their servants and furniture, I think is best observed by meals within doors. When you are tired of eating strawberries in the garden, there shall be cold meat in the house.'

The dramatic issue of the novel is in a sense whether or not Emma, as she herself fears just before the episode at Box Hill, is to be considered 'of Mrs Elton's party'. This, like every phrase in the episode, has an unmistakable resonance. To be 'of Mrs Elton's party' is a metaphor for submitting to social forms in which Mrs Elton's false, affected, and pretentious ideas of the 'natural' predominate, much as similar ideas fully control the society of *Huckleberry Finn*. Indeed, to be thought 'natural' by society in Twain's novel means that you must have acted artificially or imitated a prescribed role. The stakes for Jane Austen and her heroine are very high indeed – to prevent society from *becoming* what it is condemned for *being* in *Huckleberry Finn*.

Mark Twain cannot imagine a society in which his hero has any choice, if he is to remain in society at all, but to be 'of Tom Sawyer's party'. The evidence for such a comparative limitation on the hero – and, indeed, a justification for making a comparison to the greater freedom allowed Emma – is in the similarity between the situations of the two characters at the central crisis in each book. Beside the

famous picnic scene at Box Hill in *Emma*, when the heroine insults
Miss Bates, we can place the corresponding scene in *Huckleberry
Finn* when, in chapter 15, Huck also insults a social inferior who is
at the same time a trusting friend. The process by which each of
these insults comes about is roughly the same. Emma gradually
surrenders what is called her 'self-command' at Box Hill to the
theatrical urgings and flatteries of Frank Churchill, much as Huck
often acts in imitation of the 'style' of Tom Sawyer even when it ill
befits his own feelings and necessities. Emma literally forgets who
she is and therefore the identity of Miss Bates in relation to her, and
her witty retort to one of the older lady's simplicities expresses not
her true relationship to Miss Bates so much as the theatrical and
self-aggrandizing role which Churchill has encouraged her to play to
the whole group. Her social and psychological situation – and the
literary problem thus created – is much like Huck's at the similar
moment when imitation of Tom's role has led to his violation of the
bond between him and Jim. The central character in each novel has
violated a social contract by being artificial. Both recognize what
has happened and both make amends. But at this point there
appears an important and essential difference between the situations
of these two, and the difference is indicative of the problem in
American nineteenth-century fiction of imagining personal relationships within the context of social manners. Huck's recognition
cannot involve a choice, as can Emma's, against some forms of social
expression in favor of others: against the Frank Churchills, Mrs
Eltons (and Tom Sawyers) of this world, and for the Mr Knightleys.
Mark Twain simply cannot provide Huck with an alternative to
'games' that has any social viability or acceptance within the society
of the novel. Huck's promise to do Jim 'no more mean tricks' is, in
effect, a rejection of the only modes of expression understood by that
society. At a similar point Emma recognizes and rejects social
artifice and is then in a position to accept her natural place in society
as Knightley's wife.

Huck chooses at the end 'to light out for the Territory ahead of the
rest', while Emma, joined to Knightley in 'the perfect happiness of
the union', is both more firmly within the social group and yet saved
from all the false kinds of undiscriminating 'amiability' practised at
Box Hill. The ceremony is witnessed, significantly, not by the whole
community but by a 'small band of true friends'. 'Marriageable-
ness', as Emerson scornfully puts it, emphatically is Jane Austen's

subject. Marriage represents for her what he cannot imagine – not merely the act of choice within society but, more importantly, the union of social with natural inclinations. Naturalness and social form are fused in her work in a way that I do not think Emerson, Mark Twain of *Huckleberry Finn*, or even Henry James were able to recognize. It is no wonder that Mark Twain's difficulties begin at a comparable point where Jane Austen most brilliantly succeeds. *Huckleberry Finn* cannot dramatize the meaning accumulated at the moment of social crisis because the crisis itself reveals the inadequacy of the terms by which understandings can be expressed between the hero and the other members of his society. There is no publicly accredited vocabulary which allows Huck to reveal his inner self to others.

SOURCE: From 'Mark Twain, Jane Austen and the Imagination of Society', in *In Defense of Reading* (Dutton, 1962) pp. 282–309.

NOTE

1. In *Following the Equator* (1897) Mark Twain remarked of a ship's library: 'Jane Austen's books . . . are absent from this library. Just that one omission alone would make a fairly good library out of a library that hadn't a book in it.' His low opinion was developed at greater length in an unpublished manuscript entitled 'Jane Austen', described by Ian Watt in his Introduction to *Jane Austen: a collection of twentieth-century views* (New York, 1963) p. 7. [Ed.]

PART THREE

Modern Studies

Arnold Kettle   Emma   (1951)

> My strong point is those little things which are more important than big
> ones, because they make up life. It seems that big ones do not do that, and I
> daresay it is fortunate.
>
> I. Compton-Burnett: *A Family and a Fortune*

The subject of *Emma* is marriage. Put that way the statement seems
ludicrously inadequate, for *Emma* – we instinctively feel – is not
about anything that can be put into one word. And yet it is as well to
begin by insisting that this novel does have a subject. There is no
longer, especially after Mrs Leavis's articles, any excuse for thinking
of Jane Austen as an untutored genius or even as a kind aunt with a
flair for telling stories that have somehow or other continued to
charm. She was a serious and conscious writer, absorbed in her art,
wrestling with its problems. Casting and re-casting her material,
transferring whole novels from letter to narrative form, storing her
subject-matter with meticulous economy, she had the great artist's
concern with form and presentation. There is nothing soft about
her.[1]

Emma is about marriage. It begins with one marriage, that of
Miss Taylor, ends with three more and considers two others by the
way. The subject is marriage; but not marriage in the abstract.
There is nothing of the moral fable here; indeed it is impossible to
conceive of the subject except in its concrete expression, which is the
plot. If then, one insists that the subject of *Emma* is important it is
not in order to suggest that the novel can be read in the terms of
Jonathan Wild, but rather to counteract the tendency to treat plot or
story as self-sufficient. If it is not quite adequate to say that *Emma* is
about marriage it is also not adequate to say it is about Emma.

The concrete quality of the book, that is what has to be emphasized. We have no basic doubts about *Emma*. It is there, a living
organism, and it survives in the vibrations of its own being. In
Clarissa time and again our attention is shifted in a particular
direction not because it *must* be so directed but because Richardson
wishes to give his reader an 'exquisite sensation'; in *Tom Jones* the
happenings are too often contrived, so that we sense Fielding's
presence behind the scenes, pulling a string. But *Emma* lives with

the inevitable, interlocking logic of life itself; no part of it is separable
from any other part. Even those episodes of the plot which seem at
first mere contrivances to arouse a little suspense and keep the story
going (such as the mystery of the pianoforte, Jane's letters at the
post office, the confusion as to whether Harriet referred to Mr
Knightley or to Frank Churchill), such passages all have a more
important purpose. They reveal character, or they fail to reveal it.
This latter function is subtle and important.

Jane Austen, like Henry James, is fascinated by the complexities
of personal relationships. What is a character *really* like? Is Frank
Churchill *really* a bounder? She conveys the doubt, not in order to
trick, but in order to deepen. The more complex characters in
Emma, like people in life, reveal themselves gradually and not
without surprises. Putting aside for the moment certain minor faults
which we will return to, it is not an exaggeration to say that *Emma* is
as convincing as our own lives and has the same kind of concreteness.

It is for this reason that the subject of *Emma*, its generalized
significance, is not easily or even usefully abstracted from the story.
Just as in real life 'marriage' (except when we are considering it in a
very theoretical and probably not very helpful way) is not a problem
we abstract from the marriages we know, so marriage in *Emma* is
thought of entirely in terms of actual and particular personal relationships. If we learn more about marriage in general from Jane
Austen's novel it is because we have learned more – that is to say
experienced more – about particular marriages. We do, in fact, in
reading *Emma* thus enrich our experience. We become extremely
closely involved in the world of Highbury so that we experience the
precise quality of, say, Mr Woodhouse's affection for his daughters,
or Harriet's embarrassment at meeting the Martins in the draper's.
When Emma is rude to Miss Bates on Box Hill we *feel* the flush rise
to Miss Bates's cheek.

The intensity of Jane Austen's novels is inseparable from their
concreteness, and this intensity must be stressed because it is so
different from the charming and cosy qualities with which these
novels are often associated. Reading *Emma* is a delightful experience, but it is not a soothing one. On the contrary our faculties are
aroused, we are called upon to participate in life with an awareness,
a fineness of feeling, and a moral concern more intense than most of
us normally bring to our everyday experiences. Everything matters

in *Emma*. When Frank Churchill postpones his first visit to Randalls it matters less finely to Mr Weston than to his wife, but the reader gauges precisely the difference in the two reactions and not only appreciates them both but makes a judgment about them. We do not 'lose ourselves' in *Emma* unless we are the kind of people who lose ourselves in life. For all the closeness of our participation we remain independent.

Jane Austen does not demand (as Richardson tends to) that our subjective involvement should prejudice our objective judgment. On the contrary a valid objective judgment is made possible just because we have been so intimately involved in the actual experience. This seems to me a very valuable state of mind. How can we presume to pass judgment on the Emma Woodhouses of the world unless we have known them, and how can we valuably know them without bringing to bear our critical intelligence?

Because the critical intelligence is everywhere involved, because we are asked continuously, though not crudely, to judge what we are seeing, the prevailing interest in *Emma* is not one of mere 'aesthetic' delight but a moral interest. And because Jane Austen is the least theoretical of novelists, the least interested in Life as opposed to living, her ability to involve us intensely in her scene and people is absolutely inseparable from her moral concern. The moral is never spread on top; it is bound up always in the quality of feeling evoked.

Even when a moral conclusion is stated explicitly, as Mr Knightley states it after the Box Hill incident or while he reads Frank Churchill's letter of explanation, its force will depend not on its abstract 'correctness' but on the emotional conviction it carries, involving of course our already acquired confidence in Mr Knightley's judgment and character. Some of Mr Knightley's remarks, out of their context, might seem quite intolerably sententious. 'My Emma, does not everything serve to prove more and more the beauty of truth and sincerity in all our dealings with one another?' (III.XV).[2] The sentiment, abstracted, might serve for the conclusion of one of Hannah More's moral tales. In fact, in the novel, it is a moment of great beauty, backed as it is (even out of context the 'my Emma' may reveal something of the quality) by a depth of feeling totally convincing.

How does Jane Austen succeed in thus combining intensity with precision, emotional involvement with objective judgment? Part of the answer lies, I think, in her almost complete lack of idealism, the

delicate and unpretentious materialism of her outlook. Her judgment
is based never on some high-falutin irrelevancy but always on the
actual facts and aspirations of her scene and people. The clarity of her
social observation (the Highbury world is scrupulously seen and
analysed down to the exact incomes of its inmates) is matched by the
precision of her social judgments and all her judgments are, in the
broadest sense, social. Human happiness not abstract principle is her
concern. Such precision – it is both her incomparable strength and her
ultimate limitation – is unimaginable except in an extraordinarily
stable corner of society. The precision of her standards emerges in her
style. Each word – 'elegance', 'humour', 'temper', 'ease' – has a precise
unambiguous meaning based on a social usage at once subtle and
stable. Emma is considering her first view of Mrs Elton:

> She did not really like her. She would not be in a hurry to find fault, but
> she suspected that there was no elegance; – ease, but not elegance. – She
> was almost sure that for a young woman, a stranger, a bride, there was too
> much ease. Her person was rather good; her face not unpretty; but neither
> feature, nor air, nor voice, nor manner, were elegant. Emma thought at
> least it would turn out so.   (II. XIV)

The exquisite clarity, the sureness of touch, of Jane Austen's prose
cannot be recaptured because in different and quickly changing
society the same sureness of values cannot exist.

But to emphasize the stability and, inevitably too, the narrowness
of Jane Austen's society may lead us to a rather narrow and
mechanical view of the novels. *Emma* is *not* a period-piece. It is *not*
what is sometimes called a 'comedy of manners'. We read it not just
to illuminate the past, but also the present. And we must here face
in both its crudity and its importance the question: exactly what
relevance and helpfulness does *Emma* have for us today? In what
sense does a novel dealing (admittedly with great skill and realism)
with a society and its standards dead and gone for ever have value in
our very different world today? The question itself – stated in such
terms – is not satisfactory. If *Emma* today captures our imagination
and engages our sympathies (as in fact it does) then either it has
some genuine value for us, or else there is something wrong with the
way we give our sympathy, and our values are pretty useless.

Put this way, it is clear that anyone who enjoys *Emma* and then
remarks 'but of course it has no relevance today' is in fact debasing
the novel, looking at it not as the living work of art which he has just

enjoyed, but as something he does not even think it is – a mere dead picture of a past society. Such an attitude is fatal both to art and to life. The more helpful approach is to enquire why it is that this novel does in fact still have the power to move us today.

One has the space only to suggest one or two lines of considera-tion. The question has, I hope, been partly answered already. An extension of human sympathy and understanding is never irrelevant and the world of *Emma* is not presented to us (at any rate in its detail) with complacency. Emma faced with what she has done to Harriet, the whole humiliating horror of it, or Emma finding – the words are not minced – that, save for her feeling for Mr Knightley, 'every other part of her mind was disgusting': these are not insights calculated to decrease one's moral awareness. And in none of the issues of conduct arising in the novel is Jane Austen morally neutral. The intensity with which everything matters to us in *Emma* is the product of this lack of complacency, this passionate concern of Jane Austen for human values. Emma is the heroine of this novel only in the sense that she is its principal character and that it is through her consciousness that the situations are revealed; she is no heroine in the conventional sense. She is not merely spoilt and selfish, she is snobbish and proud, and her snobbery leads her to inflict suffering that might ruin happiness. She has, until her experience and her feeling for Mr Knightley brings her to a fuller, more humane under-standing, an attitude to marriage typical of the ruling class. She sees human relationships in terms of class snobbery and property qualifications: Harriet, for the sake of social position, she would cheerfully hand over to the wretched Elton and does in fact reduce to a humiliating misery; her chief concern about Mr Knightley is that his estate should be preserved for little Henry. It is only through her own intimate experiences (which we share) that she comes to a more critical and more fully human view.

The question of Jane Fairfax is relevant here. Many readers find her and her relationship with Frank Churchill less than fully convincing. Does she quite bear the full weight of admiration which clearly we are supposed to feel for her? If she is indeed the person she is intended to be, would she love Frank Churchill? Has not Jane Austen here failed, perhaps, completely to reconcile the character she has created and the plot and pattern to which she is committed?

I think it is worth pausing for a moment on these criticisms, in order to consider not only their justice (which can be fairly objectively tested by careful reading) but their relevance. May we not here be slipping into the undisciplined habit of judging a novel according to rather vague criteria of 'probability' or 'character'? We all know the old lady who doesn't like *Wuthering Heights* because it's so improbable and the old gentleman who reads Trollope for the characters (not to mention the 'Janeites' whose chief interest in *Emma* is to determine how many nursemaids Isabella Knightley brought with her to Hartfield); and we all know how unsatisfactory such criteria are when it comes to the point.

It is worth emphasizing, therefore, that a just criticism of Jane Fairfax has nothing to do with the question of whether we should like to meet her at dinner or even whether we think she acted rightly or wrongly. Jane Fairfax is a character in a novel. We know nothing of her except what we gather in the course of the novel. What we learn while we read (and we learn, of course, more than mere 'facts'), is that, although unduly reserved (for reasons which when revealed make the fault pardonable) she is a young woman of singular refinement and 'true elegance', a phrase carrying great significance ('elegance of mind' involves a genuine sensibility to human values as well as the more superficial refinements of polished manner). She is, moreover, especially singled out for commendation by Mr Knightley (whose judgment is recommended as invariably sound) and warmly liked (e.g. the very, very earnest shake of the hand) by Emma herself.

Now the critical question is whether the reader can be convinced that this Jane Fairfax would in fact play her essential part in the novel and marry Frank Churchill, a young man whose total quality is a good deal less than admirable. Many readers are not convinced. Are they right?

I think they are not right. It is true that Jane Fairfax is – we have been convinced – as good as she is clever and as clever as she is beautiful. But it is also true that Jane Fairfax is an unprovided woman with no prospects in life beyond those of earning her living as governess at Mrs Smallridge's (and how well the nature of that establishment has been revealed to us though Mrs Elton!) and passing her hard-earned holiday with Miss Bates. The quality of Jane's reaction to such a future has been clearly indicated:

'I am not at all afraid [she says to Mrs Elton] of being long unemployed. There are places in town, offices, where enquiry would soon produce something – Offices for the sale – not quite of human flesh – but of human intellect.'

'Oh! my dear, human flesh! You quite shock me; if you mean a fling at the slave-trade I assure you Mr Suckling was always rather a friend to the abolition.'

'I did not mean, I was not thinking of the slave-trade' replied Jane; 'governess-trade, I assure you, was all that I had in view; widely different certainly as to the guilt of those who carry it on; but as to the greater misery of the victims, I do not know where it lies. . .'   (II. XVII)

It is her horror of this alternative (notice the extraordinary force of the word 'offices'; the sentence is broken in the sense of degradation) that those who are unconvinced by Jane's decision to marry Frank Churchill have, I think, overlooked. Perhaps all this makes Jane Fairfax less 'good' than Emma thought her; but it does not make her less convincing to us. On the contrary a good deal of the moral passion of the book, as of her other novels, does undoubtedly arise from Jane Austen's understanding of and feeling about the problems of women in her society. It is this realistic, unromantic, and indeed, by orthodox standards, subversive concern with the position of women that gives the tang and force to her consideration of marriage. Jane Fairfax's marriage has not, indeed, been made in heaven, and it is unlikely that Frank Churchill will turn out to be an ideal husband; but is that not precisely Jane Austen's point?

More vulnerable is the marrying-off of Harriet Smith and Robert Martin. Here it is not the probability that is to be questioned but the manner. The treatment is altogether too glib and the result is to weaken the pattern of the novel. Since the experiences of Emma – her blunders and romanticisms – are the core of the book, and what most intimately illuminate the theme of marriage, it is essential to Jane Austen's plan that these experiences should be in no way muffled or sentimentalized. We must feel the whole force of them. The marriage of Harriet is presented in a way which does, to some extent, sentimentalize. Emma is allowed too easy a way out of her problem and the emotional force of the situation is thereby weakened. The objection is too conventional a sense of happy ending is not that it is happy (we do not question that) but that it is conventional and so lulls our feelings into accepting it too easily.

Sufficient has perhaps been said to suggest that what gives *Emma* its power to move us is the realism and depth of feeling behind Jane Austen's attitudes. She examines with a scrupulous yet passionate and critical precision the actual problems of her world. That this world is narrow cannot be denied. How far its narrowness matters is an important question.

Its *smallness* does not matter at all. There is no means of measuring importance by size. What is valuable in a work of art is the depth and truth of the experience it communicates, and such qualities cannot be identified with the breadth of the panorama. We may find out more about life in a railway carriage between Crewe and Manchester than in making a tour round the world. A conversation between two women in the butcher's queue may tell us more about a world war than a volume of despatches from the front. And when Emma says to Mr Knightley: 'Nobody, who has not been in the interior of a family, can say what the difficulties of any individual of that family may be', she is dropping a valuable hint about Jane Austen's method. The silliest of all criticisms of Jane Austen is the one which blames her for not writing about the battle of Waterloo and the French Revolution. She wrote about what she understood and no artist can do more.

But did she understand enough? The question is not a silly one, for it must be recognized that her world was not merely small but narrow. Her novels are sometimes referred to as miniatures, but the analogy is not apt. We do not get from *Emma* a condensed and refined sense of a larger entity. Neither is it a symbolic work suggesting references far beyond its surface meaning. The limitations of the Highbury world, which are indeed those of Surrey in about 1814, are likely therefore to be reflected in the total impact of the novel.

The limitation and the narrowness of the Highbury world is the limitation of class society. And the one important criticism of Jane Austen (we will suspend judgment for the moment on its truth) is that her vision is limited by her unquestioning acceptance of class society. That she did not write about the French Revolution or the Industrial Revolution is as irrelevant as that she did not write about the Holy Roman Empire; they were not her subjects. But Highbury is her subject and no sensitive contemporary reader can fail to sense here an inadequacy (again, we will suspend judgment on its validity). It is necessary to insist, at this point, that the question at issue is not Jane Austen's failure to suggest a *solution* to the problem of class divisions but her apparent failure to notice the *existence* of the problem.

The values and standards of the Highbury world are based on the assumption that it is right and proper for a minority of the community to live at the expense of the majority. No amount of sophistry can get away from this fact and to discuss the moral concern of Jane Austen without facing it would be hypocrisy. It is perfectly true that, within the assumptions of aristocratic society, the values recommended in *Emma* are sensitive enough. Snobbery, smugness, condescension, lack of consideration, unkindness of any description, are held up to our disdain. But the fundamental condescension, the basic unkindness which permits the sensitive values of *Emma* to be applicable only to one person in ten or twenty, is this not left unscathed? Is there not here a complacency which renders the hundred little incomplacencies almost irrelevant?

Now this charge, that the value of *Emma* is seriously limited by the class basis of Jane Austen's standards, cannot be ignored or written off as a nonliterary issue. If the basic interest of the novel is indeed a moral interest, and if in the course of it we are called upon to re-examine and pass judgment on various aspects of human behaviour, then it can scarcely be considered irrelevant to face the question that the standards we are called upon to admire may be inseparably linked with a particular form of social organization.

That the question is altogether irrelevant will be held, of course, by the steadily decreasing army of aesthetes. Those who try to divorce the values of art from those of life and consequently morality will not admit that the delight we find in reading *Emma* has in fact a moral basis. It is a position, I think, peculiarly hard to defend in the case of a Jane Austen novel, because of the obvious preoccupation of the novelist with social morality. If *Emma* is *not* concerned with the social values involved in and involving personal relationships (and especially marriage) it is difficult to imagine what it *is* about.

That the question though relevant is trivial will be held by those readers who consider class society either good or inevitable. Clearly, to those who think aristocracy today a morally defensible form of society, and are prepared to accept (with whatever modifications and protestations of innocence) the inevitability of a cultural *élite* whose superior standards depend on a privileged social position based on the exploitation of their inferiors, clearly such readers will not feel that Jane Austen's acceptance of class society weakens or limits her moral perspicacity. The suspicion that the true elegance which Emma so values could not exist in Highbury without the condemnation to servility and poverty of hundreds of unnamed (though not necessarily unpitied) human beings will not trouble their minds as they admire the civilized sensibility of Jane Austen's social standards. The position of such readers cannot of course be objected to on logical grounds so long as all its implications are accepted.

At the other extreme of critical attitudes will be found those readers whose sense of the limitations of Jane Austen's social consciousness makes it impossible for them to value the book at all. How can I feel sympathy, such a reader will say, for characters whom I see to be, for all their charm and politeness, parasites and exploiters? How can I feel that the problems of such a society have a relevance to me? Now if art were a matter of abstract morality it would be impossible to argue against this puritan attitude; but in truth it misses the most essential thing of all about *Emma*, that it is a warm and living work of art. To reject *Emma* outright is to reject the humanity in *Emma*, either to dismiss the delight and involvement that we feel as we read it as an unfortunate aberration, or else to render ourselves immune to its humanity by imposing upon it an attitude narrower than itself.

More sophisticated than this philistine attitude to the problem is that which will hold that *Emma* does indeed reflect the class basis and limitations of Jane Austen's attitudes, but that this really does not matter very much or seriously affect its value. This is a view, plausible at first sight, held by a surprisingly large number of readers who want to have their novel and yet eat it. Yes indeed, such a reader will say, the moral basis of Jane Austen's novels is, for us, warped by her acceptance of class society; her standards obviously can't apply in a democratic society where the Emmas and Knightleys would have to work for their living like anyone else. But, after all, we must remember when Jane Austen was writing; we must approach the novels with sympathy in their historical context. Jane Austen, a genteel bourgeoise of the turn of the eighteenth century, could scarcely be expected to analyse class society in modern terms. We must make a certain allowance, reading the book with a willing suspension of our own ideas and prejudices.

This represents a view of literature which, behind an apparently historical approach, debases and nullifies the effects of art. It invites us to read *Emma* not as a living, vital novel, relevant to our own lives and problems, but as a dead historical 'document'. A work of art which has to be read in such a way is not a work of art. The very concept of 'making allowances' of this sort for an artist is both insulting and mechanical. It has something of the puritan's contempt for those who have not seen the light, but it lacks the puritan's moral courage, for it is accompanied by a determination not to be done out of what cannot be approved. The final result is generally to come to terms with the aesthetes. For if *Emma* is morally undesirable and yet Art, then Art can have little to do with morality and some new, necessarily idealist, criteria must be found.

It is important, I believe, to realize the weakness of this pseudo-historical view of *Emma*. If, in whatever century she happened to live, Jane Austen were indeed nothing but a genteel bourgeoise 'reflecting' the views of her day, she would not be a great artist and she could not have written *Emma*. The truth is that in so far as *Emma* does reveal her as a conventional member of her class, blindly accepting its position and ideology, the value of *Emma* is indeed limited, not just relatively, but objectively and always. But the truth is also that this is not the principal or most important revelation of *Emma*.

The limitation must not be ignored or glossed over. There can be no doubt that there *is* an inadequacy here, an element of complacency that does to some extent limit the value of *Emma*. The nature of the inadequacy is fairly illustrated by this description of Emma's visit, with Harriet, to a sick cottager:

They were now approaching the cottage, and all idle topics were superseded. Emma was very compassionate; and the distresses of the poor were as sure of relief from her personal attention and kindness, her counsel and her patience, as from her purse. She understood their ways, could allow for their ignorance and their temptations, had no romantic expectations of extraordinary virtue from those, for whom education had done so little; entered into their troubles with ready sympathy, and always gave her assistance with as much intelligence as good-will. In the present instance, it was sickness and poverty together which she came to visit; and after remaining there as long as she could give comfort or advice, she quitted the cottage with such an impression of the scene as made her say to Harriet, as they walked away,

'These are the sights, Harriet, to do one good. How trifling they make every thing else appear! – I feel now as if I could think of nothing but these poor creatures all the rest of the day; and yet, who can say how soon it may all vanish from my mind?'

'Very true,' said Harriet. 'Poor creatures! one can think of nothing else.'

'And really, I do not think the impression will soon be over,' said Emma, as she crossed the low hedge and tottering footstep which ended the narrow, slippery path through the cottage garden, and brought them into the lane again. 'I do not think it will,' stopping to look once more at all the outward wretchedness of the place, and recall the still greater within.

'Oh! dear, no,' said her companion. They walked on. The lane made a slight bend; and when that bend was passed, Mr Elton was immediately in sight; and so near as to give Emma time only to say farther,

'Ah! Harriet, here comes a very sudden trial of our stability in good thoughts. Well, (smiling), I hope it may be allowed that if compassion has produced exertion and relief to the sufferers, it has done all that is truly important. If we feel for the wretched, enough to do all we can for them, the rest is empty sympathy, only distressing to ourselves.'

Harriet could just answer. 'Oh! dear, yes,' before the gentleman joined them.   (I.x)

Now there can be no doubt about the quality of the feeling here. Harriet's silly responses underline most potently the doubt that Emma herself feels as to the adequacy of her own actions. There can be no point in this passage (for it has no inevitable bearing on the plot) save to give a sense of the darker side of the moon, the aspect of Highbury that will not be dealt with. And it does indeed to a great extent answer the doubt in the reader's mind that an essential side of the Highbury world is being conveniently ignored. But the doubt is not entirely answered. After all, the important question is not whether Emma recognizes the existence of the poor at Highbury, but whether she recognizes that her own position depends on their existence. 'Comfort or advice' moreover remain the positives in Emma's attitudes and one's doubts as to their sufficiency are in fact, like Emma's, swept away by the arrival of Mr Elton and the plot. The essential moral issue is shelved; and it is, in general, the supreme merit of Jane Austen, that essential moral issues are *not* shelved.

But that the inadequacy is not crippling the passage just quoted will also suggest. That final remark of Emma's is very significant. The parenthesized 'smiling' and the idiocy of Harriet's comment have the effect of throwing into doubt the whole aristocratic philosophy that Emma is expounding and that doubt, though it does not balance the shelving of the problem, does at least extenuate it. We are not wholly lulled.

Against the element of complacency other forces, too, are at work. We should not look merely to the few specific references to the poor to confirm our sense that the inadequacies of Jane Austen's social philosophy are overtopped by other, more positive vibrations. Among these positive forces are, as we have seen, her highly critical concern over the fate of women in her society, a concern which involves a reconsideration of its basic values. Positive also are her materialism and her unpretentiousness. If aristocracy is implicitly defended it is at least on rational grounds; no bogus philosophical sanctions are called in to preserve the *status quo* from reasonable examination. And no claim is made, explicit or implicit, that we are being presented with a revelation of a fundamental truth. Highbury is offered to us as Highbury, not as Life.

And this is ultimately, I think, the strength of *Emma*: this rejection of Life in favour of living, the actual, concrete problems of behaviour and sensibility in an actual, concrete society. It is Jane Austen's sensitive vitality, her genuine concern (based on so large an honesty) for human feelings in a concrete situation, that captures our imagination. It is this concern that gives her such delicate and precise insight into the problems of personal relationships (how will a group of individuals living together best get on, best find happiness?). And the concern does not stop at what, among the ruling class at Highbury, is pleasant and easily solved.

It gives us glimpses of something Mr Woodhouse never dreamed of – the world outside the Highbury world and yet inseparably bound up with it: the world Jane Fairfax saw in her vision of offices and into which Harriet in spite of (no, *because of*) Emma's patronage, was so nearly plunged: the world for which Jane Austen had no answer. It is this vital and unsentimental concern which defeats, to such a very large extent, the limitations. So that when we think back on *Emma* we do not think principally of the narrow inadequacies of Highbury society but of the delight we have known in growing more intimately and wisely sensitive to the way men and women in a particular, given situation, work out their problems of living.

SOURCE: 'Jane Austen: *Emma*' from *An Introduction to the English Novel*, I (Hutchinson, 1951) pp. 90–104.

NOTES

1. Mrs Leavis has emphasized, too, how strong a part in Jane Austen's novels is played by her conscious war on the romance. She did to the romance of her day (whether the domestic romance of Fanny Burney or the Gothic brand of Mrs Radcliffe) what Cervantes had done in his. *Pride and Prejudice* is as much an anti-*Cecilia* as *Northanger Abbey* is an anti-*Udolpho*.

2. Parenthetical references are to the part and chapter numbers in the Chapman edition of *Emma* (Oxford, 1926).

Marvin Mudrick   Irony as Form: Emma   (1952)

Emma is a throwing off of chains. The author and her characters move with a freedom and assurance unparalleled in Jane Austen's earlier work, and all the more astonishing by contrast with the uneasy stiffness of *Mansfield Park*. The new impetus is her old familiar one, but – from our first impression of *Emma* – purely assimilated to the medium as, in *Northanger Abbey* or even in *Pride and Prejudice*, it is not: the impetus is irony. In *Emma*, the sense of strain and anxiety is purged altogether. This time the author is in her novel and never out of it, never imposing upon us as in *Northanger Abbey* with her condescension or in *Pride and Prejudice* with her occasional prim moral reminders; and she is there for the comic artist's purpose only – to embody and direct our laughter.

The relaxation of an achieved technique is the very climate of *Emma*. Certainly, no other of Jane Austen's novels offers so pleasant and comfortable an atmosphere, so much the effect of an uncomplex and immediate art: wit, irony, light laughter shining in a triumph of surface. Its surface is, in fact, unmarred by a trace of self-justification, ill humor, or back-sliding into morality. The story tells itself, and nothing seems more superfluous than inquiry or deep thought about it.[1]

Emma, like *Pride and Prejudice*, is a story of self-deception, and the problem of each heroine is to undeceive herself. Yet Emma needs, not facts, but people, to help her. If Elizabeth Bennet is self-deceived under a set of special, doubtful circumstances, if she waits mainly for facts, Emma Woodhouse is a girl absolutely self-deceived, who takes and refashions whatever circumstances may arise, who can be checked only by a personality as positive as her own. We follow Emma's comic train of misunderstandings in the happy conviction that she cannot act otherwise until someone with will and intelligence takes her in hand – someone like Mr Knightley, for example. We sympathize with Emma because she *must* fall in love, and we are relaxed because we know that she will. The love story in *Emma* is, then, predetermined to a degree unimaginable in *Pride and Prejudice*; for all Elizabeth needs in order to see is to have the facts before her, while Emma – in spite of her will and intelligence – cannot even begin to see clearly or steadily until Mr Knightley tells her what is there.

Everything, it seems, is made as easy for us as for Mr Woodhouse. Emma is provided from the beginning with a man not only admirable, but indispensable to her education. We need not worry about that. We have no financial anxiety: Emma is an 'heiress of thirty thousand pounds.' Rank is no problem: Emma is herself of an 'ancient family', and her potential lover has an ancestry equally antique. Precedence is no problem: for Emma reigns alone at Hartfield and over Highbury, unencumbered by sisters, aunts, tyrannical parents or guardians, or petty nobility. Emma is, of course, habitually self-deceived; yet Mr Knightley will come to the rescue: and we can read the novel, with no discomfort and only a pleasant minimum of suspense, as the ironic portrait of a girl who falls into mild self-deception and whose trustworthy friend always and finally helps her out.

Emma likes to manage things. Brought up by a doting governess, mistress of her father's house, almost from her childhood obliged to manage her invalid father, Emma – not surprisingly – wishes to dominate elsewhere as well; and the wish to dominate, unimpeded by anxieties over wealth or rank, quickly translates itself into action. It is not surprising that, after her governess leaves to be married, Emma takes on a protégée, especially one so malleable as Harriet Smith, and that in her extension of self-conceit she persuades herself that Harriet can trap into marriage men whose rank and ambition would lead them to aspire even to Emma. It is not surprising that Emma feels confident of her ability to manage Mr Elton or Frank Churchill – everyone, in fact, except Mr Knightley.

It is Mr Knightley who sets us at ease. His acute and decisive mind circumscribes Emma always, keeps her from the gravest consequences of her mistakes, enlightens her when she commits a particularly flagrant snobbery or stupidity, as at Box Hill after her brutal insult to Miss Bates:

'Her situation should secure your compassion. It was badly done, indeed! – You, whom she had known from an infant, whom she has seen grow up from a period when her notice was an honour, to have you now, in thoughtless spirits, and the pride of the moment, laugh at her, humble her – and before her niece, too – and before others, many of whom (certainly *some*,) would be entirely guided by *your* treatment of her. – This is not pleasant to you,

Emma – and it is very far from pleasant to me; but I must, I will – I will tell
you truths while I can, satisfied with proving myself your friend by very
faithful counsel, and trusting that you will some time or other do me greater
justice than you can do now.'   (375)[2]

We know that this will bring Emma up sharply, as it very satisfactorily does. Through all of Emma's self-deceptions, we feel Mr
Knightley's reassuring nearness; and we know that nothing can go
crucially wrong.

Nowhere else is Jane Austen so relaxed, so certain, skilled, and
exact in her effects. There is no excess; almost no sense of plot in this
delicate ordering of a small calm world, the miniature world of the
English rural gentry at the start of the nineteenth century. The ease
of style and setting predisposes us to an easy response, prepares us
for a mellowing, even a softening, of Jane Austen's newly reasserted
irony. The characters of *Emma* seem our familiars at once, in what
has been called – with a dangerous patness – 'the absolute triumph
of that reliance on the strictly ordinary which has been indicated as
Miss Austen's title to pre-eminence in the history of the novel'.[3]

Emma herself seems one of the most attractive of all heroines:
beautiful, cultivated, intelligent; solicitous of her father; inclined to
snobbery and to rash judgment, but appealing even in her errors
and caprices. There is more, but it does not bear out our preconcep-
tion. Mr Knightley is a man of integrity, of force, wit, and high
sense, and – we suspect – rather too good for Emma; but this is just
a suspicion. Frank Churchill is an elegant and engaging trifler,
whose secret courtship of Jane Fairfax, the worthy girl in unworthy
circumstances, comes finally to light as his only recommendation.
The yielding Mrs Weston, as Emma's sympathetic confidante,
recalls to us the yielding Miss Taylor who could only have given way
before her pupil's precocious wilfulness; so that with her we add to
our stock of good reasons why Emma is what she is. The author
provides us with five varieties of nonentity, will-less comic foils to
Emma's wilfulness: Harriet, the obliging; Mr Woodhouse, the
gently querulous; Mr Weston the congenial; Isabella, the domestic;
and Miss Bates, the interminably talkative. John Knightley sets off
his brother's forthrightness by presenting the same quality with a
bristly manner and a touch of misanthropy. For villains – harmless enough to be only amusing – the author gives us the Eltons:
Mr Elton, a pillar of meanly aspiring egotism; and his perfectly
appropriate wife, Augusta, radiating that field of monomaniac

affectation and self-deceit which no sarcasm or earthly judgment can penetrate.

These are Jane Austen's creatures in her new mild climate, and at the end she placidly disposes of them all: nobody left out, no strand left unwoven, nobody unhappy. The plot is fulfilled when the characters are placed where they wish to be: Emma with Mr Knightley, Frank Churchill with Jane Fairfax, Mr Elton with his Augusta, motherly Mrs Weston with her first child; everybody at Hartfield, Donwell, Randalls, and Highbury comfortably settled.

Still, as we follow her attentively, Emma comes to appear less and less an innocuous figure in a novel of simply irony. She begins as a representative young gentlewoman of her age: snobbish, half-educated, wilful, possessive; and, certainly, her consciousness of rank accounts for a good many of her prejudices and cruelties. The fact remains that Emma has unpleasant qualities, which persist in operating and having effect. Whether we try to explain these qualities on the ground of upbringing or youth or personal impulse, we cannot blind ourselves to them. They are there, embedded in the novel.

Emma is, of course, an inveterate snob. Having defined her attitude toward the yeomanry,

'precisely the order of people with whom I feel I can have nothing to do. A degree or two lower, and a creditable appearance might interest me; I might hope to be useful to their families in some way or other. But a farmer can need none of my help, and is therefore in one sense as much above my notice as in every other he is below it.'   (29)

she advises (or, more accurately, commands) Harriet to decline Robert Martin's proposal:

'Dear affectionate creature! – *You* banished to Abbey-Mill Farm! – *You* confined to the society of the illiterate and vulgar all your life! I wonder how the young man would have the assurance to ask it.'   (54)

Without having seen Mrs Elton, Emma dismisses her at once upon learning that she

brought no name, no blood, no alliance. Miss Hawkins was the youngest of the two daughters of a Bristol – merchant, of course, he must be called; but, as the whole of the profits of his mercantile life appeared so very moderate, it was not unfair to guess the dignity of his line of trade had been very moderate also.   (183)

She decides to turn down an invitation from the Coles because, though they

were very respectable in their way . . . they ought to be taught that it was not for them to arrange the terms on which the superior families would visit them. This lesson, she very much feared, they would receive only from herself; she had little hope of Mr Knightley, none of Mr Weston.   (207)

Her first thought is always of rank and family. She regards Mr Knightley's possible attachment to Jane Fairfax as a 'very shameful and degrading connection'; and although here she has other reasons, yet unknown to herself, for objecting, it is significant that her first target is Jane's family. She thinks with satisfaction of the Knightleys as a 'family of . . . true gentility, untainted in blood and understanding'. When Harriet turns out to be only the daughter of a tradesman, 'Such was the blood of gentility', Emma reflects, which she

had formerly been so ready to vouch for! – It was likely to be as untainted, perhaps, as the blood of many a gentleman: but what a connexion had she been preparing for Mr Knightley – or for the Churchills – or even for Mr Elton! – The stain of illegitimacy, unbleached by nobility or wealth, would have been a stain indeed.   (482)

Nor are we allowed to charge these snobberies wholly to the temper of her class and age, since they draw rebukes for her not only from Mrs Weston, on the subject of Jane's suitableness for Mr Knightley, but, on her attitude toward Robert Martin as well as toward Miss Bates (375), from the impeccably pure-blooded Mr Knightley himself.

Emma has neglected the genteel feminine accomplishments, and cannot endure being reminded of her neglect. Shamed by Jane's superior playing on the piano, she detests her more unjustly than ever. She sketches a fair likeness of Harriet; and the immoderate praise of her subject and Mr Elton, though it cannot delude her, is enough to flatter her ego into silence:

She was not much deceived as to her own skill either as an artist or a musician, but she was not unwilling to have others deceived, or sorry to know her reputation for accomplishment often higher than it deserved. (44)

Yet Mr Knightley remarks, 'I do not think her personally vain. Considering how very handsome she is, she appears to be little occupied with it' (39). She lacks, that is, the customary vanity that

springs from the desire to please a suitor or lover; Mr Knightley
adds: 'her vanity lies another way. Mrs Weston, I am not to be
talked out of my dislike of her intimacy with Harriet Smith, or my
dread of its doing them both harm' (39).

It is true that much of Emma's unpleasantness can be attributed
to her consciousness of rank. In her class, family is the base,
property the outward symbol, and suitable marriage the goal; and
family and property are the chief criteria of acceptability for Emma.
Marriage, however, she dismisses as a goal for herself:

> 'Were I to fall in love, indeed, it would be a different thing! but I never have
> been in love; it is not my way, or my nature; and I do not think I ever shall.
> And, without love, I am sure I should be a fool to change such a situation as
> mine. Fortune I do not want; employment I do not want; consequence I do
> not want: I believe few married women are half as much mistress of their
> husband's house as I am of Hartfield; and never, never could I expect to be
> so truly beloved and important; so always first and always right in any
> man's eyes as I am in my father's.'   (84)

Emma deals only in measurable quantities: anything uncertain is to
be dismissed, avoided; and marriage, however neatly and by a
balance of tangibles she may arrange it for others, seems for her both
an uncertainty and an abasement.

Emma is an arranger, a manager of other people's affairs.
Accustomed to look after her father's every whim and to forestall his
every possible discomfort, she tries to extend this duty over her circle
of friends and acquaintances as well. Yet she prophesies only what
she wills, and she is always wrong. She will never admit what she
herself has not contrived, until the truth strikes her in the face. She is
wrong about Mr Elton's feelings toward Harriet. She quite miscon-
ceives her own feelings toward Mr Knightley. Baffled and angered
by Jane Fairfax's reserve, she creates without a shred of evidence the
most outrageous slander about an affair she imagines Jane to have
had with another woman's husband; and she is even ready to pass
her slander on to Churchill:

> I do not mean to reflect upon the good intentions of either Mr Dixon or Miss
> Fairfax, but I cannot help suspecting either that, after making his proposals
> to her friend, he had the misfortune to fall in love with *her,* or that he
> became conscious of a little attachment on her side. One might guess twenty
> things without guessing exactly the right; but I am sure there must be a
> particular cause for her chusing to come to Highbury instead of going with
> the Campbells to Ireland. Here, she must be leading a life of privation and
> penance; there it would have been all enjoyment.   (217)

She is wrong about Harriet's feelings toward Churchill. She complacently fabricates an entire love affair between Churchill and
herself – including its decline and dissolution – with no more
encouragement than the gentleman's adroit and uncommitting
flirtation; yet throughout this imaginary affair she reiterates her
'resolution ... of never marrying' (206): for though Emma can
imagine everything else, she cannot imagine her own commitment.
She is wrong about Mr Knightley's feelings toward both Harriet and
herself. Even when she has recognized her own love for Mr
Knightley and heard his declaration joyfully, she finds the duty of
remaining with her father superior to the claim of love: 'a very short
parley with her own heart produced the most solemn resolution of
never quitting her father'. She is ready, then, to alter everyone's life
but her father's, which is after all only a shadowy extension of her
own.

   Emma is occupied in altering, as she sees fit, the lives of others;
and to this end any means will do. If, to save Harriet for gentility,
Robert Martin must be made unhappy, he is merely another
obstacle to be set aside with no more than a moment's uneasiness;
so, after Emma's quarrel with Mr Knightley over her intervention:

'... I only want to know that Mr Martin is not very, very bitterly
disappointed.'
   'A man cannot be more so,' was his short, full answer.
   'Ah! – Indeed I am very sorry. – Come, shake hands with me.'
                                                              (99)

Even death, the death of Mrs Churchill, is for Emma a means,
serving to freshen her wholly fanciful hope for a match between
Churchill and Harriet:

The character of Mrs Churchill, the grief of her husband – her mind
glanced over them both with awe and compassion – and then rested with
lightened feelings on how Frank might be affected by the event, how
benefited, how freed. She saw in a moment all the possible good. Now, an
attachment to Harriet Smith would have nothing to encounter.   (388)

The personal, as personal, cannot engage Emma for more than a
moment: her mind cannot rest upon it without making it over
altogether into a means.

   Emma claims the role of adviser, but denies its responsibility. She
delights in bullying anyone who will yield – poor Harriet most of all:

'Dear Harriet, I give myself joy of this. It would have grieved me to
lose your acquaintance, which must have been the consequence of
your marrying Mr Martin' (53) yet at the last, unwilling to face
Harriet after her own disastrous series of errors in her protégée's
affairs, she limits her compunction and their relationship to letters:

Harriet expressed herself very much as might be supposed, without
reproaches, or apparent sense of ill usage; and yet Emma fancied there was
a something of resentment, a something bordering on it in her style, which
increased the desirableness of their being separate. – It might be only her
own consciousness; but it seemed as if an angel only could have been quite
without resentment under such a stroke.   (451)

and Emma is utterly relieved when Harriet falls into the patient
arms of Robert Martin: 'She must laugh at such a close! Such an end
of the doleful disappointment of five weeks back! Such a heart – such
a Harriet!' (475). Far from examining the past, Emma absolves herself of it. Even when Harriet's confession of love for Mr Knightley
has roused Emma to the pitch of self-analysis, Emma's outcry sinks
easily into the luxury of an acknowledged defeat – 'She was most
sorrowfully indignant; ashamed of every sensation but the one
revealed to her – her affection for Mr Knightley. – Every other part
of her mind was disgusting' (412) – the act of self-abasement that
claims sin, in order to avoid the responsibility of self-knowledge.
     Emma and Harriet are the most unexpected companions in all of
Jane Austen's work. Nor may we pass off their intimacy – at least
from Emma's side – as the effect of blind adolescent exuberance.
Emma is already a worldly twenty-one; and she is aware enough of
Harriet's intellectual limitations to comment ironically on Mr
Elton's charade: 'Harriet's ready wit! All the better. A man must be
very much in love indeed, to describe her so' (72). Emma has no
intellectual ties with the unalterably sheeplike Harriet, and she can
gain no material advantage from her friendship. Of course, Emma
likes to manage people, and Harriet is manageable. But why
Harriet, of all people; and why so tenaciously Harriet, at least until
every trick has failed?
     Emma observes Harriet's beauty with far more warmth than
anyone else: 'She was so busy in admiring those soft blue eyes, in
talking and listening, and forming all these schemes in the in-
betweens, that the evening flew away at a very unusual rate' (24).
This is the clever and sophisticated Emma, transported by the

presence of the most insipid girl imaginable. Moreover, Emma's
attention never falls so warmly upon a man; against this feeling for
Harriet, her good words for Mr Knightley's appearance seem pale
indeed. Emma will excuse low birth in no one else, but Harriet's
parentless illegitimacy she will talk away with nonsense about gentle
lineage:

> 'The misfortune of your birth ought to make you particularly careful as to
> your associates. There can be no doubt of your being a gentleman's
> daughter, and you must support your claim to that station by every thing
> within your own power, or there will be plenty of people who would take
> pleasure in degrading you.'   (30)

To Mr Knightley, Emma maintains heatedly that since men are
attracted by pretty faces Harriet will have all she wants of handsome
offers:

> 'she is . . . a beautiful girl, and must be thought so by ninety-nine out of
> a hundred; and till it appears that men are much more philosophic on the
> subject of beauty than they are generally supposed; till they do fall in love
> with well-informed minds instead of handsome faces, a girl, with such
> loveliness as Harriet, has a certainty of being admired and sought after, of
> having the power of choosing from among many, consequently a claim to be
> nice.'   (63)

Nor is she moved, except to discomfort, by Mr Knightley's natural
objection:

> 'Miss Harriet Smith may not find offers of marriage flow in so fast, though
> she is a very pretty girl. Men of sense, whatever you may chuse to say, do
> not want silly wives. Men of family would not be very fond of connecting
> themselves with a girl of such obscurity – and most prudent men would be
> afraid of the inconvenience and disgrace they might be involved in, when
> the mystery of her parentage came to be revealed.'   (64)

Emma merely lies about her hopes for Harriet with Mr Elton, and
keeps her opinion intact. Yet – with the exception of the young
farmer, Robert Martin – not one man through the range of the novel
ever shows the slightest interest in Harriet. When Emma tries to
cool the ardent Mr Elton in the coach by asserting that his
attentions have been directed not toward her but toward Harriet, he
rejects the very notion with horror:

> 'Good heaven! . . . what can be the meaning of this? – Miss Smith! – I
> never thought of Miss Smith in the whole course of my existence – never

paid her any attentions, but as your friend: never cared whether she were dead or alive, but as your friend.'   (130)

No one, it seems, is attracted by *this* pretty face except Emma.

Harriet draws her unqualified confidence as only one other person does: Mrs Weston. Mrs Weston has been her affectionate governess, and continued affection between them is natural enough. But Emma's regard reaches the same noteworthy excess as with Harriet. Emma has imagined herself to be falling in love with Frank Churchill; now he and Mrs Weston, who is his stepmother, come upon her together:

She was wanting to see him again, and especially to see him in company with Mrs Weston, upon his behaviour to whom her opinion of him was to depend. If he were deficient there, nothing should make amends for it. (196)

One assumes that not even imagining herself in love with him could impel Emma to forgive Churchill's possible coolness toward his stepmother.

Emma's attitude toward young men – when she is not trying to drive them into Harriet's arms – touches now and then upon the thought of a suitable marriage for herself. With Churchill she can sustain the idea of marriage just as long as it remains an idea, a neat, appropriate, socially approved arrangement:

She had frequently thought – especially since his father's marriage with Miss Taylor – that if she *were* to marry, he was the very person to suit her in age, character and condition. He seemed, by this connection between the families, quite to belong to her. She could not but suppose it to be a match that everybody who knew them must think of.   (119)

The direct threat of marriage, however, she always thrusts aside, indignantly with Mr Elton – 'I have no thoughts of matrimony at present' – after long deliberation (which has nothing to feed on but itself), with respects to Churchill – 'Her own attachment had really subsided into a mere nothing; it was not worth thinking of' – even, for a time, in answer to Mr Knightley. Meanwhile, her involvement with Harriet – until the culminating error – remains steady and strong.

The fact is that Emma prefers the company of women, more particularly of women whom she can master and direct; the fact is that this preference is intrinsic to her whole dominating and un-committing personality. The same tendency has been recognized by

Edmund Wilson; but Mr Wilson adds that it is 'something outside
the picture which is never made explicit'.[4] The tendency is certainly
never made explicit; but is it for that reason external? The myth of
Jane Austen's simplicity persists; and its corollary, that in her work
the unexplicit is an error of tone: for surface must tell all.

Emma needs to dominate, she can of course – in her class and
time – most easily dominate women; and her need is urgent enough
to forgo even the pretense of sympathetic understanding. She feels
affection only towards Harriet, Mrs Weston, and her father: instances, not of tenderness, but rather of satisfied control. She feels
affection only toward those immediately under her command, and
all of them are women. Mr Woodhouse is no exception. The effect of
decayed gentlemanliness that he produces is a *tour de force* of Jane
Austen's, nothing else; for Mr Woodhouse is really an old woman, of
the vacuous, mild-natured, weakly selfish sort very common to
novels and (possibly) to life. He has no single masculine trait, and
his only distinction lies in the transfer of sex. He is Mrs Bates
elevated to the dignity of Hartfield.

As she herself admits, Emma has no tenderness:

> There is no charm equal to tenderness of heart. . . . There is nothing to be
> compared to it. Warmth and tenderness of heart, with an affectionate, open
> manner, will beat all the clearness of head in the world, for attraction. I am
> sure it will. It is tenderness of heart which makes my dear father so generally
> beloved – which gives Isabella all her popularity. – I have it not – but I
> know how to prize and respect it.   (269)

This last is already a misjudgment, for Emma does *not* know how to
prize and respect tenderness in anyone who rejects her domination.
Still, she recognizes her defect. Emma is a beautiful and clever girl,
with every grace but tenderness. Without it, she exhibits the strong
need to dominate, the offhand cruelty, the protective playfulness, the
malice of Jane Austen, the candid Jane Austen of the letters – in
which miscarriage is a joke:

> Mrs Hall, of Sherborne, was brought to bed yesterday of a dead child, some
> weeks before she expected, owing to a fright. I suppose she happened
> unawares to look at her husband.[5]

and death equally amusing:

> Only think of Mrs Holder's being dead! Poor woman, she has done the only
> thing in the world she could possibly do to make one cease to abuse her.[6]

recalling the more literary echo in *Emma*, on Mrs Churchill's death:

Goldsmith tells us, that when lovely woman stoops to folly, she has nothing
to do but to die; and when she stoops to be disagreeable, it is equally to be
recommended as a clearer of ill fame.   (387)

and marriage also, as – anticipating Emma on Churchill – she
shrugs off the fading interest of an eligible young man:

This is rational enough; there is less love and more sense in it than
sometimes appeared before, and I am very well satisfied. It will all go on
exceedingly well, and decline away in a very reasonable manner.[7]

Emma, of course, is only an 'imaginist' and twenty-one; creating
her, Jane Austen is an artist and thirty-nine. In the assurance of
mastery – with a quarter-century of writing behind her, a portion of
fame, and a congenial subject isolated from moral qualms[8] – Jane
Austen could be freely aware of the Emma in herself, she could
convert her own personal limitations into the very form of her novel.
All she had to discard for the character of Emma was her own
overarching artist's awareness, her unresting irony, which even in
life, in her letters at least, directed and used her need to dominate,
her fear of commitment: which made her coldly right where Emma
is coldly wrong.

Emma is moved to play God, but without tenderness or social
caution (or the artist's awareness) she falls into every conceivable
mistake and misjudgment. She must feel herself to be central and
centripetal, the confidante and adviser of all. Without tenderness or
caution, she makes the worst of every situation: imagines evil when
there is good – because Jane Fairfax is 'disgustingly reserved' or has
an 'odious composure' – and good where there is nothing but an
extension of self.

Mrs Elton – for all of Emma's heartfelt aversion to her – is
Emma's true companion in motive. Both must dominate every
situation. Both must have admirers to confirm their position. Both
are profoundly wanting in altruism and sympathy. The chief
difference is that Mrs Elton's motive lies bare, without ornament of
intelligence, beauty, or rank. Mrs Elton is 'vulgar' (Emma's favorite
word for her and her friends) – 'A little upstart, vulgar being, with
her Mr E., and her *caro sposo*, and her resources, and all her airs of
pert pretension and under-bred finery' (279) – and Emma is
'refined'.[9] Mrs Elton has no brake of intelligence or breeding upon

her egocentrism; she can rattle on and give herself away without self-consciousness:

'I honestly said that *the world* I could give up – parties, balls, plays – for I had no fear of retirement. Blessed with so many resources within myself, the world was not necesary to *me*. I could do very well without it. To those who had no resources it was a different thing; but my resources made me quite independent. And as to smaller-sized rooms than I had been used to, I really could not give it a thought. I hoped I was perfectly equal to any sacrifice of that description. Certainly I had been accustomed to every luxury of Maple Grove; but I did assure him that two carriages were not necessary to my happiness, nor were spacious apartments.'   (277)

Since she is happy as long as she is allowed to condescend:

'My dear Jane, what is this I hear? – Going to the post-office in the rain! – This must not be, I assure you. – You sad girl, how could you do such a thing? – It is a sign I was not there to take care of you.'   (295)

Jane Fairfax's mere politeness she can accept as homage. Emma, though, is neither fatuous nor unperceptive. She must play the idol and the confidante, but she requires some evidence of idolatry; and she builds up a vindictive dislike of Jane Fairfax precisely because it is clear that Jane will worship or trust neither her nor anyone else.

Emma can fall back on the nonentities of her world, those vessels of neutral purpose that are always governed from the outside: Harriet, Mr Woodhouse, Mr Weston, Isabella, and Miss Bates. Not that they have anything to offer beyond agreeableness: Mr Weston, happy with his son, ready to be satisfied with everyone, even Mr Elton; Isabella, dwindling pleasantly in hypochondria and her husband's shadow; Harriet, with her infinite pliancy; Miss Bates, spreading her obsessive good cheer: 'It is such a happiness when good people get together – and they always do' (175).

Mr Woodhouse has not even this recommendation. He is not agreeable. He is, in fact, an annoyance, with his gruel, his hypochondria, his often-quoted friend Perry, his feeble but effective insistence that nothing, nothing at all, be changed in his life or in the lives of the people around him; and we can sympathize with John Knightley when he looses his hot temper against the nagging solicitations of his father-in-law. Mr Woodhouse – after long years of invalidism, of being coddled by his daughter, of scarcely stirring from his house or seeing a new person – is an idiot. He is quite incapable of thought or judgment. Miss Bates, Jane Fairfax, Mr

Knightley, Frank Churchill – all are agreeable persons, as long as
the young ladies dry their stockings after a rain and the young men
do not insist on opening windows. Even on Mrs Elton, 'considering
we never saw her before', he remarks that 'she seems a very obliging,
pretty-behaved young lady wife. Though I think he had better not
have married' (279–80). When Emma, in a rare mood of almost
irritable playfulness with him, tries to point out the contradiction
between his respect for brides and his dislike of marriage, she only
makes him nervous without making him at all understand (280).
Anything is satisfactory as long as it does not require change; and
there is no distinction between satisfactory things. As he has no taste
for people, so he has no taste for food – except for thin, smooth gruel
and soft-boiled eggs – or for Mr Knightley's objects of art: 'Mrs
Weston had been showing them all to him, and now he would show
them all to Emma; – fortunate in having no other resemblance to a
child, than in a total want of taste for what he saw, for he was slow,
constant, and methodical' (362). He has his habits, his advice, his
fears, his small worn-out courtesies – without a touch of discriminating thought or feeling except between what is familiar and what is
alien. His tenacious clinging to Emma, to his acquaintances, to the
seen boundaries of his world comes to resemble the clinging of a
parasitic plant, which must be now or sometime shaken off. Mr
Woodhouse is the living – barely living – excuse for Emma's refusal
to commit herself to the human world.

He is also, like the other governable characters and like Mrs
Weston (whom Emma, at least, can govern), the kind of person
whom Emma can most easily persuade of her supremacy; and it is
significant that she treats them all – except one – with the utmost
kindness and solicitude. The exception is Miss Bates, whom Emma
mimics in company and shockingly ridicules to her face:

> 'Oh very well,' exclaimed Miss Bates, 'then I need not be uneasy. "Three
> things very dull indeed." That will just do for me, you know. I shall be sure
> to say three dull things as soon as ever I open my mouth, shan't I? –
> (looking round with the most good-humoured dependence on every body's
> assent) – Do not you all think I shall?'
>   Emma could not resist.
>   'Ah! ma'am, but there may be a difficulty. Pardon me – but you will be
> limited as to number – only three at once.'   (370)

since Miss Bates, unluckily for her, has no greater pleasure than
chattering the praises of her niece, Jane Fairfax.

The only character in the story who sees Emma at all clearly is Frank Churchill. He is as egoistic and calculating as she, but he beats her at her own game because he is far less self-deluded. Emma's prodigious self-deception springs at least partly from inexperience. With experience, with the especially valuable experience of pampering a cross and dictatorial old woman, Churchill has learned to be cautious, to blunt the edge of his ego with careless charm. He has learned to use people more successfully than Emma, but he is not less destructive. His playing at love with Emma is required, perhaps, in order to keep the secret of his engagement to Jane; but he takes cynical delight in tormenting the latter and mystifying the former. He convinces Emma that he wholly accepts her slander about Jane and Mr Dixon, and her view that it is Mr Dixon who has sent the piano: 'Indeed you injure me if you suppose me unconvinced . . . now I can see it in no other light than as an offering of love' (218–19). Allusion to Mr Dixon and Ireland becomes, in fact, his favorite method of simultaneously hurting Jane and amusing Emma while he laughs at both. He jokes with Emma about Jane's hair-do:

'Those curls! – This must be a fancy of her own. I see nobody else looking like her! – must go and ask her whether it is an Irish fashion. Shall I? – Yes, I will – I declare I will – and you shall see how she takes it; – whether she colours.'   (222)

Concerning the gift piano, he baits Jane openly, over Emma's feeble objection:

'It is not fair,' said Emma in a whisper, 'mine was a random guess. Do not distress her.'
He shook his head with a smile, and looked as if he had very little doubt and very little mercy. Soon afterwards he began again,
'How much your friends in Ireland must be enjoying your pleasure on this occasion, Miss Fairfax. I dare say they often think of you, and wonder which will be the day, the precise day of the instrument's coming to hand.'   (241)

He persists, though Emma is 'half ashamed':

Emma wished he would be less pointed, yet could not help being amused. . . .
'You speak too plain. She must understand you.'
'I hope she does. I would have her understand me. I am not in the least ashamed of my meaning.'

'But really, I am half ashamed, and wish I had never taken up the idea.'
'I am very glad you did, and that you communicated it to me. I have now
a key to all her odd looks and ways. Leave shame to her. If she does wrong,
she ought to feel it.'   (243)

At Hartfield, Mr Knightley, with considerable suspicion of
Churchill's deceit, watches the word-game in progress:

He saw a short word prepared for Emma, and given to her with a look sly
and demure. He saw that Emma had soon made it out, and found it highly
entertaining, though it was something which she judged it proper to appear
to censure; for she said, 'Nonsense! for shame!' He heard Frank Churchill
next say, with a glance towards Jane, 'I will give it to her – shall I?' – and as
clearly heard Emma opposing it with eager laughing warmth. 'No, no, you
must not; you shall not, indeed.'
   It was done, however. This gallant young man, who seemed to love
without feeling, and to recommend himself without complaisance, directly
. . . handed over the word to Miss Fairfax, and, with a particular degree of
sedate civility entreated her to study it. Mr Knightley's excessive curiosity
to know what this word might be, made him seize every possible moment for
darting his eye towards it, and it was not long before he saw it to be
Dixon.   (348)

In the strained and heavy atmosphere at Box Hill, with the
company separating into small sullen parties, with Jane bitterly
jealous (though no one but Churchill knows) of Churchill's attentions to Emma, he flirts defiantly with Emma and directs his scorn
at everyone else: 'Our companions are excessively stupid. What
shall we do to rouse them? Any nonsense will serve. They *shall* talk'
(369). Through his unsuspecting dupe, Emma, Churchill recalls to
Jane their meeting at a resort and baits her cruelly about her family;

'as to any real knowledge that Bath, or any public place, can give – it is all
nothing; there can be no knowledge. It is only by seeing women in their own
homes, among their own set, just as they always are, that you can form any
just judgment. Short of that, it is all guess and luck – and will generally be
ill-luck. How many a man has committed himself on a short acquaintance,
and rued it all the rest of his life.'   (372)

And all the while he makes Jane sick with shame, jealousy,
bitterness, and fear: uncertain of his affection, uncertain even
whether she desires it, sick with the burden of a clandestine
engagement,[10] bitterly resigned to sinking her talent, her taste, her
intelligence into the governess-role by which – if Churchill fails her
– she must live: 'There are places in town, offices, where inquiry

would soon produce something – Offices for the sale – not quite of human flesh – but of human intellect' (300). Moreover, Churchill does all this consciously and with relish, enjoying his duplicity: 'I am the wretchedest being in the world at a civil falsehood' (234). He has no scruples, for he needs none: charm and wealth excuse everything. One wonders whether Emma – even under the vigilance of Mr Knightley – will not be polished into the same engaging ruthlessness after several years of marriage.

Emma accepts Mr Knightley doubtless because she loves and admires him. She has failed so discouragingly with Harriet as to give up all thought of protégées for the present; and Mr Knightley is after all a very impressive and admirable man. He is even the most likable and most heroic of Jane Austen's heroes: unlike Darcy, he is a frank and social man; he is not a prig like Edmund Bertram, or a wary ironist like Henry Tilney. He is intelligent, perceptive, mature – but not so indivertibly as to save his judgment altogether from the effects of love:

> He had found her agitated and low. – Frank Churchill was a villain. – He heard her declare that she had never loved him. Frank Churchill's character was not desperate. – She was his own Emma, by hand and word, when they returned into the house; and if he could have thought of Frank Churchill then, he might have deemed him a very good sort of fellow.   (433)

That he should continue to love Emma at all, after observing her through all her misdemeanors, is in fact a tribute to the power of love; for Mr Knightley is quite capable of recognizing and pointing out the implications of her conduct, with Harriet, with Churchill and Jane Fairfax, with Miss Bates – implications he vigorously points out to Emma herself. Success in love, though, overthrows him. As for Emma, she has been defeated. All her dreams of fruitful dominion have been at least temporarily dissipated; and, for the time being, she is willing to be dominated by a man of whom her intelligence and her snobbery can approve (though even now she accepts only on condition that he move into her father's home!). The flood of repentance has not yet subsided. Yet there is no sign that Emma's motives have changed, that there is any difference in her except her relief and temporary awareness. Later on, the story may turn back again: it is hard to think of Emma undominant for any length of time.

Emma plays God because she cannot commit herself humanly.

Her compulsion operates in the absence of one quality: a quality which Emma, Frank Churchill, and Mrs Elton – the only destructive figures in the novel – are all without. The quality is tenderness. For Emma, there is no communication of feeling. She can esteem, loathe, praise, censure, grieve, rejoice – but she cannot feel like anyone else in the world. Her ego will admit nothing but itself. Frank Churchill and Mrs Elton fall under the same charge: but Mrs Elton is too transparently vulgar to be effective; and Churchill, too astute to be caught playing God, keeps his own counsel, trifles, observes, and makes use of people by the less imposing and less dangerous tactic of charm. Of the three, only Emma is both foolish enough to play God and dazzling enough to blind anyone even for a short time.

The primary large irony of the novel is, then, the deceptiveness of surface. Charm is the chief warning-signal of Jane Austen's world, for it is most often the signal of wit adrift from feeling. The brilliant façades of Emma and Frank Churchill have no door. Indeed, the only charming person in all of Jane Austen's novels whom both she and the reader fully accept is Elizabeth Bennet, and Elizabeth has obvious virtues – a clear head and good intentions – to lend depth and steadiness to her charm. The other heroines – Elinor Dashwood, Catherine Morland, Fanny Price, Anne Elliot – are presented in the quietest colors. And Willoughby, Wickham, Mary Crawford, Frank Churchill – the charming interlopers – always betray.

In *Emma*, Jane Austen has given surface the benefit of every alluring quality in the persons of the heroine and of Frank Churchill. She has given them beauty, wealth, position, and immediate circumstances most favorable to the exercise of their wills. The only results have been confusion and unhappiness, on the reduced scale appropriate to the people and the society involved.

Of course, the denouement brushes aside confusion and unhappiness, and brings Emma and Churchill into ostensibly happy marriages. *Emma* can be read as the story of a spoiled rich girl who is corrected by defeat and love, and who lives happily ever after. This is a limited vision, but it is not a false one; for Jane Austen does succeed on her primary levels in achieving her 'ripest and kindliest',[11] her most perfect love comedy. On these levels, Emma is 'faultless in spite of all her faults' (433), Frank Churchill's frivolity will be tempered by the sense and grave sweetness of his wife, even Mrs Elton can do little harm, and everyone else is comfortably settled – with the exception of poor Mrs Churchill, who had to die to clear the way for her nephew's marriage. The conditions are almost standard for romantic comedy: two love-affairs, one complicated by self-deception, the other by secrecy, both turning out well; no strong issue, no punishment.

Emma can be read so; but it has more to give, and not easily. Reginald Farrer, one of the few critics of Jane Austen who have taken the trouble to read her carefully, has observed that *Emma* 'is not an easy book to read; it should never be the beginner's primer, nor be published without a prefatory synopsis. Only when the story has been thoroughly assimilated, can the infinite delights and subtleties of its workmanship begin to be appreciated, as you realize the manifold complexity of the book's web, and find that every sentence, almost every epithet, has its definite reference to equally unemphasized points before and after in the development of the plot. Thus it is that, while twelve readings of *Pride and Prejudice* give you twelve periods of pleasure repeated, as many readings of *Emma* give you that pleasure, not repeated only, but squared and squared again with each perusal, till at every fresh reading you feel anew that you never understood anything like the widening sum of its delights.'[12]

It is this multiplicity and sureness of reference that most immediately distinguishes *Emma* from the rest of Jane Austen's work: the total confident control of all her resources, without intrusion of derivativeness or fatigue or morality. The author's vision and instrument is, of course, irony: the widening sum of delights in *Emma* is, first of all, our widening recognition of the decisive pertinence with which every word, every action, and every response of Emma's establish her nature, confirm her self-deception, and prepare for her downfall. The ironic reverberations, rather than conflicting with one another or passing out of context – as they do sometimes in *Pride and Prejudice* and often in *Northanger Abbey* – remain internal and interdependent, they reinforce one another in a structure whose apparent lightness is less remarkable only than its compact and powerful density.

When we first observe Emma's maneuverings with Harriet, it is with the consciousness of her urge to dominate. Soon, though, this urge has become inextricable from Emma's own snobbery and her vicarious snobbery for Harriet, which drive it even farther from the possibility of caution or rational direction. Why does Emma want Harriet to marry? Harriet begins to seem a kind of proxy for Emma, a means by which Emma – too reluctant, too fearful of involvement, to consider the attempt herself – may discover what marriage is like. If Harriet is a proxy for Emma, she must serve as a defense also. Emma is outraged by Mr Elton's proposal, not merely because she has not expected it (the basis of the simple irony here), but because Mr Elton dares to circumvent the buffer she has so carefully set up. Harriet is to experience for her what she refuses to commit herself to, but cannot help being curious about. Yet Harriet is a very pretty girl, and being infinitely stupid and unperceptive, may be used in other uncommitting ways. Emma's interest in Harriet is not merely mistress-and-pupil, but quite emotional and particular: for a time at least – until Harriet becomes slightly resentful of the yoke after Emma's repeated blunders – Emma is in love with her: a love unphysical and inadmissible, even perhaps undefinable in such a society; and therefore safe. And in all this web of relations, by no means exhausted here, we return always to Emma's overpowering motive: her fear of commitment.

The simple irony of Emma's flirtation with Frank Churchill rises, of course, from the fact that Churchill is in love with someone else and uses Emma as a decoy. More than this, however, Churchill uses Emma so successfully only because he knows her so well. Emma is a perfect decoy for a man in love with someone else. She enjoys and invites admiration, but will draw away from any sign of serious attachment. Churchill does not use Emma merely for want of other dupes: he knows her, and exploits her with a ruthless thoroughness, not making a fool of her but revealing her as she is. 'But is it possible,' he asks Emma blandly, later, 'that you had no suspicion?' (477). He knows that she neither did nor could have had. She took part so eagerly in the flirtation because there she could be at once admired and unengaged, there she could smugly exchange scandal in the guise of wit, and be cynically and most delicately stroked into a pleasant (though wary) submissiveness by flattery without feeling, by assurances of her Olympian superiority.

The one quality which Mr Knightley may regard as Emma's saving grace is her honesty. It is a very circumscribed honesty, it operates characteristically in the trough of failure and disaster, before the next rise of confidence and self-delusion; and it is another inextricable strand in the complex ironic web. Emma can recognize how badly her matchmaking schemes have turned out and resolve never to attempt them again – but without recognizing why she

attempts them at all and keeps coming back to them. She can set her
calculating nature against Harriet's simple and lachrymose one,
without understanding the motives behind either, or anticipating
the author's charge of sentimentality: 'It was rather too late in the
day to set about being simple-minded and ignorant' (142). Most
crucially, after the conventional settling of accounts, after Mr
Knightley has secured his Emma and Churchill his Jane, Emma for
the first time can judge herself and Churchill as they must have
seemed together in their flirtation, as they have been and are now
alike:

Emma could not help saying,
   'I do suspect that in the midst of your perplexities at that time, you had
very great amusement in tricking us all. – I am sure you had. – I am sure it
was a consolation to you.'
   'Oh! no, no, no – how can you suspect me of such a thing? – I was the
most miserable wretch!'
   'Not quite so miserable as to be insensible to mirth. I am sure it was a
source of high entertainment to you, to feel that you were taking us all in. –
Perhaps I am the readier to suspect, because, to tell you the truth, I think it
might have been some amusement to myself in the same situation. I think
there is a little likeness between us.'
   He bowed.
   'If not in our dispositions,' she presently added, with a look of true
sensibilty, 'there is a likeness in our destiny; the destiny which bids fair to
connect us with two characters so much superior to our own.'   (478)

   This is honesty, and very acute. In an interlude with the man who
most completely understands her, Emma recognizes and gives us the
truth; and it is no mistake that Jane Austen places this clarifying
exchange so close to the end of her book. Emma has finally – almost
– got to know herself; but only because the knowledge is here
painless and may be discarded in a little while with Mr Knightley
again, where she may resume, however self-amusedly for the
present, her characteristic role:

   'Do you dare say this?' cried Mr Knightley. 'Do you dare to suppose me
so great a blockhead, as not to know what a man is talking of? – What do
you deserve?'
   'Oh! I always deserve the best treatment, because I never put up with any
other. . .'   (474)

Emma knows that she is moving toward a happy ending. Emma and
Churchill are very lucky in the irony that finds them a Mr Knightley

and a Jane Fairfax to sober and direct them: this much Emma sees. So Mr Knightley, not yet accepted by Emma, speaks bitterly of Churchill:

'Frank Churchill is, indeed, the favourite of fortune. Every thing turns out for his good. – He meets with a young woman at a watering-place, gains her affection, cannot even weary her by negligent treatment – and had he and all his family sought round the world for a perfect wife for him, they could not have found her superior. – His aunt is in the way. – His aunt dies. – He has only to speak. – His friends are eager to promote his happiness. – He has used every body ill – and they are all delighted to forgive him. – He is a fortunate man indeed!'   (428)

Still, Churchill – as Mr Knightley knows – and Emma are lucky not by luck (except the luck of an invalid aunt's dying), but because in their social milieu charm conquers, even as it makes every cruel and thoughtless mistake; because, existing apart from and inevitably denying emotion and commitment, it nevertheless finds committed to it even the good and the wise, even when it is known and evaluated. The irony of *Emma* is multiple; and its ultimate aspect is that there is no happy ending, easy equilibrium, if we care to project confirmed exploiters like Emma and Churchill into the future of their marriages.

Emma's and Frank Churchill's society, which makes so much of surface, guarantees the triumph of surface. Even Mr Knightley and Jane Fairfax succumb. Jane Austen, however, does not ask us to concern ourselves beyond the happy ending: she merely presents the evidence, noncommittally.

SOURCE: From 'Irony as Form: *Emma*' in *Jane Austen: Irony as Defense and Discovery* (University of California Press, 1952) pp. 181–206.

NOTES

1. Far from thinking about it, some critics seem to drift out of it into a warm, irrelevant daydream of their own, in which they discover in the book a 'good-natured, placid, slightly dispersed and unoccupied quality . . . pleasantly reflected in the character of its heroine'. O. W. Firkins, *Jane Austen* (New York, 1920) p. 96.

2. Parenthetical references are to page numbers in the Chapman edition of *Emma* (Oxford, 1926).

3. G. Saintsbury, *The English Novel* (1919) p. 198.

4. E. Wilson, 'A Long Talk About Jane Austen', in the *New Yorker*, xx (24 June 1944) 69.

5. *Jane Austen's Letters to her sister Cassandra and others*, collected and edited by R. W. Chapman (Oxford, 1932) i no. 24 (27 Oct 1798).

6. Ibid. ii no. 350 (14 Oct 1813).

7. Ibid. i no. 28 (17 Nov 1798).

8. Anticipating objections to Emma, Jane Austen said: 'I am going to take a heroine whom no one but myself will much like' (J. E. Austen-Leigh, *A Memoir of Jane Austen* (Oxford, 1926) p. 157); the moral finickiness of *Mansfield Park* is put decisively behind.

9. Emma 'is the type in fiction of a whole race of English ladies ... for whom refinement is religion. Her claim to oversee and order the social things about her consisted in being refined.' G. K. Chesterton, 'The Evolution of Emma', in *Living Age*, ccxciv (25 Aug 1917) 504.

10. Mr Chapman documents 'the enormity of Jane Fairfax's deviation from right' in her particular social context (512–13).

11. R. Farrer, 'Jane Austen, *ob*. July 18, 1817', in *Quarterly Review*, ccxxviii (July 1917) 26.

12. Ibid., 23–4. The fact that great novels require frequent re-experience to produce their full effect is perhaps less insisted upon than it should be. The same fact is taken for granted with respect to lyric poetry and 'absolute' music. In a work of art, one can arrive at form only by apprehending specifically – and in a great work this is always difficult – all the individual relationships, implications, and resolutions that together make up form. In a novel, one is tempted to stop at narrative and plot, and to imagine that these – plus several lively characters – constitute all the form of which a novel is capable. *Novel* and *story* become nearly interchangeable, especially when the technique is superficially as simple and traditional as Jane Austen's.

Lionel Trilling Emma and the Legend of Jane Austen (1957)

I

It is possible to say of Jane Austen, as perhaps we can say of no other writer, that the opinions which are held of her work are almost as interesting, and almost as important to think about, as the work itself. This statement, even with the qualifying 'almost', ought to be, on its face, an illegitimate one. We all know that the reader should come to the writer with no preconceptions, taking no account of any previous opinion. But this, of course, he cannot do. Every established writer exists in the aura of his legend – the accumulated opinion that we cannot help being aware of, the image of his personality that has been derived, correctly or incorrectly, from what he has written. In the case of Jane Austen, the legend is of an unusually compelling kind. Her very name is a charged one. The homely quaintness of the Christian name, the cool elegance of the surname, seem inevitably to force upon us the awareness of her sex, her celibacy, and her social class. 'Charlotte Brontë' rumbles like thunder and drowns out any such special considerations. But 'Jane Austen' can by now scarcely fail to imply femininity, and, at that, femininity of a particular kind and in a particular social setting. It dismays many new readers that certain of her admirers call her Jane, others Miss Austen. Either appellation suggests an unusual, and questionable, relation with this writer, a relation that does not consort with the literary emotions we respect. The new reader perceives from the first that he is not to be permitted to proceed in simple literary innocence. Jane Austen is to be for him not only a writer but an issue. There are those who love her; there are those – no doubt they are fewer but they are no less passionate – who detest her; and the new reader understands that he is being solicited to a fierce partisanship, that he is required to make no mere literary judgment but a decision about his own character and personality, and about his relation to society and all of life.

And indeed the nature of the partisanship is most intensely personal and social. The matter at issue is: What kind of people like Jane Austen? What kind of people dislike her? Sooner or later the characterization is made or implied by one side or the other, and with extreme invidiousness. It was inevitable that there should arise a third body of opinion, which holds that it is not Jane Austen herself who is to be held responsible for the faults that are attributed to her by her detractors, but rather the people who admire her for the wrong reasons and in the wrong language and thus create a false image of her. As far back as 1905 Henry James was repelled by what a more recent critic, Professor Marvin Mudrick, calls 'gentle-Janeism' and he spoke of it with great acerbity. James admired Jane Austen; his artistic affinity with her is clear, and he may be thought to have shared her social preferences and preoccupations. Yet James could say of her reputation that it had risen higher than her intrinsic

interest warranted: the responsibility for this, he said, lay with 'the
body of publishers, editors, illustrators, producers of magazines,
which have found their "dear", our dear, everybody's dear Jane so
infinitely to their material purpose'.[1] In our own day, Dr Leavis's
admiration for Jane Austen is matched in intensity by his impatience
with her admirers. Mr D. W. Harding in a well-known essay[2] has
told us how the accepted form of admiration of Jane Austen kept
him for a long time from reading her novels, and how he was able to
be at ease with them only when he discovered that they were
charged with scorn of the very people who set the common tone of
admiration. And Professor Mudrick, in the preface to his book on
Jane Austen,[3] speaks of the bulk of the criticism of her work as being
'a mere mass of cozy family adulation, self-glorif[ication] ... and
nostalgic latterday enshrinements of the gentle-hearted chronicler of
Regency order'. It is the intention of Professor Mudrick's book to
rescue Jane Austen from coziness and nostalgia by representing her
as a writer who may be admired for her literary achievement, but
who is not to be loved, and of whom it is to be said that certain
deficiencies of temperament account for certain deficiencies of her
literary practice.

The impatience with the common admiring view of Jane Austen is
not hard to understand and sympathize with, the less so because (as
Mr Harding and Professor Mudrick say) admiration seems to stimu-
late self-congratulation in those who give it, and to carry a reproof of
the deficient sensitivity, reasonableness, and even courtesy, of those
who withhold their praise. One may refuse to like almost any author
and incur no other blame from his admirers than that of being
wanting in taste in that one respect. But not to like Jane Austen is to
put oneself under suspicion of a general personal inadequacy and
even – let us face it – of a want of breeding.

This is absurd and distasteful. And yet we cannot deal with this
unusual – this extravagantly personal – response to a writer simply
in the way of condemnation. No doubt every myth of a literary
person obscures something of the truth. But it may also express
some part of the truth as well. If Jane Austen is carried outside the
proper confines of literature, if she has been loved in a fashion that
some temperaments must find objectionable and that a strict criticism must call illicit, the reason is perhaps to be found not only in the
human weakness of her admirers, in their impulse to self-flattery, or
in whatever other fault produces their deplorable tone. Perhaps a

reason is also to be found in the work itself, in some unusual promise
that it seems to make, in some hope that it holds out.

II

Of Jane Austen's six great novels *Emma* is surely the one that is most
fully representative of its author. *Pride and Prejudice* is of course
more popular. It is the one novel in the canon that 'everybody'
reads, the one that is most often reprinted. *Pride and Prejudice*
deserves its popularity, but it is not a mere snobbery, an affected
aversion from the general suffrage, that makes thoughtful readers of
Jane Austen judge *Emma* to be the greater book – not the more
delightful but the greater. It cannot boast the brilliant, unimpeded
energy of *Pride and Prejudice*, but that is because the energy which it
does indeed have is committed to dealing with a more resistant
matter. In this it is characteristic of all three novels of Jane Austen's
mature period, of which it is the second. *Persuasion*, the third and
last, has a charm that is traditionally, and accurately, called
'autumnal', and it is beyond question a beautiful book. But *Persuasion*, which was published posthumously and which may not
have been revised to meet the author's full intention, does not have
the richness and substantiality of *Emma*. As for *Mansfield Park*, the
first work of the mature period, it quite matches *Emma* in point of
substantiality but it makes a special and disturbing case. Greatly
admired in its own day – far more than *Emma* – *Mansfield Park* is
now disliked by many readers who like everything else that Jane
Austen wrote. They are repelled by its heroine and by all that she
seems to imply of the author's moral and religious preferences at this
moment of her life, for Fanny Price consciously devotes herself to
virtue and piety, which she achieves by a willing submissiveness that
goes against the modern grain. What is more, the author seems to be
speaking out against wit and spiritedness (while not abating her
ability to represent these qualities), and virtually in praise of dullness
and acquiescence, and thus to be condemning her own peculiar
talents. *Mansfield Park* is an extraordinary novel, and only Jane
Austen could have achieved its profound and curious interest, but its
moral tone is antipathetic to contemporary taste, and no essay I
have ever written has met with so much resistance as the one in
which I tried to say that it was not really a perverse and wicked

book. But *Emma*, as richly complex as *Mansfield Park*, arouses no
such antagonism, and the opinion that holds it to be the greatest of
all Jane Austen's novels is, I believe, correct.

Professor Mudrick says that everyone has misunderstood *Emma*,
and he may well be right, for *Emma* is a very difficult novel. We in
our time are used to difficult books and like them. But *Emma* is more
difficult than any of the hard books we admire. The difficulty of
Proust arises from the sheer amount and complexity of his thought,
the difficulty of Joyce from the brilliantly contrived devices of representation, the difficulty of Kafka from a combination of doctrine and
mode of communication. With all, the difficulty is largely literal; it
lessens in the degree that we attend closely to what the books say;
after each sympathetic reading we are the less puzzled. But the
difficulty of *Emma* is never overcome. We never know where to have
it. If we finish it at night and think we know what it is up to, we wake
the next morning to believe it is up to something quite else; it has
become a different book. Reginald Farrer speaks at length of the
difficulty of *Emma* and then goes on to compare its effect with that of
Pride and Prejudice. 'While twelve readings of *Pride and Prejudice*
give you twelve periods of pleasure repeated, as many readings of
Emma give you that pleasure, not repeated only, but squared and
squared again with each perusal, till at every fresh reading you feel
anew that you never understood anything like the widening sum of
its delights.'[4] This is so, and for the reason that none of the twelve
readings permits us to flatter ourselves that we have fully understood what the novel is doing. The effect is extraordinary, perhaps
unique. The book is like a person – not to be comprehended fully
and finally by any other person. It is perhaps to the point that it is
the only one of Jane Austen's novels that has for its title a person's
name.

For most people who recognize the difficulty of the book, the
trouble begins with Emma herself. Jane Austen was surely aware of
what a complexity she was creating in Emma, and no doubt that is
why she spoke of her as 'a heroine whom no one but myself will
much like'. Yet this puts it in a minimal way – the question of
whether we will like or not like Emma does not encompass the
actuality of the challenge her characters offers. John Henry Newman
stated the matter more accurately, and very charmingly, in a letter
of 1837. He says that Emma is the most interesting of Jane Austen's
heroines, and that he likes her. But what is striking in his remark is

this sentence: 'I feel kind to her whenever I think of her.' This does indeed suggest the real question about Emma, whether or not we will find it in our hearts to be kind to her.

Inevitably we are attracted to her, we are drawn by her energy and style, and by the intelligence they generate. Here are some samples of her characteristic tone:

'Never mind, Harriet, I shall not be a poor old maid; it is poverty only which makes celibacy contemptible to a generous public!'

Emma was sorry; to have to pay civilities to a person she did not like through three long months! – to be always doing more than she wished and less than she ought!

'I do not know whether it ought to be so, but certainly silly things do cease to be silly if they are done by sensible people in an impudent way. Wickedness is always wickedness, but folly is not always folly.'

'Oh! I always deserve the best treatment, because I never put up with any other. . . .'

[On an occasion when Mr Knightley comes to a dinner party in his carriage, as Emma thinks he should, and not on foot:] '. . . There is always a look of consciousness or bustle when people come in a way which they know to be beneath them. You think you carry it off very well, I dare say, but with you it is a sort of bravado, an air of affected unconcern; I always observe it whenever I meet you under these circumstances. *Now* you have nothing to try for. You are not afraid of being supposed ashamed. You are not striving to look taller than any body else. *Now* I shall really be happy to walk into the same room with you.'

We cannot be slow to see what is the basis of this energy and style and intelligence. It is self-love. There is a great power of charm in self-love, although, to be sure, the charm is an ambiguous one. We resent it and resist it, yet we are drawn by it, if only it goes with a little grace or creative power. Nothing is easier to pardon than the mistakes and excesses of self-love: if we are quick to condemn them, we take pleasure in forgiving them. And with good reason, for they are the extravagance of the first of virtues, the most basic and biological of the virtues, that of self-preservation.

But we distinguish between our response to the self-love of men and the self-love of women. No woman could have won the forgiveness that has been so willingly given (after due condemnation) to the self-regard of, say, Yeats and Shaw. We understand self-love to be part of the moral life of all men; in men of genius we expect it to appear in unusual intensity and we take it to be an essential element of their power. The extraordinary thing about Emma is that she has a moral life as a man has a moral life. And she doesn't have it as a special instance, as an example of a new kind of woman, which is the way George Eliot's Dorothea Brooke has her moral life, but quite as a matter of course, as a given quality of her nature.

And perhaps that is what Jane Austen meant when she said that no one would like her heroine – and what Newman meant when he said that he felt kind to Emma whenever he thought of her. She needs kindness if she is to be accepted in all her exceptional actuality. Women in fiction only rarely have the peculiar reality of the moral life that self-love bestows. Most commonly they exist in a moonlike way, shining by the reflected moral light of men. They are 'convincing' or 'real' and sometimes 'delightful', but they seldom exist as men exist – as genuine moral destinies. We do not take note of this; we are so used to the reflected quality that we do not observe it. It is only on the rare occasions when a female character like Emma confronts us that the difference makes us aware of the usual practice. Nor can we say that novels are deficient in realism when they present women as they do: it is the presumption of our society that women's moral life is not as men's. No change in the modern theory of the sexes, no advance in status that women have made, has yet contradicted this. The self-love that we do countenance in women is of a limited and passive kind, and we are troubled if it is as assertive as the self-love of men is permitted, and expected, to be. Not men alone, but women as well, insist on this limitation, imposing the requirement the more effectually because they are not conscious of it.

But there is Emma, given over to self-love, wholly aware of it and quite cherishing it. Mr Knightley rebukes her for heedless conduct and says, 'I leave you to your own reflections.' And Emma wonderfully replies: 'Can you trust me with such flatterers? Does my vain spirit ever tell me I am wrong?' She is 'Emma, never loth to be first', loving pre-eminence and praise, loving power and frank to say so.

Inevitably we are drawn to Emma. But inevitably we hold her to be deeply at fault. Her self-love leads her to be a self-deceiver. She can be unkind. She is a dreadful snob.

Her snobbery is of the first importance in her character, and it is of a special sort. The worst instance of it is very carefully chosen to put her thoroughly in the wrong. We are on her side when she mocks Mrs Elton's vulgarity, even though we feel that so young a woman

(Emma is twenty) ought not set so much store by manners and tone – Mrs Elton, with her everlasting barouche-landau and her '*caro sposo*' and her talk of her spiritual 'resources', is herself a snob in the old sense of the word, which meant a vulgar person aspiring to an inappropriate social standing. But when Emma presumes to look down on the young farmer, Robert Martin, and undertakes to keep little Harriet Smith from marrying him, she makes a truly serious mistake, a mistake of nothing less than national import.

Here it is to be observed that *Emma* is a novel that is touched – lightly but indubitably – by national feeling. Perhaps this is the result of the Prince Regent's having expressed his admiration for *Mansfield Park* and his willingness to have the author dedicate her next book to him:[5] it is a circumstance which allows us to suppose that Jane Austen thought of herself, at this point in her career, as having, by reason of the success of her art, a relation to the national ethic. At any rate, there appears in *Emma* a tendency to conceive of a specifically English ideal of life. Knightley speaks of Frank Churchill as falling short of the demands of this ideal: 'No, Emma, your amiable young man can be amiable only in French, not in English. He may be very "aimable", have very good manners, and be very agreeable; but he can have no English delicacy towards the feelings of other people: nothing really amiable about him.' Again, in a curiously impressive moment in the book, we are given a detailed description of the countryside as seen by the party at Donwell Abbey, and this comment follows: 'It was a sweet view – sweet to the eye and the mind. English verdure, English culture [agriculture, of course, is meant], English comfort, seen under a sun bright without being oppressive.' This is a larger consideration than the occasion would appear to require; there seems no reason to expect this vision of 'England's green and pleasant land'. Or none until we note that the description of the view closes thus: '. . . and at the bottom of this bank, favourably placed and sheltered, rose the Abbey-Mill Farm, with meadows in front, and the river making a close and handsome curve around it'. Abbey-Mill Farm is the property of young Robert Martin, for whom Emma has expressed a principled social contempt, and the little burst of strong feeling has the effect, among others, of pointing up the extremity of Emma's mistake.

It is often said, sometimes by way of reproach, that Jane Austen took no account in her novels of the great political events of her lifetime, nor of the great social changes that were going on in England. 'In Jane Austen's novels', says Arnold Hauser in his *Social History of Art*, 'social reality was the soil in which characters were rooted but in no sense a problem which the novelist made any attempt to solve or interpret.' The statement, true in some degree, goes too far. There is in *some* sense an interpretation of social problems in Jane Austen's contrivance of the situation of Emma and Robert Martin. The yeoman class had always held a strong position in English class feeling, and, at this time especially, only stupid or ignorant people felt privileged to look down upon it. Mr Knightley, whose social position is one of the certainties of the book, as is his freedom from any trace of snobbery, speaks of young Martin, who is his friend, as a 'gentleman farmer', and it is clear that he is on his way to being a gentleman pure and simple. And nothing was of greater importance to the English system at the time of the French Revolution than the relatively easy recruitment to the class of gentlemen. It made England unique among European nations. Here is Tocqueville's view of the matter as set forth in the course of his explanation of why England was not susceptible to revolution as France was:

It was not merely parliamentary government, freedom of speech, and the jury system that made England so different from the rest of contemporary Europe. There was something still more distinctive and more far-reaching in its effects. England was the only country in which the caste system had been totally abolished, not merely modified. Nobility and commoners joined forces in business enterprises, entered the same professions, and – what is still more significant – intermarried. The daughter of the greatest lord in the land could marry a 'new' man without the least compunction. . . .

Though this curious revolution (for such in fact it was) is hidden in the mists of time, we can detect traces of it in the English language. For several centuries the word 'gentleman' has had in England a quite different application from what it had when it originated. . . . A study of the connection between the history of language and history proper would certainly be revealing. Thus if we follow the mutation in time and place of the English word 'gentleman' (a derivative of our *gentilhomme*), we find its connotation being steadily widened in England as the classes draw nearer to each other and intermingle. In each successive century we find it being applied to men a little lower in the social scale. Next, with the English, it crosses to America. And now in America, it is applicable to all male citizens, indiscriminately. Thus its history is the history of democracy itself.[6]

Emma's snobbery, then, is nothing less than a contravention of the best – and safest – tendency of English social life. And to make matters worse, it is a principled snobbery. 'A young farmer . . . is the very last sort of person to raise my curiosity. The yeomanry are precisely the order of people with whom I feel that I can have nothing to do. A degree or two lower, and a creditable appearance might interest me; I might hope to be useful to their families in some way or other. But a farmer can need none of my help, and is therefore in one sense as much above my notice as in every other he is below it.' This is carefully contrived by the author to seem as dreadful as possible; it quite staggers us, and some readers will even feel that the author goes too far in permitting Emma to make this speech.

Snobbery is the grossest fault that arises from Emma's self-love, but it is not the only fault. We must also take account of her capacity for unkindness. This can be impulsive and brutal, as in the witticism directed to Miss Bates at the picnic, which makes one of the most memorable scenes in the whole range of English fiction; or extended and systematic, as in her conspiracy with Frank Churchill to quiz Jane Fairfax. Then we know her to be a gossip, at least when she is tempted by Frank Churchill. She finds pleasure in dominating and has no compunctions about taking over the rule of Harriet Smith's life. She has been accused, on the ground of her own estimate of herself, of a want of tenderness, and she has even been said to be without sexual responsiveness.

Why, then, should anyone be kind to Emma? There are several reasons, of which one is that we come into an unusual intimacy with her. We see her in all the elaborateness of her mistakes, in all the details of her wrong conduct. The narrative technique of the novel brings us very close to her and makes us aware of each misstep she will make. The relation that develops between ourselves and her becomes a strange one – it is the relation that exists between our ideal self and our ordinary fallible self. We become Emma's helpless conscience, her unavailing guide. Her fault is the classic one of *hubris*, excessive pride, and it yields the classic result of blindness, of an inability to interpret experience to the end of perceiving reality, and we are aware of each false step, each wrong conclusion, that she will make. Our hand goes out to hold her back and set her straight, and we are distressed that it cannot reach her.

There is an intimacy anterior to this. We come close to Emma because, in a strange way, she permits us to – even invites us to – by being close to herself. When we have said that her fault is *hubris* or self-love, we must make an immediate modification, for her self-love,

though it involves her in self-deception, does not lead her to the
ultimate self-deception – she believes she is clever, she insists she is
right, but she never says she is good. A consciousness is always at
work in her, a sense of what she ought to be and do. It is not an
infallible sense, anything but that, yet she does not need us, or the
author, or Mr Knightley, to tell her, for example, that she is jealous
of Jane Fairfax and acts badly to her; indeed, 'she never saw [Jane
Fairfax] without feeling that she had injured her'. She is never
offended – she never takes the high self-defensive line – when once
her bad conduct is made apparent to her. Her sense of her
superiority leads her to the 'insufferable vanity' of believing 'herself
in the secret of everybody's feelings' and to the 'unpardonable
arrogance' of 'proposing to arrange everybody's destiny', yet it is an
innocent vanity and an innocent arrogance which, when frustrated
and exposed, do not make her bitter, but only ashamed. That is
why, bad as her behavior may be, we are willing to be implicated in
it. It has been thought that in the portrait of Emma there is 'an air of
confession', that Jane Austen was taking account of 'something
offensive' that she and others had observed in her own earlier
manner and conduct, and whether or not this is so, it suggests the
quality of intimacy which the author contrives that we shall feel with
the heroine.

   Then, when we try to explain our feeling of kindness to Emma, we
ought to remember that many of her wrong judgments and actions
are directed to a very engaging end, a very right purpose. She
believes in her own distinction and vividness and she wants all
around her to be distinguished and vivid. It is indeed unpardonable
arrogance, as she comes to see, that she should undertake to arrange
Harriet Smith's destiny, that she plans to 'form' Harriet, making
her, as it were, the mere material or stuff of a creative act. Yet the
destiny is not meanly conceived, the act is meant to be truly creative
– she wants Harriet to be a distinguished and not a commonplace
person, she wants nothing to be commonplace, she requires of life
that it be well shaped and impressive, and alive. It is out of her
insistence that the members of the picnic shall cease being dull and
begin to be witty that there comes her famous insult to Miss Bates.
Her requirement that life be vivid is too often expressed in terms of
social deportment – she sometimes talks like a governess or a
dowager – but it is, in its essence, a poet's demand.

   She herself says that she lacks tenderness, although she makes the self-accusation in her odd belief that Harriet possesses this quality; Harriet is soft and 'feminine', but she is not tender. Professor Mudrick associates the deficiency with Emma's being not suscepti-ble to men. This is perhaps so; but if it is, there may be found in her apparent sexual coolness something that is impressive and right. She makes great play about the feelings and about the fineness of the feelings that one ought to have; she sets great store by literature (although she does not read the books she prescribes for herself) and makes it a condemnation of Robert Martin that he does not read novels. Yet although, like Don Quixote and Emma Bovary, her mind is shaped and deceived by fiction, she is remarkable for the actuality and truth of her sexual feelings. Inevitably she expects that Frank Churchill will fall in love with her and she with him, but others are more deceived in the outcome of this expectation than she is – it takes but little time for her to see that she does not really respond to Churchill, that her feeling for him is no more than the lively notice that an attractive and vivacious girl takes of an attractive vivacious young man. Sentimental sexuality is not part of her nature, however much she feels it ought to be part of Harriet Smith's nature. When the right time comes, she chooses her husband wisely and seriously and eagerly.

There is, then, sufficient reason to be kind to Emma, and perhaps for nothing so much as the hope she expresses when she begins to understand her mistakes, that she will become 'more acquainted with herself'. And, indeed, all through the novel she has sought better acquaintance with herself, not wisely, not adequately, but assiduously. How modern a quest it is, and how thoroughly it confirms Dr Leavis's judgment that Jane Austen is the first truly modern novelist of England. 'In art,' a critic has said, 'the decision to be revolutionary usually counts for very little. The most radical changes have come from personalities who were conservative and even conventional. . .'[7] Jane Austen, conservative and even conventional as she was, perceived the nature of the deep psycho-logical change which accompanied the establishment of democratic society – she was aware of the increase of the psychological burden of the individual, she understood the new necessity of con-scious self-definition and self-criticism, the need to make private judgments of reality.[8] And there is no reality about which the modern person is more uncertain and more anxious than the reality of himself.

III

But the character of Emma is not the only reason for the difficulty of the novel. We must also take into account the particular genre to which the novel in some degree belongs – the pastoral idyll. It is an archaic genre which has the effect of emphasizing by contrast the brilliant modernity of Emma, and its nature may be understood through the characters of Mr Woodhouse and Miss Bates.

These two people proved a stumbling-block to one of Jane Austen's most distinguished and devoted admirers, Sir Walter Scott. In his review of *Emma* in the *Quarterly Review*, Scott said that 'characters of folly and simplicity, such as old Woodhouse and Miss Bates' are 'apt to become tiresome in fiction as in real society'. But Scott is wrong. Mr Woodhouse and Miss Bates are remarkably interesting, even though they have been created on a system of character portrayal that is no longer supposed to have validity – they exist by reason of a single trait which they display whenever they appear. Miss Bates is possessed of continuous speech and of a perfectly free association of ideas which is quite beyond her control; once launched into utterance, it is impossible for her to stop. Mr Woodhouse, Emma's father, has no other purpose in life than to preserve his health and equanimity, and no other subject of conversation than the means of doing so. The commonest circumstances of life present themselves to him as dangerous – to walk or to drive is to incur unwarrantable risk, to eat an egg not coddled in the prescribed way is to invite misery; nothing must ever change in his familial situation; he is appalled by the propensity of young people to marry, and to marry *strangers* at that.

Of the two 'characters of folly and simplicity', Mr Woodhouse is the more remarkable because he so entirely, so extravagantly, embodies a principle – of perfect stasis, of entire inertia. Almost in the degree that Jane Austen was interested in the ideal of personal energy, she was amused and attracted by persons capable of extreme inertness. She does not judge them harshly, as we incline to do – we who scarcely recall how important a part in Christian feeling the dream of *rest* once had. Mr Woodhouse is a more extreme representation of inertness than Lady Bertram of *Mansfield Park*. To say that he represents a denial of life would not be correct. Indeed, by his fear and his movelessness, he affirms life and announces his naked unadorned wish to avoid death and harm. To life, to mere life, he sacrifices almost everything.

But if Mr Woodhouse has a more speculative interest than Miss Bates, there is not much to choose between their achieved actuality as fictional characters. They are, as I have said, created on a system of character portrayal that we regard as primitive, but the reality of existence which fictional characters may claim does not depend only upon what they do, but also upon what others do to or about them, upon the way they are regarded and responded to. And in the community of Highbury, Miss Bates and Mr Woodhouse are sacred. They are fools, to be sure, as everyone knows. But they are fools of a special and transcendent kind. They are innocents – of such is the kingdom of heaven. They are children, who have learned nothing of the guile of the world. And their mode of existence is the key to the nature of the world of Highbury, which is the world of the pastoral idyll. London is but sixteen miles away – Frank Churchill can ride there and back for a haircut – but the proximity of the life of London serves but to emphasize the spiritual geography of Highbury. The weather plays a great part in *Emma*; in no other novel of Jane Austen's is the succession of the seasons, and cold and heat, of such consequence, as if to make the point which the pastoral idyll characteristically makes, that the only hardships that man ought to have to endure are meteorological. In the Forest of Arden we suffer only 'the penalty of Adam, / The seasons' difference', and Amiens' song echoes the Duke's words:

> Here shall he see
> No enemy
> But winter and rough weather.

Some explicit thought of the pastoral idyll is in Jane Austen's mind, and with all the ambivalence that marks the attitude of *As You Like It* toward the dream of man's life in nature and simplicity. Mrs Elton wants to make the strawberry party at Donwell Abbey into a *fête champêtre*: 'It is to be a morning scheme, you know, Knightley; quite a simple thing. I shall wear a large bonnet, and bring one of my little baskets hanging on my arm. Here, – probably this basket with pink ribbon. Nothing can be more simple, you see. And Jane will have such another. There is to be no form or parade – a sort of gipsy party. – We are to walk about your gardens, and gather the strawberries ourselves, and sit under trees; – and whatever else you may like to provide, it is to be all out of doors – a table spread in the shade, you know. Every thing as natural and simple as possible. Is not that your idea?' To which Knightley replies: 'Not quite. My idea of the simple and natural will be to have the table spread in the dining-room. The nature and the simplicity of gentlemen and ladies, with their servants and furniture, I think is best observed by meals within doors. When you are tired of eating strawberries in the garden, there will be cold meat in the house.'

That the pastoral idyll should be mocked as a sentimentality by its association with Mrs Elton, whose vulgarity in large part consists in flaunting the cheapened version of high and delicate ideals, and that Knightley should answer her as he does – this is quite in accordance with our expectation of Jane Austen's judgment. Yet it is only a few pages later that the members of the party walk out to see the view and we get that curious passage about the sweetness of the view, 'sweet to the eye and to the mind'. And we cannot help feeling that 'English verdure, English culture, English comfort, seen under a sun bright without being oppressive' make an England seen – if but for the moment – as an idyll.

The idyll is not a genre which nowadays we are likely to under-stand. Or at least not in fiction, the art which we believe must always address itself to actuality. The imagination of felicity is difficult for us to exercise. We feel that it is a betrayal of our awareness of our world of pain, that it is politically inappropriate. And yet one considerable critic of literature thought otherwise. Schiller is not exactly of our time, yet he is remarkably close to us in many ways and he inhabited a world scarcely less painful than ours, and he thought that the genre of the idyll had an important bearing upon social and political ideas. As Schiller defines it, the idyll is the literary genre that 'presents the idea and description of an innocent and happy humanity'.[9] This implies remoteness from the 'artificial refinements of fashionable society'; and to achieve this remoteness poets have commonly set their idylls in actually pastoral surround-ings and in the infancy of humanity. But the limitation is merely accidental – these circumstances 'do not form the object of the idyll, but are only to be regarded as the most natural means to attain this end. The end is essentially to portray man in a state of innocence, which means a state of harmony and peace with himself and the external world.' And Schiller goes on to assert the political import-ance of the genre: 'A state such as this is not merely met with before the dawn of civilization; it is also the state to which civilization aspires, as to its last end, if only it obeys a determined tendency in its progress. The idea of a similar state, and the belief in the possible reality of this state, is the only thing that can reconcile man with all the evils to which he is exposed in the path of civilization. . . .'

It is the poet's function – Schiller makes it virtually the poet's political duty – to represent the idea of innocence in a 'sensuous' way, that is, to make it seem real. This he does by gathering up the elements of actual life that do partake of innocence, and that the predominant pain of life leads us to forget, and forming them into a coherent representation of the ideal. [10]

But the idyll as traditionally conceived has an aesthetic deficiency of which Schiller is quite aware. Works in this genre, he says, appeal to the heart but not to the mind. 'We can only seek them and love them in moments in which we need calm, and not when our faculties aspire after movement and exercise. A morbid mind will find its *cure* in them, a sound soul will not find its *food* in them. They cannot vivify, they can only soften.' For the idyll excludes the idea of activity, which alone can satisfy the mind – or at least the idyll as it has been traditionally conceived makes this exclusion, but Schiller goes on to imagine a transmutation of the genre in which the characteristic calm of the idyll shall be 'the calm that follows accomplishment, not the calm of indolence – the calm that comes from the equilibrium re-established between the faculties and not from the suspending of their exercise.'

It is strange that Schiller, as he projects this new and as yet unrealized idea, does not recur to what he has previously said about comedy. To the soul of the writer of tragedy he assigns the adjective 'sublime', which for him implies reaching greatness by intense effort and strength of will; to the soul of the writer of comedy he assigns the adjective 'beautiful', which implies the achievement of freedom by an activity which is easy and natural. 'The noble task of comedy', he says, 'is to produce and keep up in us this freedom of mind.' Comedy and the idyll, then, would seem to have a natural affinity with each other. Schiller does not observe this, but Shakespeare knew it – the curious power and charm of *As You Like It* consists of bringing the idyll and comedy together, of making the idyll the subject of comedy, even of satire, yet without negating it. The mind teases the heart, but does not mock it. The unconditioned freedom that the idyll hypothecates is shown to be impossible, yet in the demonstration a measure of freedom is gained.

So in *Emma* Jane Austen contrives an idyllic world, or the closest approximation of an idyllic world that the genre of the novel will permit, and brings into contrast with it the actualities of the social world, of the modern self. In the precincts of Highbury there are no bad people, and no adverse judgments to be made. Only a modern critic, Professor Mudrick, would think to call Mr Woodhouse an idiot and an old woman: in the novel he is called 'the kindhearted, polite old gentleman'. Only Emma, with her modern consciousness, comes out with it that Miss Bates is a bore, and only Emma can give herself to the thought that Mr Weston is *too* simple and openhearted, that he would be a 'higher character' if he were not quite so friendly with everyone. It is from outside Highbury that the peculiarly modern traits of insincerity and vulgarity come, in the person of Frank Churchill and Mrs Elton. With the exception of Emma herself, every person in Highbury lives in harmony and peace – even Mr Elton would have been all right if Emma had let him alone! – and not merely because they are simple and undeveloped: Mr Knightley and Mrs Weston are no less innocent than Mr Woodhouse and Miss Bates. If they please us and do not bore us by a perfection of manner and feeling which is at once lofty and homely, it is because we accept the assumptions of the idyllic world which they inhabit – we have been led to believe that man may actually live 'in harmony and peace with himself and the external world'.

The quiet of Highbury, the unperturbed spirits of Mr Woodhouse and Miss Bates, the instructive perfection of Mr Knightley and Mrs Weston, constitute much of the charm of *Emma*. Yet the idyllic stillness of the scene and the loving celebration of what, for better or worse, is fully formed and changeless, is of course not what is decisive in the success of the novel. On the contrary, indeed: it is the idea of activity and development that is decisive. No one has put better and more eloquently what part this idea plays in Jane Austen's work than an anonymous critic writing in the *North British Review* in 1870:[11]

Even as a unit, man is only known to [Jane Austen] in the process of his formation by social influences. She broods over his history, not over his individual soul and its secret workings, nor over the analysis of its faculties and organs. She sees him, not as a solitary being completed in himself, but only as completed in society. Again, she contemplates virtues, not as fixed quantities, or as definable qualities, but as continual struggles and conquests, as progressive states of mind, advancing by repulsing their contraries, or losing ground by being overcome. Hence again the individual mind can only be represented by her as a battle-field where contending hosts are marshalled, and where victory inclines now to one side and now to another. A character therefore unfolded itself to her, not in statuesque repose, not as a model without motion, but as a dramatic sketch, a living history, a composite force, which could only exhibit what it was by exhibiting what it did. Her favourite poet Cowper taught her,

'By ceaseless action all that is subsists.'

The mind as a battlefield: it does not consort with some of the views of Jane Austen that are commonly held. Yet this is indeed how she understood the mind. And her representation of battle is the truer because she could imagine the possibility of victory – she did not shrink from the idea of victory – and because she could represent harmony and peace.

The anonymous critic of the *North British Review* goes on to say a strange and startling thing – he says that the mind of Jane Austen was 'saturated' with a 'Platonic idea'. In speaking of her ideal of 'intelligent love' – the phrase is perfect – he says that it is based on the 'Platonic idea that the giving and receiving of knowledge, the active formation of another's character, or the more passive growth under another's guidance, is the truest and strongest foundation of love'.[12] It is an ideal that not all of us will think possible of realization and that some of us will not want to give even a theoretical assent to. Yet most of us will consent to think of it as one of the most attractive of the idyllic elements of the novel. It proposes to us the hope of victory in the battle that the mind must wage, and it speaks of the expectation of allies in the fight, of the possibility of community – not in actuality, not now, but perhaps again in the future, for do we not believe, or almost believe, that there was community in the past?

The impulse to believe that the world of Jane Austen really did exist leads to notable error. 'Jane Austen's England' is the thoughtless phrase which is often made to stand for the England of the years in which our author lived, although any serious history will make it sufficiently clear that the England of her novels was not the real England, except as it gave her the license to imagine the England which we call hers. This England, especially as it is represented in *Emma*, is an idyll. The error of identifying it with the actual England ought always to be remarked. Yet the same sense of actuality that corrects the error should not fail to recognize the remarkable force of the ideal that leads many to make the error. To represent the

possibility of controlling the personal life, of becoming acquainted
with ourselves, of creating a community of 'intelligent love' – this is
indeed to make an extraordinary promise and to hold out a rare
hope. We ought not be shocked and repelled if some among us think
there really was a time when such promises and hopes were realized.
Nor ought we be entirely surprised if, when they speak of the person
who makes such promises and holds out such hopes, they represent
her as not merely a novelist, if they find it natural to deal with her as
a figure of legend and myth.

SOURCE: '*Emma* and the Legend of Jane Austen', introduction to
the Riverside Edition of *Emma* (Houghton Mifflin, 1957).

NOTES

1. *The Question of Our Speech; The Lesson of Balzac: Two Lectures*
(Boston, New York and London, 1905).

2. 'Regulated Hatred: An Aspect of the Work of Jane Austen', *Scrutiny*
VIII (March 1940); [reprinted in part in this volume, pp. 69–73].

3. *Jane Austen: Irony as Defense and Discovery* (Princeton, 1952).

4. 'Jane Austen', in *Quarterly Review*, CCXXVIII (July 1917).

5. [Editor's Note. This is doubtful, as Jane Austen finished *Emma* on 29
March 1815, and did not learn of the Regent's interest in her work until the
autumn of that year. See R. W. Chapman, *Facts and Problems* (Oxford,
1948) pp. 81 and 138.]

6. Alexis de Tocqueville, *The Old Régime and the French Revolution*
(Anchor ed. 1955) pp. 82–3. Tocqueville should not be understood as
saying that there was no class system in England but only that there was no
caste system, caste differing from class in its far greater rigidity. In his sense
of the great advantage that England enjoyed, as compared with France, in
having no caste system, Tocqueville inclines to represent the class feelings of
the English as being considerably more lenient than in fact they were. Still,
the difference between caste and class and the social and political importance of the 'gentleman' are as great as Tocqueville says.

7. Harold Rosenberg, 'Revolution and the Idea of Beauty', in *Encounter*,
Dec 1953.

8. See Abram Kardiner, *The Psychological Frontiers of Society* (New York
and London, 1945) p. 410. In commenting on the relatively simple society
which is described in James West's *Plainville, U.S.A.*, Dr Kardiner touches
on a matter which is dear, and all too dear, to Emma's heart – speaking of
social mobility in a democratic, but not classless, society, he says that the
most important criterion of class is 'manners', that 'knowing how to behave'
is the surest means of rising in the class hierarchy. Nothing is more
indicative of Jane Austen's accurate awareness of the mobility of her society

than her concern not so much with manners themselves as with her characters' concern with manners.

9. 'On Simple and Sentimental Poetry', in *Essays Aesthetical and Philosophical* (1875).

10. Schiller, in speaking of the effectiveness that the idyll should have, does not refer to the pastoral-idyllic element of Christianity which represents Christ as an actual shepherd.

11. Vol. XXCII (April) 129–52. I am grateful to Professor Joseph Duffy for having told me of this admirable study. [Editor's note. The anonymous critic has been identified as Richard Simpson. Extracts from his article are given on pp. 53–7.)

12. Emma's attempt to form the character of Harriet is thus a perversion of the relation of Mrs Weston and Mr Knightley to herself – it is a perversion, says the *North British* critic, adducing Dante's '*amoroso uso de sapienza*', because it is without love.

Wayne Booth   Control of Distance in Jane Austen's *Emma*   (1961)

Sympathy and judgment in Emma

Henry James once described Jane Austen as an instinctive novelist whose effects, some of which are admittedly fine, can best be explained as 'part of her unconsciousness'. It is as if she 'fell-a-musing' over her work-basket, he said, lapsed into 'wool-gathering', and afterward picked up 'her dropped stitches' as 'little master-strokes of imagination'.[1] The amiable accusation has been repeated in various forms, most recently as a claim that Jane Austen creates characters towards whom we cannot react as she consciously intends.[2]

Although we cannot hope to decide whether Jane Austen was entirely conscious of her own artistry, a careful look at the technique of any of her novels reveals a rather different picture from that of the unconscious spinster with her knitting needles. In *Emma* especially, where the chances for technical failure are great indeed, we find at work one of the unquestionable masters of the rhetoric of narration.

At the beginning of *Emma*, the young heroine has every requirement for deserved happiness but one. She has intelligence, wit, beauty, wealth, and position, and she has the love of those around

her. Indeed, she thinks herself completely happy. The only threat to
her happiness, a threat of which she is unaware, is herself: charming
as she is, she can neither see her own excessive pride honestly nor
resist imposing herself on the lives of others. She is deficient both in
generosity and in self-knowledge. She discovers and corrects her
faults only after she has almost ruined herself and her closest friends.
But with the reform in her character, she is ready for marriage with
the man she loves, the man who throughout the book has stood in
the reader's mind for what she lacks.

It is clear that with a general plot of this kind Jane Austen gave
herself difficulties of a high order. Though Emma's faults are comic,
they constantly threaten to produce serious harm. Yet she must
remain sympathetic or the reader will not wish for and delight
sufficiently in her reform.

Obviously, the problem with a plot like this is to find some way to
allow the reader to laugh at the mistakes committed by the heroine
and at her punishment, without reducing the desire to see her reform
and thus earn happiness. In *Tom Jones* this double attitude is
achieved, as we have seen, partly through the invention of episodes
producing sympathy and relieving any serious anxiety we might
have, and partly through the direct and sympathetic commentary.
In *Emma*, since most of the episodes must illustrate the heroine's
faults and thus increase either our emotional distance or our anxiety,
a different method is required. If we fail to see Emma's faults as
revealed in the ironic texture from line to line, we cannot savor to the
full the comedy as it is prepared for us. On the other hand, if we fail
to love her, as Jane Austen herself predicted we would[3] – if we fail to
love her more and more as the book progresses – we can neither
hope for the conclusion, a happy and deserved marriage with
Knightley following upon her reform, nor accept it as an honest one
when it comes.[4] Any attempt to solve the problem by reducing
either the love or the clear view of her faults would have been fatal.

Sympathy through control of inside views

The solution to the problem of maintaining sympathy despite almost
crippling faults was primarily to use the heroine herself as a kind of
narrator, though in third person, reporting on her own experience.
So far as we know, Jane Austen never formulated any theory to
cover her own practice; she invented no term like James's 'central

intelligence' or 'lucid reflector' to describe her method of viewing the world of the book primarily through Emma's own eyes. We can thus never know for sure to what extent James's accusation of 'unconsciousness' was right. But whether she was inclined to speculate about her method scarcely matters; her solution was clearly a brilliant one. By showing most of the story through Emma's eyes, the author insures that we shall travel with Emma rather than stand against her. It is not simply that Emma provides, in the unimpeachable evidence of her own conscience, proof that she has many redeeming qualities that do not appear on the surface; such evidence could be given with authorial commentary, though perhaps not with such force and conviction. Much more important, the sustained inside view leads the reader to hope for good fortune for the character with whom he travels, quite independently of the qualities revealed.

Seen from the outside, Emma would be an unpleasant person, unless, like Mr Woodhouse and Knightley, we knew her well enough to infer her true worth. Though we might easily be led to laugh at her, we could never be made to laugh sympathetically. While the final unmasking of her faults and her humiliation would make artistic sense to an unsympathetic reader, her marriage with Knightley would become irrelevant if not meaningless. Unless we desire Emma's happiness and her reform, which alone can make that happiness possible, a good third of this book will seem irredeemably dull.

Yet sympathetic laughter is never easily achieved. It is much easier to set up a separate fool for comic effects and to preserve your heroine for finer things. Sympathetic laughter is especially difficult with characters whose faults do not spring from sympathetic virtues. The grasping but witty Volpone can keep us on his side so long as his victims are more grasping and less witty than he, but as soon as the innocent victims, Celia and Bonario, come on stage, the quality of the humor changes; we no longer delight unambiguously in his triumphs. In contrast to this, the great sympathetic comic heroes often are comic largely because their faults, like Uncle Toby's sentimentality, spring from an excess of some virtue. Don Quixote's madness is partly caused by an excess of idealism, an excess of loving concern for the unfortunate. Every crazy gesture he makes gives further reason for loving the well-meaning old fool, and we can thus laugh at him in somewhat the same spirit in which we laugh at our own faults – in a benign, forgiving spirit. We may be contemptible for doing so; to persons without a sense of humor such laughter often seems a wicked escape. But self-love being what it is, we laugh at ourselves in a thoroughly forgiving way, and we laugh in the same way at Don Quixote: we are convinced that his heart, like ours, is in the right place.

Nothing in Emma's comic misunderstandings can serve for the same effect. Her faults are not excesses of virtue. She attempts to manipulate Harriet not from an excess of kindness but from a desire for power and admiration. She flirts with Frank Churchill out of vanity and irresponsibility. She mistreats Jane Fairfax because of Jane's *good* qualities. She abuses Miss Bates because of her own essential lack of 'tenderness' and 'good will'.

We have only to think of what Emma's story would be if seen through Jane Fairfax' or Mrs Elton's or Robert Martin's eyes to recognize how little our sympathy springs from any natural view, and to see how inescapable is the decision to use Emma's mind as a reflector of events – however beclouded her vision must be. To Jane Fairfax, who embodies throughout the book most of the values which Emma discovers only at the end, the early Emma is intolerable.

But Jane Austen never lets us forget that Emma is not what she might appear to be. For every section devoted to her misdeeds – and even they are seen for the most part through her own eyes – there is a section devoted to her self-reproach. We see her rudeness to poor foolish Miss Bates, and we see it vividly. But her remorse and act of penance in visiting Miss Bates after Knightley's rebuke are experienced even more vividly. We see her successive attempts to mislead Harriet, but we see at great length and in high color her self-castigation (chs. 16, 17, 48). We see her boasting proudly that she does not need marriage, boasting almost as blatantly of her 'resources' as does Mrs Elton (ch. 10). But we know her too intimately to take her conscious thoughts at face value. And we see her, thirty-eight chapters later, chastened to an admission of what we have known all along to be her true human need for love. 'If all took place that might take place among the circle of her friends, Hartfield must be comparatively deserted; and she left to cheer her father with the spirits only of ruined happiness. The child to be born at Randalls must be a tie there even dearer than herself; and Mrs Weston's heart and time would be occupied by it. . . . All that were good would be withdrawn' (ch. 48).

Perhaps the most delightful effects from our sustained inside view of a very confused and very charming young woman come from her frequent thoughts about Knightley. She is basically right all along about his pre-eminent wisdom and virtue, and she is our chief authority for taking *his* authority so seriously. And yet in every thought about him she is misled. Knightley rebukes her; the reader knows that Knightley is in the right. But Emma?

> Emma made no answer, and tried to look cheerfully unconcerned, but was really feeling uncomfortable, and wanting him very much to be gone. She did not repent what she had done; she still thought herself a better judge of such a point of female right and refinement than he could be; but yet she had a sort of habitual respect for his judgment in general, which made her dislike having it so loudly against her; and to have him sitting just opposite to her in angry state, was very disagreeable. (ch. 8)

Even more striking is the lack of self-knowledge shown when Mrs Weston suggests that Knightley might marry Jane Fairfax.

> Her objections to Mr Knightley's marrying did not in the least subside. She could see nothing but evil in it. It would be a great disappointment to Mr John Knightley [Knightley's brother]; consequently to Isabella. A real injury to the children – a most mortifying change, and material loss to them all; – a very great deduction from her father's daily comfort – and, as to herself, she could not at all endure the idea of Jane Fairfax at Donwell Abbey. A Mrs Knightley for them all to give way to! – No, Mr Knightley must never marry. Little Henry must remain the heir of Donwell. (ch. 26)

Self-deception could hardly be carried further, at least in a person of high intelligence and sensitivity.

Yet the effect of all this is what our tolerance for our own faults produces in our own lives. While only immature readers ever really identify with any character, losing all sense of distance and hence all chance of an artistic experience, our emotional reaction to every event concerning Emma tends to become like her own. When she feels anxiety or shame, we feel analogous emotions. Our modern awareness that such 'feelings' are not identical with those we feel in our own lives in similar circumstances has tended to blind us to the fact that aesthetic form can be built out of patterned emotions as well as out of other materials. It is absurd to pretend that because our emotions and desires in responding to fiction are in a very real sense disinterested, they do not or should not exist. Jane Austen, in developing the sustained use of a sympathetic inside view, has mastered one of the most successful of all devices for inducing a parallel emotional response between the deficient heroine and the reader.

Sympathy for Emma can be heightened by withholding inside views of others as well as by granting them of her. The author knew, for example, that it would be fatal to grant any extended inside view of Jane Fairfax. The inadequacies of impressionistic criticism are nowhere revealed more clearly than in the suggestion often made about such minor characters that their authors would have liked to make them vivid but didn't know how.[5] Jane Austen knew perfectly well how to make such a character vivid; Anne in *Persuasion* is a kind of Jane Fairfax turned into heroine. But in *Emma*, Emma must shine supreme. It is not only that the slightest glance inside Jane's mind would be fatal to all of the author's plans for mystification about Frank Churchill, though this is important. The major problem is that any extended view of her would reveal her as a more sympathetic person than Emma herself. Jane is superior to Emma in most respects except the stroke of good fortune that made Emma the heroine of the book. In matters of taste and ability, of head and of heart, she is Emma's superior, and Jane Austen, always in danger of losing our sympathy for Emma, cannot risk any degree of distraction. Jane could, it is true, be granted fewer virtues, and *then* made more vivid. But to do so would greatly weaken the force of Emma's mistakes of heart and head in her treatment of the almost faultless Jane.

Control of judgment

But the very effectiveness of the rhetoric designed to produce sympathy might in itself lead to a serious misreading of the book. In reducing the emotional distance, the natural tendency is to reduce – willy-nilly – moral and intellectual distance as well. In reacting to Emma's faults from the inside out, as if they were our own, we may very well not only forgive them but overlook them.

There is, of course, no danger that readers who persist to the end will overlook Emma's serious mistakes; since she sees and reports those mistakes herself, everything becomes crystal clear at the end. The real danger inherent in the experiment is that readers will overlook the mistakes as they are committed and thus miss much of the comedy that depends on Emma's distorted view from page to page. If readers who dislike Emma cannot enjoy the preparation for the marriage to Knightley, readers who do not recognize her faults with absolute precision cannot enjoy the details of the preparation for the comic abasement which must precede that marriage.

It might be argued that there is no real problem, since the conventions of her time allowed for reliable commentary whenever it was needed to place Emma's faults precisely. But Jane Austen is not operating according to the conventions, most of which she had long since parodied and outgrown; her technique is determined by the needs of the novel she is writing. We can see this clearly by contrasting the manner of *Emma* with that of *Persuasion*, the next, and last-completed, work. In *Emma* there are many breaks in the point of view, because Emma's beclouded mind cannot do the whole job. In *Persuasion*, where the heroine's viewpoint is faulty only in her ignorance of Captain Wentworth's love, there are very few. Anne Elliot's consciousness is sufficient, as Emma's is not, for most of the needs of the novel which she dominates. We can never rely completely on Emma. It is hardly surprising that Jane Austen has provided many correctives to insure our placing her errors with precision.

The chief corrective is Knightley. His commentary on Emma's errors is a natural expression of his love; he can tell the reader and Emma at the same time precisely how she is mistaken. Thus, nothing Knightley says can be beside the point. Each affirmation of a value, each accusation of error is in itself an action in the plot. When he rebukes Emma for manipulating Harriet, when he attacks her for superficiality and false pride, when he condemns her for gossiping and flirting with Frank Churchill, and finally when he attacks her for being 'insolent' and 'unfeeling' in her treatment of Miss Bates, we have Jane Austen's judgment on Emma, rendered dramatically. But it has come from someone who is essentially sympathetic toward Emma, so that his judgments against her are presumed to be temporary. His sympathy reinforces ours even as he criticizes, and her respect for his opinion, shown in her self-abasement after he has criticized, is one of our main reasons for expecting her to reform.

If Henry James had tried to write a novel about Emma, and had cogitated at length on the problem of getting her story told dramatically, he could not have done better than this. It is possible, of course, to think of *Emma* without Knightley as *raisonneur*, just as it is possible to think of *The Golden Bowl*, say, without the Assinghams as *ficelles* to reflect something not seen by the Prince or Princess. But Knightley, though he receives less independent space than the Assinghams and is almost never seen in an inside view, is clearly more useful for Jane Austen's purposes than any realistically limited *ficelle* could possibly be. By combining the role of commentator with the role of hero, Jane Austen has worked more economically than James, and though economy is as dangerous as any other criterion when applied universally, even James might have profited from a closer study of the economies that a character like Knightley can be made to achieve. It is as if James had dared to make one of the four main characters, say the Prince, into a thoroughly good, wise, perceptive man, a thoroughly clear rather than a partly confused 'reflector'.

Since Knightley is established early as completely reliable, we need no views of his secret thoughts. He has no secret thoughts, except for the unacknowledged depths of his love for Emma and his jealousy of Frank Churchill. The other main characters have more to hide, and Jane Austen moves in and out of minds with great freedom, choosing for her own purposes what to reveal and what to withhold. Always the seeming violation of consistency is in the consistent service of the particular needs of Emma's story. Sometimes a shift is made simply to direct our suspense, as when Mrs Weston suggests a possible union of Emma and Frank Churchill, at the end of her conversation with Knightley about the harmful effects of Emma's friendship with Harriet (ch. 5). 'Part of her meaning was to conceal some favourite thoughts of her own and Mr Weston's on the subject, as much as possible. There were wishes at Randalls respecting Emma's destiny, but it was not desirable to have them suspected.'

One objection to this selective dipping into whatever mind best serves our immediate purposes is that it suggests mere trickery and inevitably spoils the illusion of reality. If Jane Austen can tell us what Mrs Weston is thinking, why not what Frank Churchill and Jane Fairfax are thinking? Obviously, because she chooses to build a mystery, and to do so she must refuse, arbitrarily and obtrusively, to grant the privilege of an inside view to characters whose minds would reveal too much. But is not the mystery purchased at the price of shaking the reader's faith in Jane Austen's integrity? If she simply withholds until later what she might as well relate now – if her procedure is not dictated by the very nature of her materials – why should we take her seriously?

If a natural surface were required in all fiction, then this objection would hold. But if we want to read *Emma* in its own terms, the real question about these shifts cannot be answered by an easy appeal to general principles. Every author withholds until later what he 'might as well' relate now. The question is always one of desired effects, and the choice of any one effect always bans innumerable other effects. There is, indeed, a question to be raised about the use of mystery in *Emma*, but the conflict is not between an abstract end that Jane Austen never worried about and a shoddy mystification that she allowed to betray her. The conflict is between two effects, both of which she cares about a good deal. On the one hand she cares about maintaining some sense of mystery as long as she can. On the other, she works at all points to heighten the reader's sense of dramatic irony, usually in the form of a contrast between what Emma knows and what the reader knows.

As in most novels, whatever steps are taken to mystify inevitably decrease the dramatic irony, and, whenever dramatic irony is increased by telling the reader secrets the characters have not yet suspected, mystery is inevitably destroyed. The longer we are in doubt about Frank Churchill, the weaker our sense of ironic contrast between Emma's views and the truth. The sooner we see through Frank Churchill's secret plot, the greater our pleasure in observing Emma's innumerable misreadings of his behavior and the less interest we have in the mere mystery of the situation. And we all find that on second reading we discover new intensities of dramatic irony resulting from the complete loss of mystery; knowing what abysses of error Emma is preparing for herself, even those of us who may on first reading have deciphered nearly all the details of the Churchill mystery find additional ironies.

But it is obvious that these ironies could have been offered even on a first reading, if Jane Austen had been willing to sacrifice her mystery. A single phrase in her own name – 'his secret engagement to Jane Fairfax' – or a short inside view of either of the lovers could have made us aware of every ironic touch.

The author must, then, choose whether to purchase mystery at the expense of irony. For many of us Jane Austen's choice here is perhaps the weakest aspect of this novel. It is a commonplace of our

criticism that significant literature arouses suspense not about the
'what' but about the 'how'. Mere mystification has been mastered
by so many second-rate writers that her efforts at mystification seem
second-rate.

But again we must ask whether criticism can be conducted
effectively by balancing one abstract quality against another. Is
there a norm of dramatic irony for all works, or even for all works of
a given kind? Has anyone ever formulated a 'law of first and second
readings' that will tell us just how many of our pleasures on page one
should depend on our knowledge of what happens on page the last?
We quite properly ask that the books we call great be able to stand
up under repeated reading, but we need not ask that they yield
identical pleasures on each reading. The modern works whose
authors pride themselves on the fact that they can never be read but
only re-read may be very good indeed, but they are not *made* good
by the fact that their secret pleasures can only be wrested from them
by repeated readings.

In any case, even if one accepted the criticism of Jane Austen's
efforts at mystification, the larger service of the inside views is clear:
the crosslights thrown by other minds prevent our being blinded by
Emma's radiance.

The reliable narrator and the norms of Emma

If mere intellectual clarity about Emma were the goal in this work,
we should be forced to say that the manipulation of inside views and
the extensive commentary of the reliable Knightley are more than is
necessary. But for maximum intensity of the comedy and romance,
even these are not enough. The 'author herself' – not necessarily the
real Jane Austen but an implied author, represented in this book by
a reliable narrator – heightens the effects by directing our intellectual, moral, and emotional progress. She performs, of course, most
of the functions described in chapter 7. But her most important role
is to reinforce both aspects of the double vision that operates
throughout the book: our inside view of Emma's worth and our
objective view of her great faults.

The narrator opens *Emma* with a masterful simultaneous presentation of Emma and of the values against which she must be judged:
'Emma Woodhouse, handsome, clever, and rich, with a comfortable
home and happy disposition, seemed to unite some of the best

blessings of existence, and had lived nearly twenty-one years in the world with very little to distress or vex her.' This 'seemed' is immediately reinforced by more directly stated reservations. 'The real evils of Emma's situation were the power of having rather too much her own way, and a disposition to think a little too well of herself; these were the disadvantages which threatened alloy to her many enjoyments. The danger, however, was at present so unperceived, that they did not by any means rank as misfortunes with her.'

None of this could have been said by Emma, and if shown through her consciousness, it could not be accepted, as it must be, without question. Like most of the first three chapters, it is non-dramatic summary, building up, through the ostensible business of getting the characters introduced, to Emma's initial blunder with Harriet and Mr Elton. Throughout these chapters we learn much of what we must know from the narrator, but she turns over more and more of the job of summary to Emma as she feels more and more sure of our seeing precisely to what degree Emma is to be trusted. Whenever we leave the 'real evils' we have been warned against in Emma, the narrator's and Emma's views coincide: we cannot tell which of them, for example, offers the judgment on Mr Woodhouse that 'his talents could not have recommended him at any time', or the judgment on Mr Knightley that he is 'a sensible man', 'always welcome' at Hartfield, or even that 'Mr Knightley, in fact, was one of the few people who could see faults in Emma Woodhouse, and the only one who ever told her of them'.

But there are times when Emma and her author are far apart, and the author's direct guidance aids the reader in his own break with Emma. The beautiful irony of the first description of Harriet, given through Emma's eyes (ch. 3) could no doubt be grasped intellectually by many readers without all of the preliminary commentary. But even for the most perceptive its effect is heightened, surely, by the sense of standing with the author and observing with her precisely how Emma's judgment is going astray. Perhaps more important, we ordinary, less perceptive readers have by now been raised to a level suited to grasp the ironies. Certainly, most readers would overlook some of the barbs directed against Emma if the novel began, as a serious modern novelist might well begin it, with this description:

[Emma] was not struck by any thing remarkably clever in Miss Smith's conversation, but she found her altogether very engaging – not inconveniently shy, not unwilling to talk – and yet so far from pushing, shewing so proper and becoming a deference, seeming so pleasantly grateful for being admitted to Hartfield, and so artlessly impressed by the appearance of every thing in so superior a style to what she had been used to, that she must have good sense and deserve encouragement. Encouragement should be given. Those soft blue eyes ... should not be wasted on the inferior society of Highbury. . . .

And so Emma goes on, giving herself away with every word, pouring out her sense of her own beneficence and general value; Harriet's past friends, 'though very good sort of people, must be doing her harm'. Without knowing them, Emma knows that they 'must be coarse and unpolished, and very unfit to be the intimates of a girl who wanted only a little more knowledge and elegance to be quite perfect'. And she concludes with a beautiful burst of egotism: '*She* would notice her; she would improve her; she would detach her from her bad acquaintance, and introduce her into good society; she would form her opinions and her manners. It would be an interesting, and certainly a very kind undertaking; highly becoming her own situation in life, her leisure, and powers.' Even the most skilful reader might not easily plot an absolutely true course through these ironies without the prior direct assistance we have been given. Emma's views are not so outlandish that they could never have been held by a female novelist writing in her time. They cannot serve effectively as signs of *her* character unless they are clearly disavowed as signs of Jane Austen's views. Emma's unconscious catalogue of her egotistical uses for Harriet, given under the pretense of listing the services *she* will perform, is thus given its full force by being framed explicitly in a world of values which Emma herself cannot discover until the conclusion of the book.

The full importance of the author's direct imposition of an elaborate scale of norms can be seen by considering that conclusion. The sequence of events is a simple one: Emma's faults and mistakes are brought home to her in a rapid and humiliating chain of rebukes from Knightley and blows from hard fact. These blows to her self-esteem produce at last a genuine reform (for example, she brings herself to apologize to Miss Bates, something she could never have done earlier in the novel). The change in her character removes the only obstacle in the way of Knightley's proposal, and the marriage follows. 'The wishes, the hopes, the confidence, the predictions of

the small band of true friends who witnessed the ceremony, were
fully answered in the perfect happiness of the union.'

It may be that if we look at Emma and Knightley as real people,
this ending will seem false. G. B. Stern laments, in *Speaking of Jane
Austen*, 'Oh, Miss Austen, it was *not* a good solution; it was a bad
solution, an unhappy ending, could we see beyond the last pages of
the book.' Edmund Wilson predicts that Emma will find a new protégée like Harriet, since she has not been cured of her inclination to
'infatuations with women'. Marvin Mudrick even more emphatically
rejects Jane Austen's explicit rhetoric; he believes that Emma is still a
'confirmed exploiter', and for him the ending must be read as ironic.[6]

But it is precisely because this ending is neither life itself nor a
simple bit of literary irony that it can serve so well to heighten our
sense of a complete and indeed perfect resolution to all that has gone
before. If we look at the values that have been realized in this
marriage and compare them with those realized in conventional
marriage plots, we see that Jane Austen means what she says: this
will be a happy marriage because there is simply nothing left to
make it anything less than perfectly happy. It fulfils every value
embodied in the world of the book – with the possible exception that
Emma may never learn to apply herself as she ought to her reading
and her piano! It is a union of intelligence: of 'reason', of 'sense', of
'judgment'. It is a union of virtue: of 'good will', of generosity, of
unselfishness. It is a union of feeling: of 'taste', 'tenderness', 'love',
'beauty'.[7]

In a general way, then, this plot offers us an experience superficially like that offered by most tragicomedy as well as by much of
the cheapest popular art: we are made to desire certain good things
for certain good characters, and then our desires are gratified. If we
depended on general criteria derived from our justified boredom
with such works, we should reject this one. But the critical difference
lies in the precise quality of the values appealed to and the precise
quality of the characters who violate or realize them. All of the cheap
marriage plots in the world should not lead us to be embarrassed
about our pleasure in Emma and Knightley's marriage. It is more
than just the marriage: it is the *rightness* of *this* marriage, as a
conclusion to all of the comic wrongness that has gone before. The
good for Emma includes both her necessary reform and the resulting
marriage. Marriage to an intelligent, amiable, good, and attractive

man is the best thing that can happen to this heroine, and the
readers who do not experience it as such are, I am convinced, far
from knowing what Jane Austen is about – whatever they may say
about the 'bitter spinster's' attitude towards marriage.

Our modern sensibilities are likely to be rasped by any such
formulation. We do not ordinarily like to encounter perfect endings
in our novels – even in the sense of 'perfectedness' or completion, the
sense obviously intended by Jane Austen. We refuse to acept it when
we see it: witness the many attempts to deny Dostoevski's success
with Alyosha and Father Zossima in *The Brothers Karamazov*. Many
of us find it embarrassing to talk of emotions based on moral
judgment at all, particularly when the emotions have any kind of
affirmative cast. Emma herself is something of a 'modern' in this
regard throughout most of the book. Her self-deception about
marriage is as great as about most other important matters. Emma
boasts to Harriet of her indifference to marriage, at the same time
unconsciously betraying her totally inadequate view of the sources of
human happiness.

'If I know myself, Harriet, mine is an active, busy mind, with a great
many independent resources; and I do not perceive why I should be more in
want of employment at forty or fifty than one-and-twenty. Woman's usual
occupations of eye and hand and mind will be as open to me then, as they
are now; or with no important variation. If I draw less, I shall read more; if
I give up music, I shall take to carpet-work.'

Emma at carpet-work! If she knows herself indeed.

'And as for objects of interest, objects for the affections, which is, in truth,
the great point of inferiority, the want of which is really the great evil to be
avoided in *not* marrying [a magnificent concession, this] I shall be very well
off, with all the children of a sister I love so much, to care about. There will
be enough of them, in all probability, to supply every sort of sensation that
declining life can need. There will be enough for every hope and every fear;
and though my attachment to none can equal that of a parent, it suits my
ideas of comfort better than what is warmer and blinder. My nephews and
nieces! – I shall often have a niece with me.'   (ch. 10)

Without growing solemn about it – it is wonderfully comic – we can
recognize that the humor springs here from very deep sources
indeed. It can be fully enjoyed, in fact, only by the reader who has
attained to a vision of human felicity far more profound than
Emma's 'comfort' and 'want' and 'need'. It is a vision that includes

not simply marriage, but a kind of loving converse not based, as is Emma's here, on whether the 'loved' person will serve one's irreducible needs.

The comic effect of this repudiation of marriage is considerably increased by the fact that Emma always thinks of marriage for others as *their* highest good, and in fact unconsciously encourages her friend Harriet to fall in love with the very man she herself loves without knowing it. The delightful denouement is thus what we want not only because it is a supremely good thing for Emma, but because it is a supremely comic outcome of Emma's profound misunderstanding of herself and of the human condition. In the schematic language of chapter 5, it satisfies both our practical desire for Emma's well-being and our appetite for the qualities proper to these artistic materials. It is thus a more resounding resolution than either of these elements separately could provide. The other major resolution of the work – Harriet's marriage with her farmer – reinforces this interpretation. Emma's sin against Harriet has been something far worse than the mere meddling of a busybody. To destroy Harriet's chances for happiness – chances that depend entirely on her marriage – is as close to viciousness as any author could dare to take a heroine designed to be loved. We can laugh with Emma at this mistake (ch. 54) only because Harriet's chance for happiness is restored.

Other values, like money, blood, and 'consequence', are real enough in *Emma*, but only as they contribute to or are mastered by good taste, good judgment, and good morality. Money alone can make a Mrs Churchill, but a man or woman 'is silly to marry without it'. Consequence untouched by sense can make a very inconsequential Mr Woodhouse; untouched by sense or virtue it can make the much more contemptible Mr and Miss Elliot of *Persuasion*. But it is a pleasant thing to have, and it does no harm unless, like the early Emma, one takes it too seriously. Charm and elegance without sufficient moral force can make a Frank Churchill; unschooled by morality it can lead to the baseness of Henry Crawford in *Mansfield Park* or of Wickham in *Pride and Prejudice*. Even the supreme virtues are inadequate in isolation: good will alone will make a comic Miss Bates or a Mr Weston, judgment with insufficient good will a comic Mr John Knightley, and so on.

I am willing to risk the commonplace in such a listing because it is only thus that the full force of Jane Austen's comprehensive view can

be seen. There is clearly at work here a much more detailed ordering
of values than any conventional public philosophy of her time could
provide. Obviously, few readers in her own time, and far fewer in
our own, have ever approached this novel in full and detailed
agreement with the author's norms. But they were led to join her as
they read, and so are we.

Explicit judgments on Emma Woodhouse

We have said in passing almost enough of the other side of the coin –
the judgment of particular actions as they relate to the general
norms. But something must be said of the detailed 'placing' of
Emma, by direct commentary, in the hierarchy of values established
by the novel. I must be convinced, for example, not only that
tenderness for other people's feelings is an important trait but also
that Emma's particular behavior violates the true standards of
tenderness, if I am to savor to the full the episode of Emma's insult
to Miss Bates and Knightley's reproach which follows. If I refuse to
blame Emma, I may discover a kind of intellectual enjoyment in
the episode, and I will probably think that any critic who talks of
'belief' in tenderness as operating in such a context is taking things
too seriously. But I can never enjoy the episode in its full intensity or
grasp its formal coherence. Similarly, I must agree not only that to
be dreadfully boring is a minor fault compared with the major virtue
of 'good will', but also that Miss Bates' exemplification of this fault
and of this virtue entitle her to the respect which Emma denies. If I
do not – while yet being able to laugh at Miss Bates – I can hardly
understand, let alone enjoy, Emma's mistreatment of her.

But these negative judgments must be counteracted by a larger
approval, and, as we would expect, the novel is full of direct
apologies for Emma. Her chief fault, lack of good will or tenderness,
must be read not only in relationship to the code of values provided
by the book as a whole – a code which judges her as seriously
deficient; it must also be judged in relationship to the harsh facts of
the world around her, a world made up of human beings ranging in
degree of selfishness and egotism from Knightley, who lapses from
perfection when he tries to judge Frank Churchill, his rival, down to
Mrs Elton, who has most of Emma's faults and none of her virtues.
In such a setting, Emma is easily forgiven. When she insults Miss
Bates, for example, we remember that Miss Bates lives in a world

where many others are insensitive and cruel. 'Miss Bates, neither young, handsome, rich, nor married, stood in the very worst predicament in the world for having much of the public favor; and she had no intellectual superiority to make atonement to herself, or frighten those who might hate her, into outward respect.' While it would be a mistake to see only this 'regular hatred' in Jane Austen's world, overlooking the tenderness and generosity, the hatred of viciousness is there, and there is enough vice in evidence to make Emma almost shine by comparison.

Often, Jane Austen makes this apology-by-comparison explicit. When Emma lies to Knightley about Harriet, very close to the end of the book, she is excused with a generalization about human nature: 'Seldom, very seldom, does complete truth belong to any human disclosure; seldom can it happen that something is not a little disguised, or a little mistaken; but where, as in this case, though the conduct is mistaken, the feelings are not, it may not be very material. – Mr Knightley could not impute to Emma a more relenting heart than she possessed, or a heart more disposed to accept of his.'

The implied author as friend and guide

With all of this said about the masterful use of the narrator in *Emma*, there remain some 'intrusions' unaccounted for by strict service to the story itself. 'What did she say?' the narrator asks, at the crucial moment in the major love scene. 'Just what she ought, of course. A lady always does. – She said enough to show there need not be despair – and to invite him to say more himself.' To some readers this has seemed to demonstrate the author's inability to write a love scene, since it sacrifices 'the illusion of reality'.[8] But who has ever read this far in *Emma* under the delusion that he is reading a realistic portrayal which is suddenly shattered by the unnatural appearance of the narrator? If the narrator's superabundant wit is destructive of the kind of illusion proper to this work, the novel has been ruined long before.

But we should now be in a position to see precisely why the narrator's wit is not in the least out of place at the emotional climax of the novel. We have seen how the inside views of the characters and the author's commentary have been used from the beginning to get the values straight and to keep them straight and to help direct our reactions to Emma. But we also see here a beautiful case of the dramatized author as friend and guide. 'Jane Austen', like 'Henry Fielding', is a paragon of wit, wisdom, and virtue. She does not talk about her qualities; unlike Fielding, she does not in *Emma* call direct attention to her artistic skill. But we are seldom allowed to forget about her for all that. When we read this novel we accept her as representing everything we admire most. She is as generous and wise as Knightley; in fact, she is a shade more penetrating in her judgment. She is as subtle and witty as Emma would like to think herself. Without being sentimental she is in favor of tenderness. She is able to put an adequate but not excessive value on wealth and rank. She recognizes a fool when she sees one, but unlike Emma she knows that it is both immoral and foolish to be rude to fools. She is, in short, a perfect human being, within the concept of perfection established by the book she writes; she even recognizes that human perfection of the kind *she* exemplifies is not quite attainable in real life. The process of her domination is of course circular; her character establishes the values for us according to which her character is then found to be perfect. But this circularity does not affect the success of her endeavor; in fact it insures it.

Her 'omniscience' is thus a much more remarkable thing than is ordinarily implied by the term. All good novelists know all about their characters – all that they need to know. And the question of how their narrators are to find out all that *they* need to know, the question of 'authority', is a relatively simple one. The real choice is much more profound than this would imply. It is a choice of the moral, not merely the technical, angle of vision from which the story is to be told.

Unlike the central intelligences of James and his successors, 'Jane Austen' has learned nothing at the end of the novel that she did not know at the beginning. She needed to learn nothing. She knew everything of importance already. We have been privileged to watch with her as she observes her favorite character climb from a considerably lower platform to join the exalted company of Knightley, 'Jane Austen', and those of us readers who are wise enough, good enough, and perceptive enough to belong up there too. As Katherine Mansfield says, 'the truth is that every true admirer of the novels cherishes the happy thought that he alone – reading between the lines – has become the secret friend of their author'.[9] Those who love 'gentle Jane' as a secret friend may undervalue the irony and wit; those who see her in effect as the greatest of Shaw's heroines, flashing about her with the weapons of irony, may undervalue the emphasis on tenderness and good will. But only a very few can resist her.

The dramatic illusion of her presence as a character is thus fully as important as any other element in the story. When she intrudes, the illusion is not shattered. The only illusion we care about, the illusion of traveling intimately with a hardy little band of readers whose heads are screwed on tight and whose hearts are in the right place, is actually strengthened when we are refused the romantic love scene. Like the author herself, we don't care about the love scene. We can find love scenes in almost any novelist's works, but only here can we find a mind and heart that can give us clarity without oversimplification, sympathy and romance without sentimentality, and biting irony without cynicism.

SOURCE: 'Control of Distance in Jane Austen's *Emma*', from *The Rhetoric of Fiction* (University of Chicago Press, 1961) pp. 243–66.

NOTES

1. 'The Lesson of Balzac', in *The Question of Our Speech* (Cambridge, 1905) p. 63.

2. See, for example, Mudrick, *Jane Austen: Irony as Defense and Discovery* (Princeton, 1952) pp. 91, 165; Frank O'Connor, *The Mirror in the Roadway* (1957) p. 30.

3. 'A heroine whom no one but myself will much like'; see James Edward Austen-Leigh, *Memoir of His Aunt* (London, 1870; Oxford, 1926) p. 157.

4. What is probably the best discussion of this double-edged problem is buried in Reginald Farrer's essay on 'Jane Austen', in *Quarterly Review*, CCXXVIII (July 1917) 1–30. For one critic the book fails because the problem was never recognized by Jane Austen herself: Mr E. N. Hayes, in what may well be the least sympathetic discussion of *Emma* yet written, explains the whole book as the *author's* failure to see Emma's faults. 'Evidently Jane Austen wished to protect Emma.' 'The author is therefore in the ambiguous position of both loving and scorning the heroine' – see '*Emma*: A Dissenting Opinion', in *Nineteenth-century Fiction*, IV (June 1949) 18, 19. [Extracts from these articles are reprinted in this volume, pp. 65–9 and 74–7.]

5. A. C. Bradley, for example, once argued that Jane Austen intended Jane Fairfax to be as interesting throughout as she becomes at the end, but 'the moralist in Jane Austen stood for once in her way. The secret engagement is, for her, so serious an offence, that she is afraid to win our hearts for

Jane until it has led to great unhappiness.' 'Jane Austen', in *Essays and Studies, by Members of the English Association*, II (Oxford, 1911) 23.

6. The first two quotations are from Wilson's 'A Long Talk about Jane Austen', in *A Literary Chronicle: 1920–1950* (New York, 1952). The third is from *Jane Austen* (Princeton, 1952) p. 206.

7. It has lately been fashionable to underplay the value of tenderness and good will in Jane Austen in reaction to an earlier generation that overdid the picture of 'gentle Jane'. The trend seems to have begun in earnest with D. W. Harding's 'Regulated Hatred: An Aspect of the Work of Jane Austen', in *Scrutiny*, VIII (March 1940) 346–62 [reprinted in this volume, pp. 69–73.] While I do not feel as strongly aroused against this school of readers as does R. W. Chapman – (see his *A Critical Bibliography* (Oxford, 1953) p. 52, and his review of Mudrick's work in the *Times Literary Supplement* (19 Sept 1952)) – it seems to me that another swing of the pendulum is called for: when Jane Austen praises the 'relenting heart', she means that praise, though she is the same author who can lash the unrelenting heart with 'regulated hatred'.

8. Edd Winfield Parks, 'Exegesis in Austen's Novels', in *South Atlantic Quarterly*, LI (Jan 1952) 117.

9. *Novels and Novelists*, ed. J. Middleton Murry (1930) p. 304.

Malcolm Bradbury Jane Austen's *Emma* (1962)

'Jane Austen', said Henry James in one of his few great misjudgments, 'was instinctive and charming.... For signal examples of what composition, distribution, arrangement can do, of how they intensify the life of a work of art, we have to go elsewhere.' We do not, of course; and my purpose here is to suggest something of the complexity of the structure that Jane Austen creates to express the elaborate pattern of values contained in *Emma*. 'I am going to take a heroine whom no-one but myself will much like', said Jane Austen of the novel; and one might set the remark against her comment that Anne Elliot, the heroine of *Persuasion* (surely Jane Austen's best novel) was almost too good for her. It is presumably a moral objection she fears will be brought against Emma; and it is to be by resolving this situation – by fitting Emma into the moral expectations which she projects outwards into the audience, as it were – that the book must work. The self-willed quality of Emma, in which

her attractiveness for reader and for novelist resides, must be contained and adapted, adapted to a norm which is neither social
(though it is a norm which *lives* in society) nor doctrinaire (though it
is a norm pragmatic simply in the sense that it re-establishes by
proof of value the best traditional decencies).

Jane Austen is concerned with two kinds of world – the social
world and the moral world – and their interaction, an interaction
that is intimate, but also complex. It is often complained of her that
she measured life from the conventional social standards of the
upper middle class about which she writes and to which she belongs,
and that this limits her wider relevance and 'excludes' her from the
modern novel, one of the attributes of which is a greater range in its
treatment of character and value. Leavis disposes of one aspect of
this idea in *The Great Tradition*, and it is worth stressing here the
degree to which she dissipates and tests her own predilections, and is
capable of having predilections that seem to violate the rigidities we
associate with her. Of course it is true that class attitudes are of the
greatest importance; but it is in the evaluation of these attitudes, and
the building up of a scale of them for the proper conduct of the moral
life, that she excels. She is nothing if not stringent. The whole structure of her inventions is recurrently that of a kind of moral assault
course, an extended interview in which candidates give their qualifications, undergo a succession of tests, and are finally rewarded by
the one prize that is possible and appropriate in their social context
– marriage, a marriage which is aesthetically right, morally and
humanly balanced, financially sound. (Lawrence in some of his
novels uses a similar structure, the tests here being emotional and
sexual, the final reward genital.)

What Jane Austen has to do, then, in *Emma* is to establish side by
side a social world and a moral world, the latter setting up a higher
level of action and judgment than the former. The social world is
carefully and precisely given; it is elaborate in range, though not in
class. The action takes place in Highbury, a 'large and populous
village, almost amounting to a town', sixteen miles out of London;
its life is the life of the time of writing (*Emma* was published in 1816).
The landscape of Highbury is a landscape of property; there is
Hartfield, the home of the Woodhouses, who are 'the first in consequence in Highbury'; there is Randalls, home of Mr Weston, 'a
little estate'; there is Donwell Abbey 'in the parish adjoining, the
seat of Mr Knightley'. Emma's sister lives in London, in Brunswick

Square, only relatively accessible; Highbury is a more or less self-contained social unit, and it certainly contains most of the action. Further, the upper-middle-class level of Highbury life includes most of the significant characters; and this is the level we see from. There are persons of higher rank, but they are *felt* to be high – in particular, the Churchills, the great Yorkshire family, are presented as rather 'above' the novel. There are, too, characters clearly 'below' the novel, like the tenant farmer Robert Martin and the former Miss Taylor and Mrs Goddard and Miss Bates, who come from the depressed 'professional' middle class. And then there are the socially indeterminate characters, who serve so importantly in the action – Miss Harriet Smith, illegitimate, of obscure origins, unfixed by kinship or duty; Frank Churchill, split between families; and Jane Fairfax. These figures, coming from outside the locale and existing in uncertain relation to it, are the disturbing forces; and their presence promotes most of the action. In particular Miss Harriet Smith is an anarchic force and, especially, a test of people's observations of innate quality, because she can fit in at any of a number of possible class levels; indeed, she can claim her class by her own merits, and so is in the singular position of being mobile in a largely stable society. And the novel, by concentrating on the period prior to marriage in these people, is able to show them at their most mobile; they exist in a state of uncertainty, finished by marriage, which 'fixes' them at a deserved level in the class system.

Now the central characters of the fiction are landowners with tenant farmers, persons of private income, or persons dependent on the professions or trade; they are small in number in the novel, and are concentrated in houses and families, with few points of reference outside Highbury; they live in a controlled and stable world. Most of the characters know one another before the action of the novel begins and enlarge existing relationships in the course of it; they are related by kinship or common social duties; they live most of their lives in the place where they are born. The limits of the world of the novel are, indeed, determined from the centre – all the characters exist in some kind of established relationship to the heroine or her immediate friends. In picaresque novels the relationships with the hero are usually those of casual encounter, a structure that is consonant with a pragmatic and open view of the universe; but here we have a homogeneous world, taking its standards of life from within itself, and communicating outside only rarely. The characters are inhibited by a strong sense of rank and social duty, and no real violation of rank is within the novel's probabilities. The Highbury equals are capable of intimate relationships with one another; but, as rank changes, the relation to the Woodhouses grows more distant (the vicar is not close, the schoolmistress is received, the poor are visited), while characters in mobile situations create most of the tensions – like the rising Coles: 'The Coles were very respectable in their way, but they ought to be taught that it was not for them to arrange the terms on which superior families would visit them.' (But this is by no means the *final* standard of judgment; the thought is Emma's, and the reader is invited soon to wonder, when he meets the Coles and finds their pleasantness stressed, what constitutes 'superiority'.) The constraints of a fixed society are firmly felt, and Jane Austen never tests the values that arise within this world outside the area in which they are possible (in industrial cities or in lower social brackets); there is no need to; in this agrarian and hierarchical world, subscribing by assent to a stylized system of properties and duties, she finds a context in which they can yield their full resources.

The society in which the moral action takes place is then a local, limited, stylized world, with its own operative values and its own occasions. Its social intercourse is unelaborate. When people meet they do so over dinner or at balls or in Ford's shop; encounters occur by formal arrangement; there are few accidental meetings, and so precise are the circumstances of this life that when these occur (as when Harriet meets Robert Martin in the shop) they are deeply disturbing. Persons stand out large, while the formalities make for a controlled universe, in which our own sense of propriety as readers is engaged to the degree that, when Jane Fairfax and Frank Churchill are, by a conjunction of accidents, left alone with the sleeping Miss Bates and this 'breach' goes unobserved, we alone are called on to observe it and reflect on its significance. The degree of social stability, the preciseness of social expectations, the limitations on eccentric behaviour or concealments or violent action, reinforce and make significant the moral order. They enable a concentration on the quality of the individual life. They create a high degree of consensus about behaviour – about what constitutes decent action. They provide a relatively closed and rounded world in which, once a level of adequate living has been acquired, it can be reinforced from without, for the future will be reasonably like the present.

Within these limits, though, the society throws up a broad range of values, out of which the tensions of the novel arise. The characters think about similar things, but they think differently about them. They think differently about the importance of rank, about the relative value of taste or courtesy or honour, and about the importance of reason or emotion in conduct. Certain things are commonly approved or frowned upon – frivolity is disliked and goodwill valued – while on other matters different characters take different stands. And this is the way in which we are coerced, by the novelist, into perceiving and adopting a measure, for, either through direct authorial intervention or more commonly by the relative elevation and demotion of various characters, this latter done by a complex strategy and tone, we perceive a pattern. The public values are placed according to a private and, as I've said, an interestingly pragmatic view. People define themselves by their actions, and as they act we perceive that there are in the novel superior and inferior people in moral as well as social terms. The social order yields to the moral. The morally inferior people tend in fact to be socially high, to considerable dramatic effect: Emma herself, at the beginning, is one of them and Frank Churchill another, while people of lower rank, like the Martins and the Coles, elevate themselves by their actions. In this fashion certain values emerge as positive – particularly values having to do with care and respect for others, the decent discharge of one's duties, and the scrupulous improvement of one-self. They are values associated with, but by no means intrinsic to, an upper-middle-class social position. So frivolity may be despised, but accomplishments count high, since they evidence self-discipline and self-enlargement and please others – the fact that Mr Martin reads is highly in his favour in this emergent scale, while Harriet Smith's taking a long time to choose materials at Ford's is not in hers. A friendly and social disposition is valued, but not *too* highly, since Emma's criticism of Jane Fairfax's reserve comes to tell more against Emma than it does against Jane and, what is more, it blinds her to some of the excellence of Mr Knightley. Goodwill and a contented temper are valued, but have their associated failures – Mr Weston is too easy-going for reasonable living, and Emma at once too indulgent over moral matters and not indulgent enough over social ones. To be 'open, straightforward and well judging', like Martin, is important, but not as important as the rewarding side of Mr Knightley's more closed and critical temper. All this is the

central area of the action, for it is what is at issue between Knightley
and Emma; and yet we do come to value Emma's warmth and
openness, only wanting it placed and ordered.

   Birth and good manners are important, but only when there is
something behind them. Elegance is admired, highly by Emma, less
so by others. Mr Elton is 'self-important, presuming, familiar,
ignorant and ill-bred'; the observations are Emma's, and have to be
mediated by us carefully, for they show up Mr Elton *and* Emma.
This picking up of tone is most important for the book, and we are
helped by alternative views – for instance, Jane Fairfax is more
tolerant of Mr Elton. Mr Weston is a little too open-hearted for
Emma – 'General benevolence, and not general friendship, make a
man what he ought to be. She could fancy such a man.' To Harriet
she commends 'the habit of self-command', but responds to Harriet's 'tenderness of heart' – 'There is nothing to be compared to it.
Warmth and tenderness of heart, with an affectionate, open manner,
will beat all clearness of head in the world for attraction.' But Mr
Knightley, in one of the debates in which the education of Emma –
and to a lesser extent of Knightley himself – is conducted and in
which a permissible range of *difference* of value is reconciled, offers a
more rational and mature view; he states the case for a plan of life
strictly adhered to, a sense of duty and of courtesy, and a right
realization of what one owes to one's social situation and therefore
one's function. This competition of values between Knightley and
Emma, which is one of our main guides to the direction of the book,
touches on other issues and other people, of course – an interesting
example of its method being the way in which Knightley reappraises
Emma's description of Churchill as 'amiable':

'No, Emma; your amiable young man can be amiable only in French, not in
English. He may be very 'aimable', have very good manners, and be very
agreeable; but he can have no English delicacy towards the feelings of other
people – nothing really amiable about him.'

Other issues come into these debates, to add to the dense moral
atmosphere. Thus Churchill is criticized early for being above his
connections, later for being too exuberant; while he himself criticizes
'civil falsehoods', but employs them. Emma admires elegance
highly; she has a practical, advantage-seeking view of attractive
qualities in people; she criticizes Mr Knightley for inventing lines of
conduct that are not practical. Mr Knightley reverses this case,

condemns Emma's fancy and whim, and recommends 'judging by nature'. In consequence, the moral life is in the front of the character's minds throughout; it is *linked* with class – as in the description of the estate at Donwell Abbey as belonging to 'a family of such true gentility, untainted in blood *and understanding*' – but understanding is insistently prior to blood as the notion of gentility begins to take a kind of ideal shape.

And so from the very first page of the book we are conscious of a disparity between the moral and the social scale. Emma's situation is, from the start, shown to be happy –

Emma Woodhouse, handsome, clever, and rich, with a comfortable home and happy disposition, seemed to unite some of the best blessings of existence; and had lived nearly twenty-one years in the world with little to distress or vex her.

But the complexities of the handling are already present. There is the hint, offered through nuances of diction, that the 'best blessings of existence' only *seem* to be hers; there is the point, further taken up and insisted on, that she has not been vexed but rather over-indulged. Her father is 'affectionate, indulgent'; her governess has 'a mildness of temper' that 'had hardly allowed her to impose any restraint', and presently by an explicit statement Jane Austen converts the hints into a direct moral observation – 'The real evils, indeed, of Emma's situation were the power of having rather too much of her own way, and a disposition to think a little too well of herself.'

A distinction is to be made between social and moral 'success', then; and this is reinforced when we are told, for instance, of the history of Mr Weston's previous marriage into a family of high rank, which

was an unsuitable connection, and did not produce much happiness. Mrs Weston ought to have found more in it, for she had a husband whose warm heart and sweet temper made him think everything due to her in return for the great goodness of being in love with him; but though she had one sort of spirit, she had not the best. She had resolution enough to pursue her own will in spite of her brother, but not enough to refrain from unreasonable regrets. . .

The moral scale is centred rather particularly, throughout, upon what is reasonable and desirable in a social life whose basic unit is the family, what makes for good and open dealing between people, prospers and opens their relationships and makes them dutiful and considerate in all their public actions. Jane Austen's novels are domestic novels, novels centred on marriage; most of the commentary and moral discussion is in fact directed toward defining the conditions for a good marriage, and preparing the one good marriage which contrasts with all others in the novel and so dominates it. But marriage is a social pact and so must answer to the public dimension. The general expectations of this book are that people will make the marriages they deserve, and that the climax will be Emma's marriage, made when she has answered to her faults and resolved her dilemmas.

Whom, then, will Emma marry? This is the question on which the plot turns. This plot, simply summarised, is concerned with a girl of many fine qualities, but of certain considerable errors deriving from the misuse of her own powers, who realises these errors, perceives that they have made her make false attributions of worth to the people in her circle and, repenting, marries the man who can instruct her in an accurate reaction to the world. The first part of the plot, the Aristotelian 'beginning', takes us to chapter 17. In this section Emma is a detached agent in someone else's destiny; this is that part of the novel concerned with Emma's attempt to intervene in the life of Harriet Smith by marrying her to Mr Elton, and its function is to demonstrate the nature of Emma's mistakes about the world, and the dangers of detached and desultory action. By the time we reach chapters 16 and 17, where we are presented with Emma's regrets, we have all we need in the way of moral direction for the rest of the book. Mr Knightley's interpretation of character and event has been shown to be better than Emma's, and we have a clear sense of Emma's tendency to misread what is before her, as well as of the faults, particularly snobbery and whimsy, which make her do this. The use of Harriet Smith as a device to expose the two different versions of the world espoused by Emma and Mr Knightley is singularly skilful. For Harriet's illegitimacy means that she can be judged very differently by different people; and each of them associate her with a rank that indicates the nature of their judgment. The uncertainty about Harriet's background thus becomes a dramatic delaying device, and much depends on the discovery of her true station, for then we shall see who is correct about her. The point is, as I have indicated, that her statement of herself, unlike that of any other characters in the book, depends entirely upon her *own* attributes; she is not reinforced by any class position. And so the question that arises is – is it Emma who is snobbish about Mr Martin, and damaging to Harriet in seeking to link her with Mr Elton; or is it Mr Knightley who is snobbish in his assumption that she deserves no better than Mr Martin, and that she is harmful company for Emma? The matter goes further – for to Emma Harriet has the virtues which commend a woman to men (beauty and good nature) and with these she has all she needs to win affection. But Mr Knightley sees the marriage connection as involving larger issues – 'Men of sense, whatever you may choose to say, do not want silly wives. Men of family would not be very fond of connecting themselves with a girl of such obscurity. . .'.

The beautifully managed scene where Knightley puts this to Emma, and dissipates any feeling we may have of *his* snobbery by talking of Robert Martin's 'sense, sincerity and good humour' and his 'true gentility' of mind, is quickly supported by his being proved right about Mr Elton – 'Depend upon it. Elton will not do . . . Elton may talk sentimentally, but he will act rationally. He is as well acquainted with his own claims as you can be with Harriet's.' Indeed, Knightley's criticism of Emma's behaviour has a precise moral tenor; he points to a specific fault – 'If you were as much guided by nature in your estimate of men and women, and as little under the power of fancy and whim in your dealings with them as you are where these children are concerned, we might always think alike.' That Emma *is* guided by fancy and whim we begin to see the more when, after a succession of delightfully handled comic scenes founded on the ambiguity of Mr Elton's supposed wooing of Harriet, Mr John Knightley points out to Emma that Mr Elton seems to have an interest in her. Emma's response is clearly self-deluding:

She walked on, amusing herself in the consideration of the blunders which often arise from a partial knowledge of circumstances, of the mistakes which people of high pretensions to judgment are for ever falling into; and not very well pleased with her brother for imagining her blind and ignorant, and in want of counsel.

The irony is turned directly against her; and her ignorance on the matter, her failure to perceive that it is *she* who is being courted by Mr Elton, takes on a dimension beyond the comic – takes on the status of a moral fault.

The second part of the novel, the 'middle', is that concerned with

Emma's mistakes about the nature of Frank Churchill's and Jane's characters, and her inability to infer the truth here because of her pre-judgments. The situations are now more complicated, but Emma repeats her errors without real improvement, inventing a romance before she has even met her between Jane and Mr Dixon, and another between Churchill and herself. Here the purpose of the action is to show how she behaves in events which increasingly come to involve not a protégé's but her own destiny, to show how she is capable of misusing herself. This part of the plot ends with a significant and crucial discovery. Emma's discovery that she is in love.

The 'end' of the book beautifully enforces the weight and meaning of the book; the waters clear, and all the significances are laid bare in a simple delaying action which enables Jane Austen to make clear all the inadequacies of her characters and the moral lesson to be learned from them. Repentance in Emma is delayed to the last and therefore most effective moment, and it comes after a train of thought in which we see Emma affected, involved, pressed into realisation of her follies. On top of understanding comes marriage, a right resolution to the plot in that it enforces the significance of true understanding. The preparation is over and by extending the novel indefinitely by a closing sentence referring to 'the perfect happiness of the union' Jane Austen assures us that it is an effective understanding that Emma has come to.

These final effects are so precisely controlled and placed that it is evident that we *do* have a plot in which 'composition, distribution and arrangement' are handled with the greatest finesse. It is reached through such indirect methods that one can't but wonder at the vast number of threads that need to be woven into the resolution. The most complex strategy of the novel is the device of filtering it through the eyes of a character of whom Jane Austen doesn't wholly approve, yet with whom she is strongly in sympathy. There is no unsureness about the moments of understanding and improvement that must (despite her position as heroine) come to her. The device is handled particularly by the use of Mr Knightley as a 'corrective'; but that is by no means the whole of the effect, for Mr Knightley is not always right either. Another force exists to handle this; it resides in the values that emerge when we have taken away the irony from the treatment of events seen through Emma's eyes. For we must be careful to see that Emma is right sometimes; we must know, however, precisely when she is wrong. How well this is managed! Emma judges excessively by elegance; but though her criticism of Mrs Elton is that she lacks elegance, she perceives most of her faults. Indeed Emma is by no means consistently in error; she is clever enough to be right on nearly all the occasions where she is not giving rein to her snobbery and her prejudice – or pre-judgment. It is Mrs Elton's snobbery that makes Emma's seem mild; and we need the scene where the two talk together to place Emma in that good light. The point then is that if Emma were judged by Jane Austen from 'outside', she would be unlikeable and highly criticized. In fact she is a violator of Jane Austen's moral scale to such a degree that it is hard at first to understand how she could have been made a heroine by her. And the fact that she *is* the heroine is the most remarkable thing about her – *Emma* is Jane Austen's *Tom Jones* in which the most devout expectation roused in the reader is the expectation that she will in some way come to grief; but we demand that her grief, like Tom Jones', will not be too painful, that repentance will occur, redemption be won and all the blessings of the prodigal son be given to her. This is what happens. The artistic problem of the book is then to make us care for Emma in such a way that we care about her fate, and like her, but that we in no way subdue our moral feelings about her faults.

And here another aspect of the tone is involved. For *Emma* is a comic novel, a novel concerned with comedy of manners in such a way as to make this the comedy of morals. There is comedy in various veins. There is the straightforward humorous treatment of Mr Woodhouse and Miss Bates as 'comic characters'. This, of course, does function in the moral dimension of the book – Mr Woodhouse's affectations are based on an indulgence to himself and it is an indulgence of the same order that has harmed Emma, while Miss Bates's absurdities make her a kind of test-case for Emma's power of responding to other people. But the significant action of the comedy in the management of the plot is to be found, for example, in the comic flavour of the scenes at the beginning where Emma, Harriet and Mr Elton are playing at picture-making and with riddles. These scenes are treated lightly, and they are designedly about trivial events; but they are organized to show us one thing above all, that Emma is capable of misreading radically the significance of these situations. What makes them most comic to the reader is his sense of a completely different possible explanation for

Mr Elton's actions. The operative principle is, in short, an irony that works against the heroine.

This irony dominates the novel. It is contrived through the device of an omniscient narrator who is able to offer an alternative set of values, and it concerns almost always the difference between what the character sees and comes to judgment about, and other potential readings of the incident. It refers then particularly to Emma's habit of pre-judging situations. It is offered by a variety of methods, such as the changes in point of view that – for example – let us, at the beginning of chapter 20, see Jane Fairfax independently of Emma's judging eye. Its effect is not simply to set up another set of *facts* against which Emma's foolish interpretations are judged; we have to wait a while for *those*. What, at the time, we are invited to realize is not that Emma is wrong, but that she might be – that she has pre-judged. In short, then, we are drawn away from a determined interpretation or prejudice about people and events, and towards a sense of possible variety. The irony is thus in favour of empiricism; and the pattern of the book is one in which the events presented before us are capable of more complex interpretation. And because we commonly see through Emma's eyes, and because Emma doesn't see this further interpretation, it is dramatically delayed and becomes the centre of our sustained interest. The devices which assure us that it is there are, among other things, the insistent and critical presence of Mr Knightley, the occasional movements to other points of view, and the revelation of the first part that Emma has been wrong about Harriet Smith and so can be wrong again. This tension between events as they seem and events as they might be – between the pleasing Frank Churchill that Emma sees, and the temporizing and cunning Churchill that Mr Knightley sees – is the dynamic of the book. When Churchill comes to Randalls and talks so pleasantly, pleasing everyone, we wonder, we have been prepared to wonder, whether this is because he is deeply amiable or simply cunning. Events will bear at least two interpretations. But it should be said that Emma suspects this, that her views put to Mr Knightley are views she doubts, and that to some extent she has learned from the Harriet incident. As readers, however, skilled in plots, we are put into the position of being encouraged to entertain our suspicions longer; there is a devised relationship between reader and heroine, inherent in the ironic note.

The novel closes on a final irony. One of Emma's faults has been her external view of persons, and her willingness to interfere in the destinies of others without being prepared to involve herself. Marriages are to be made only for others. In being forced into true feelings of love, she is released and opened out; love is the final testimony, in fact, of her redemption. She concludes the book by involving herself in the essential commitment of the Austen universe, which is marriage; so she has opened out into tenderness of heart, a tenderness without weakness or sentimentality. If she has still some faults to recant, these will come in time, for the fundamental liberation has taken place; she is no longer the Sleeping Beauty.

And in this way the shape of the novel is fulfilled. It has begun by delineating a variety of contesting moral viewpoints; it ends by clarification, by offering to the reader his way through the variety. We have learned this particularly through our understanding of Emma's faults, and by learning above all how significant, how *fundamental*, they are. For Emma's aloof relation to others, her willingness to treat them as toys or counters, her over-practical view of the good quality, which she sees simply as ensuring for its possessor a good match – these become significant betrayals of human possibility. 'With insufferable vanity she had believed herself in the secret of everybody's feelings; with unpardonable arrogance proposed to arrange everybody's destiny. She was proved to have been universally mistaken; and she had not quite done nothing – for she had done mischief. She had brought evil on Harriet, on herself, and, she too much feared, on Mr Knightley . . .' The social and moral universe I described at the beginning of these comments takes on all the weight of its significance here, for it provides a context in which Emma's faults are not peccadilloes to be regarded with indulgence, but total violations of a whole worthwhile universe. Jane Austen's method is to rouse our expectations and draw on our moral stringency to such an extent that this insight becomes absolutely essential, and retribution is demanded. The agents of retribution here are Mr Knightley and Jane Austen herself, and the retribution, once understanding has come, is genial – the lesson learned by Emma is that of how to commit herself fully and properly in the moral and social act of marriage, an act whose validity she has begun by denying and with which she begins her mature life. And what is rendered for us, then, is the moral horror of values we are awfully apt to associate with Jane Austen herself – snobbery, an excessive regard for the elegant and smart, a practical regard for goodness because it is such a *marriageable* trait. These are the values that are purged. We have been turned another way; we have learned of the duty of the individual to immerse himself in the events about him and to accept his obligations to his acquaintance finely and squarely; we have learned of the value of 'the serious spirit', involved and totally responsible. We have been persuaded in fact of the importance of true regard for self and others, persuaded to see the full human being as full, fine, morally serious, totally responsible, entirely involved, and to consider every human action as a crucial, committing act of self-definition.

SOURCE: 'Jane Austen's *Emma*,' in *Critical Quarterly*, IV (1962) 335–46.

Graham Hough Narrative and Dialogue in Jane Austen (1970)

1

The earliest distinction of literary styles is that made by Plato in *Republic* III, between the narrative, the dramatic and the mixed styles. It has not occupied a very large place in later discussion, but, as I hope to show, it is still fruitful of consequences. It is the mixed style with which we shall be concerned. For us the prime example of the mixed style is the novel; and it still has its problems. The problems that Plato found in it were moral ones, but we shall be concerned with a different set of questions. In the mixed style we find in the same work two diverse modes of utterance; firstly the utterance of the narrator, and second the utterances of the various characters. The sort of questions to be asked here are what contribution each makes to the whole, how they reinforce and co-operate with each other, and how they are fused together into an artistic unity, that is also an interpretation of reality.

The problem is not simply that of different *voices*. The drama, the pure dramatic style, has this too. But here the voices are all on the same plane, all of imagined characters. The conflict is a conflict between epistemological equals, and a consistent texture, though composed of diverse elements, is fairly easy to achieve. Two procedures are common in drama. One is that all the voices are reduced to a homogeneous style, as in Racine; the other is to employ two styles in some sort of alternation, that of the 'serious' and that of the 'comic' characters, as in Shakespeare.

The problem in the novel is partly that of different voices, but far more acutely that different parts of the work occupy different ontological and epistemological levels, one for which the narrator makes himself directly responsible, and in the other in which he disappears and the words of the characters are simply reproduced. This shows up far more plainly in the novel than in other kinds where the mixed style is used. In the epic, for example, the whole is uniformly stylised; the narrative voice and those of the characters tend to be assimilated to the same stylistic norm. This uniform stylisation can occur in the novel (as it does for example in *La Princesse de Clèves*), but it is not the typical procedure. Normally in the novel the speech of the characters is individual, often idiosyncratic in the highest degree. In dialogue we expect a decorum of realism that can include oddity, eccentricity, colloquialism, vulgarism, ignorance or partial insight. While the speech of the narrator generally conforms to a standard of regularity, 'correctness', intelligence and understanding. This way of working on two planes gives the novelist some of his greatest difficulties and some of his greatest opportunities. There are no rules for handling this relation, yet the total effect of a novel depends greatly on the way it is handled. And if anyone wants to say that the only interesting thing about a novel is the moral values or the quantity of felt life that it communicates, I will reply that it is only by such formal means as those indicated above that the novel can communicate life and values at all, and that it is very much to the point to ask questions about them.

2

I propose to examine the narrative-dialogue relation in Jane Austen's *Emma*. The appropriate unit of observation I take to be a single work. No doubt an author has his habitual practice, and what is true of one novel is likely to be true of other novels by the same writer. But this is not entirely so. A writer's habits may vary at different times of his career; he may vary his procedure according to the demands of his subject. Dickens changes his normal procedure in *David Copperfield* and *Great Expectations*, where he employs a first-person narrator; and more markedly in *Bleak House*, part of which, but only part, is narrated directly by Esther Summerson, the principal character. And there are more general considerations. However possible it may be to extrapolate from the observation of short passages, or to generalise about an author's total *oeuvre*, the central object of criticism must always be the individual work, and the work seen as a whole. In the case of the novel there are no insuperable difficulties: a novel is long enough to make a connected series of observations possible, and not as a rule so long as to be hopelessly unwieldy.[1]

We have made a broad distinction between narrative and dialogue; and this is considerably over-simplified, as will be seen shortly. But before going on to further discriminations we can make some general remarks about *Emma* on this simple foundation. First we might note how much of the burden of the work is carried by the dialogue. A cursory glance will show that by far the largest proportion of the book, quantitatively speaking, is either pure dialogue or dialogue interrupted by short narrative connections. Compare *Emma* with *Middlemarch*, for example, and we can observe at once that though George Eliot's dialogue is full and generous, she employs the narrative voice far more extensively than Jane Austen. Qualitatively the preponderance of dialogue in *Emma* is no less remarkable. All the big scenes, those of the greatest functional importance to the progress of the story and those of the highest emotional tension, are almost exclusively in dialogue. We may instance the scene between Emma and Harriet in Chapter 9, where Harriet is induced to believe that Mr. Elton is in love with her; the scene in the carriage at the end of Chapter 15 where Mr. Elton declares his ill-placed pretensions to Emma's hand; the long scenes of mystification about Jane Fairfax between Emma and Frank Churchill; complex scenes with much varied conversation among a number of characters, such as the dinner-party at Hartfield (Chapters 34–36), the ball (Chapter 38), and the picnic at Box Hill (Chapter 43); the climactic scene in which Frank Churchill's engagement to Jane Fairfax is revealed (Chapter 45), and that in Chapter 49 in which Mr. Knightley at last declares his love for

Emma. And there is no need to illustrate the primary importance of direct speech as the indicator of character. *Emma*, then, is very fully dramatised; Jane Austen prefers as her main instrument direct speech, direct conversational interchange between her characters. The most sustained passages of straightforward objective narrative without any dialogue occur at the beginning where the scene is to be set and the characters introduced, and again at Chapter 20, where an entirely new character, Jane Fairfax, requires the same sort of introduction.

However, though the narrative-dialogue distinction is obvious enough, we have only to ask what is behind it to see that it does not provide any very exact discrimination. It is ordinarily assumed that the narrative is that part of a work of fiction for which the author assumes immediate responsibility, and the dialogue that in which he allows his characters 'to speak for themselves'. However, in *Emma* this division of labour is by no means clear. There is indeed narrative which tells us *about* the characters, and in which they have no expressive share; the vocabulary, syntax and rhetorical ordonnance are entirely those of the narrator. There is also direct speech which is entirely mimetic, in which no trace of the narrator's voice is heard. But there is a large intermediate area, formally narrative, which in fact represents the thoughts, spoken or unspoken, of the characters, and goes far towards reproducing their actual mode of expression – their vocabulary, syntax and rhetorical ordonnance, rather than those of the narrator. Here it becomes evident that the simple distinction between narrative and dialogue is not enough. The different modes of discourse in the novel must be distinguished more exactly.

3

I distinguish five kinds of discourse in *Emma*:

(1) The authorial voice. Here we have to distinguish between the voice of the *author* and that of the *narrator*; and the authorial voice occurs in passages (usually reflective, hortatory or gnomic) that stand outside the economy of the narrative, short-circuit it, as it were, and constitute a direct address from author to reader. These are very few and very brief in *Emma* – indeed in Jane Austen generally. They are always ironical and epigrammatic, and because

they are brilliant and amusing we tend to think of them as more prominent than they are. Everyone remembers the opening lines of *Pride and Prejudice:*

It is a truth universally acknowledged, that a single man in possession of a good fortune must be in want of a wife.

Similar passages in *Emma* are:

Human nature is so well-disposed towards those who are in interesting situations, that a young person, who either marries or dies, is sure of being kindly spoken of.   (Chap. 22)

It may be possible to do without dancing entirely. Instances have been known of young people passing many, many months successively without being at a ball of any description, and no material injury to accrue either to body or mind. . .   (Chap. 29)

They tend to establish a footing of agreeable complicity between author and reader; but otherwise they are not important, and I shall say little more of them. Other writers of course use this form in other ways.

(2) Objective narrative. I mean by this passages where the facts are presented to us as facts, uncoloured, not from any particular point of view, manifestly to be accepted as true, uncontaminated either by the subjectivity of the author or that of any of the characters. We can call this if we like the voice of the narrator. Passages of this kind are fairly extensive but not dominant. There are fifteen pages at the beginning, and scattered passages of from two to five pages throughout the book. They occur, as I have said, where the scene is to be set, circumstances explained, and new characters introduced; and also though often in a less pure form, in short pieces where a sequence of events – shift of scene, change of partners – has to be presented between conversations.

(3) Coloured narrative. This is a form into which the objective narrative, after a time, very commonly modulates. I mean by it narrative or reflection or observation more or less deeply coloured by a particular character's point of view. The point of view is mainly Emma's, but this is not kept up with any Jamesian scrupulosity; most of the others also get their turn.

The longer she considered it the greater was her sense of its expediency. Mr. Elton's situation was most suitable, quite the gentleman himself, and

without low connections; at the same time, not of any family that could
fairly object to the doubtful birth of Harriet. He had a comfortable home for
her, and Emma imagined a very sufficient income; for though the vicarage
of Highbury was not large, he was known to have some independent
property; and she thought very highly of him as a good-humoured, well-
meaning, respectable young man, without any deficiency of useful understanding or knowledge of the world.   (Chap. 4)

    This kind of discourse is very extensively used. There is far more
of it than there is of pure objective narrative. Indeed, after dialogue,
it forms the staple of the book, and much of what I have to say will
be about the skill and variety with which Jane Austen uses this
method. The passage quoted hovers between impersonal narration
and virtual quotation from Emma's interior monologue: 'quite the
gentleman himself, and without low connections; at the same time,
not of any family . . .' This is manifestly coloured by the tone of
Emma herself, and it is a danger signal. The objective narrator is
always right; Emma may be wrong, as she turns out to have been
here. There is a considerable range in this type of discourse.
Sometimes it is almost indistinguishable from objective narrative,
sometimes it shades into the next, more deeply coloured type, the
free indirect style.
    (4) Free indirect style. This is a concentration of what I have
called coloured narrative. Since it was first observed it has been
the subject of a voluminous literature in French.[2] It occurs, as we
have said, when the actual mode of expression, the *ipsissima verba*,
of a fictional character are used, but embedded in the narrative,
and with the grammatical forms assimilated to those of reported
speech.

    Scarcely had they passed the sweep-gate and joined the other carriage,
than she found her subject cut up – her hand seized – her attention
demanded, and Mr. Elton actually making violent love to her: *availing
himself of the precious opportunity, declaring sentiments which must be already
well known, hoping – fearing – ready to die if she refused him; but flattering
himself that his ardent attachment and unequalled love and unexampled passion
could not fail of having some effect*, and, in short, very much resolved on
being seriously accepted as soon as possible.   (Chap. 15)

    For half an hour Mr. Weston was surprised and sorry; but then he began
to perceive that Frank's coming two or three months later *would be a much
better plan, better time of year, better weather*; and that he would be able,
without any doubt, to stay considerably longer with them than if he had
come sooner.   (Chap. 18)

It will be observed that this device occurs in short snatches, without breaking the flow of the narrative. It is used intermittently throughout the book. Since the object here is only to define the style we will postpone discussion of its effects and its varieties till later.

(5) Direct speech and dialogue. This requires no definition, and to describe Jane Austen's use of it is to go far towards describing her technique as a whole.

4

Quantitively (3) and (5), coloured narrative and direct speech, account for most of the book. (1), the authorial voice is almost negligible; the effective extremes are (2), objective narrative, and (5), direct speech. They are widely different from each other; but they are blended, stylistically harmonised, by the two intermediate forms (3) and (4), coloured narrative and *style indirect libre*. We will begin by examining the nature of the objective narrative.

How do we know that it is objective? *Emma* contains many passages of discourse – feelings, judgments, interpretations of events, which later turn out to be erroneous. They are the judgments of the actors in the drama – incomplete because the outcome of the total action is as yet unknown to them; partial because they are made solely from an individual point of view, and the relevant point of view of others has not been taken into account; misguided because they are under the sway of self regard or feeling inappropriate to the situation, or mere carelessness. We do not as a rule recognise these errors as they are made. Sometimes we do, but in the more important cases we are misled with the characters, only discovering the true state of the case when they do. If the reader judged rightly from the start the whole structure of tensions and resolutions that make up the book would be dissolved. Of that more hereafter; but I think it is true to say, of this novel as of most others, that while we go along with the characters in their experiences and their interpretation of them, we give them only a provisional assent. In the back of our minds we are prepared to have it upset or altered. But there are other passages in the book to which we give total and immediate assent. This is the objective narrative. The facts and judgments it presents are not upset or altered; if they were we should feel that we had been cheated; and in a good novel ideally this never happens.

How do we recognise, instantaneously, as I think we do, the objectivity of these passages?

The simple answer is that it is a matter of convention; what the narrator tells us is true; he has made a contract with us to this effect, and we don't do business with people who cheat. This I think is the case; such conventions in literature are very common and this one is obviously necessary. Yet it is not a sufficient answer. There are plenty of narratives in which the convention operates well enough, and we are willing enough to let it do so, but we are all the time aware that we are *being told a story*. We want to listen to a story and the narrator has engaged to tell us one, and that is all right. But in very accomplished novels like this of Jane Austen's the objective narrative seems to carry an authority beyond the conventional. It bears intrinsic signs of its objectivity; and since while the story is in progress we do not know its outcome, these signs can only be local ones, i.e. stylistic.

Let us grant all we need to the convention; the objective narrative is to a large extent concerned with facts, and the narrator is not going to deceive us about the facts.

> She was the youngest of the two daughters of a most affectionate indulgent father; and had, in consequence of her sister's early marriage, been mistress of his house from a very early period.   (Chap. 1)

The facts are presented simply and uncoloured by feeling, in a language formal and correct both in syntax and vocabulary. A language too that is quite unidiosyncratic; Fanny Burney for example presents her facts in exactly the same manner:

> Miss Evelyn, Madam, from the second to the eighteenth year of her life, was brought up under my care, and, except when at school, under my roof . . . at that period of her life we parted. Her mother, then married to Mr. Duval, then sent her to Paris.   (*Evelina*, Letter II)

The authority of the narrative is reinforced by adopting the common form of decent educated discourse. But in Jane Austen's case the objective narrative is not only concerned with facts; it is concerned as much or even more with values. The passage just quoted on Emma's circumstances goes on:

> Her mother had died too long ago for her to have more than an indistinct remembrance of her caresses; and her place had been supplied by an excellent woman as governess, who had fallen little short of a mother in affection.

We are not to doubt that Miss Taylor the governess was really an excellent woman, and we are certainly to think that a mother's affection is valuable and important. The objectivity of the narrative does not at all consist in refraining from value judgments; they are constantly made and discriminated with considerable care. Emma's condition seems favourable enough but our view of it is soon explicitly qualified:

The real evils indeed of Emma's situation were the power of having rather too much of her own way, and the disposition to think a little too well of herself: these were the disadvantages which threatened alloy to her many enjoyments.

And it is not only the heroine who has the benefit of these careful discriminations. The pages devoted to Jane Fairfax at the beginning of Chapter 20 are entirely similar:

Such was Jane Fairfax's history. She had fallen into good hands, known nothing but kindness from the Campbells, and been given an excellent education. Living constantly with right-minded and well-informed people, her heart and understanding had received every advantage of discipline and culture; and Colonel Campbell's residence being in London, every lighter talent had been done full justice to, by the attendance of first-rate masters. Her disposition and abilities were equally worthy of all that friendship could do; and at eighteen or nineteen she was, as far as such an early age can be qualified for the care of children, fully competent to the office of instruction herself.

In these passages (I must refer the reader to the relevant chapters, as to give adequate quotations would be too long) the material information is conveyed as briefly and simply as possible. That done, we find the predominant words are abstract nouns – *affection, authority, enjoyment, misfortune, friendship, discipline, heart, understanding, disposition, education*; or adjectives expressing moral and intellectual qualities – *unexceptionable, generous, self-denying, useful, right-minded, well-informed, competent*. C. S. Lewis has justly remarked that in such passages 'we still breathe the air of the *Rambler* and *Idler*'. The echoes from Johnson's moral world, even the formal resemblances to his manner are very strong. 'Living constantly with right-minded and well-informed people her heart and understanding had received every advantage of discipline and culture'. This is what Bally would have called a *fait d'évocation*; the Johnsonian cadence evokes a special social and moral ethos, one that carries

authority and weight. In places where this kind of language is used
dubieties and ironies are excluded.

The tendency of this diction is to generalise. There is no attempt
at a vivid setting of the scene, and physical detail is markedly
absent. We do not know with any degree of particularity what sort of
a house Hartfield was, any more than we know what Emma looked
like. Yet the effect is not a failure of realisation; it is rather an
assumption that many things can be taken for granted. We know
what an unpretentious old-fashioned gentleman's house is like; there
is no need to specify. We know what an attractive intelligent girl is
like. Writer and reader are presumed to share a common knowledge
and to be in natural agreement on these matters. And if this is so on
the social and material plane it is even more so on the moral plane.
The great abstract words of moral evaluation are completely
authoritative symbols. The narrator can say 'the real evil of Emma's
situation was . . .' only on the assumption that she knows what real
evils are, and that any likely reader would share her knowledge and
her judgment. The language is highly evaluative, but it is never in
the least hortatory or persuasive. Like Hamlet we sometimes doubt
a lady who protests too much; Jane Austen establishes her reliability
by never protesting at all.

The language then of the objective narrative in *Emma* is general,
abstract, evaluative and formally correct. It is general because
common knowledge is assumed, and particular illustration at this
stage is not needed. It is abstract because the appeal is not merely to
a shared sentiment, but to an explicit, formulated code of values, of
which the abstract nouns are a sufficient sign. It is evaluative
because the highest human faculty is to make right judgments. It is
formally correct because the well disposed and well informed share
allegiance to a common set of standards, and these are more
important than any mere idiosyncrasy. Such are the stylistic means
by which the objective narrative is established as objective.

5

The almost majestic impersonality of this kind of narrative is not
what the casual reader would normally associate with Jane Austen.
Quantitatively it is not dominant in the book. It is of quite fundamental importance, as I hope to show; but our ordinary impression

of a Jane Austen novel (and our ordinary impressions of novels are likely to be right, as far as they go) is derived from passages of a much livelier colouring. Many of these belong to the objective narrative too – in the sense that they are telling the simple truth. The voice is no longer that of the narrator talking on behalf of society or Dr. Johnson or God; it is that of the narrator as an individual woman, shrewd, sensible, sometimes tart and frequently amused. Yet it is just as reliable as the voice of the graver passages; the sparkle of satire or irony does not lead into error, and the fundamental characteristics of style are still the same – generality, abstraction, judgment and evaluation constantly active, constantly referring to the same code – Christian morals in a temperate English version.

Miss Bates stood in the very worst predicament in the world for having much of the public favour; and she had no intellectual superiority to make atonement to herself, or frighten those who might hate her into outward respect. She had never boasted either beauty or cleverness. Her youth had passed without distinction and her middle of life was devoted to the care of her failing mother, and the endeavour to make a small income go as far as possible. And yet she was a happy woman and a woman whom no one named without good-will. It was her own universal goodwill and contented temper which worked such wonders. She loved everybody, was interested in everybody's happiness, quick-sighted to everybody's merits; thought herself a most fortunate creature, and surrounded with blessings in such an excellent mother, and so many good neighbours and friends, and a home that wanted for nothing.   (Chap. 3)

Two kinds of colouring are visible here. First the vivid touch of the narrator, speaking the truth indeed, but speaking it as it has been seen by a sharp individual perception. 'She had no intellectual superiority to frighten those who might hate her into outward respect.' This is the perception of an observer who has seen something below the surface of life, something that cannot be acquired from the attendance of first-rate masters and the society of right-minded and well-informed people. Yet there is nothing here to cause us to doubt their lessons. The sharpness is that of a moralist, not that of a mocker. A little lower down a new shade appears. The narrative description of Miss Bates is intruded upon by the subjectivity of Miss Bates herself:

She loved everybody, was interested in everybody's happiness, quick-sighted to everybody's merits; *thought herself a most fortunate creature, and surrounded with blessings in such an excellent mother and so many good neighbours and friends and a home that wanted for nothing.*

The second part of this sentence clearly presents Miss Bates' point of view, and probably a selection of her very words. It does not present the situation as it is. Her mother is actually so far past everything that she has no particular excellence; the neighbours are ordinary; the home wants for a good deal. Yet we are not for a moment misled. The narrator's objective judgment is firmly in charge of the whole passage.

Such local effects may seem to be a small matter, but if we consult our actual experience in reading the book we shall find that they are constantly active, and make a very large contribution to the effect of the whole. When all has been said, and with perfect justice, about Jane Austen's fine discrimination and her moral insight, the general reader will be apt to feel that half his satisfaction has been left unaccounted for. And he will be right. It is the continual diversification of the surface, the sparkling slightly effervescent quality of the narrative that gives Jane Austen's work its special flavour. This is very largely a matter of continual slight shifts in the point of view; the narrator as an impersonal enunciator of facts and values; the narrator as a keen and witty observer of social oddities; the characters themselves with all their idiosyncrasies of feeling and expression. A painting cannot be adequately described by indicating only the main lines of the composition: there is also the sheer physical handling of the material. What would we know of Rubens or Watteau if we did not appreciate this? It is Jane Austen's handling that at this point I am trying to define. Lively raconteurs have two main weapons – one is their own individual wit and insight, the other is the power of mimicking, of entering into another's being, of momentarily *becoming* another character. Jane Austen has both at her disposal, and uses both in continual interplay against a background of uncoloured objective narration.

A good deal of this is commonly smothered under the blanket term irony. I am trying as far as Jane Austen is concerned to insert a few discriminations into that overloaded catch-all. Some of her sharpest effects escape from it altogether. 'She had no intellectual superiority to frighten those who might hate her into outward respect.' This is not irony at all. It is the flat statement of a devastating scepticism about the real motives of much ordinary social intercourse. And when irony does appear its purpose is not always what might be expected. 'Miss Bates thought herself the most fortunate creature, and surrounded with blessings in such an excellent mother, etc.' This is irony in the strict sense; two points of view are presented simultaneously – Miss Bates' amiable view of her circumstances and the much less rosy actuality – but its motive is wholly kindly and generous. We are apt to think of irony as a destructive weapon; it is not so here. The disparity between Miss Bates' situation as she sees it and her situation as it is does not in any way diminish her; on the contrary it enhances her simplicity and goodness.

It is hardly necessary to illustrate the numerous occasions on which irony is used for its more accustomed purpose of exposing pretensions and shams; but if Jane Austen's practice is compared with the often monotonous and mechanical employment of this figure by Dickens and Thackeray the subtlety and range of her handling will become apparent. It will not do to be too solemn about this. However serious her purpose, there is an element of sheer playfulness in Jane Austen's narrative method. By playfulness I do not imply triviality, rather the sense in which Schiller thinks of all art as play – an unselfconscious delight in virtuosity, in exercising a skill with the utmost delicacy and variety of which it is capable.

We also talk of the irony of fate and tragic irony; and here we approach a territory whose harsher reaches Jane Austen hardly cares to explore. However, the massive fact that lies behind these species of irony is simply human blindness; men act without foreseeing the consequences of their actions, they speak without realising the implications of what they say. And this, though in examples that fall far short of being tragic, lies close to the heart of Jane Austen's experience. C. S. Lewis in the essay already cited finds the theme of four of Jane Austen's novels (all except *Persuasion* and *Mansfield Park*) to be disillusionment, disenchantment – in the strict, not the popular senses of these words; the awakening from a false view of things to seeing things as they are. If this is to be the theme it is necessary that the illusions shall be fully presented first. If the theme is to be presented as effectively as possible it is even necessary for a time that we shall share in the illusions. It is here that Jane Austen's coloured narrative assumes a greater importance. It becomes not a matter of handling but a matter of structure.

The theme of illusion and disillusionment is clearly central in *Emma*. It is the story of a clever but self-willed girl who makes a whole series of misjudgments which might have had disastrous consequences, but (since this is Jane Austen's world and the world

of comedy) fortunately finds out her mistakes in time. Half the
energy of the book would be gone if the reader did not share in her
mistakes. It is by the coloured narrative that he is induced to do so.
We have seen Emma in a passage quoted earlier reflecting on Mr.
Elton's suitability for Harriet: 'quite the gentleman himself, and
without low connections; at the same time not of any family that
could fairly object to the doubtful birth of Harriet.' Of course this
train of thought turns out to be wholly mistaken; Mr. Elton isn't a
gentleman at all but a howling cad; when put to it he objects
strongly to the doubtful birth of Harriet. Yet the wrongness is mixed
up with rightness. Emma is probably right in thinking that Mr.
Elton is not of any family that *could fairly object*; she goes on to
assume that he won't object; and here she is quite wrong. The
proper word for this fragment of narrative is unreliable; it is
unreliable like most of our conjectural analyses of other people's
dispositions. The stylistic signal of this unreliability is the half-
quotation from Emma's own interior discourse, the bit of young-
ladyish slang 'quite the gentleman himself.' The objective narrator
who described Jane Fairfax's upbringing would never have allowed
herself such an expression. Yet the signal does not succeed in
flagging down the train. We go along with Emma's misconception,
though retrospectively we realise that a scintilla of doubt appeared
at this point, one of those gleams of partial illumination that
contribute so richly to the texture of Jane Austen's work.

Sometimes Emma's judgment is entirely right, but the motives for
it are partly suspect. In Chapter 32 Mrs. Elton is pestering Emma
with unwanted offers of introduction to her friends in Bath:

It was as much as Emma could bear without being impolite! The idea of her
being indebted to Mrs. Elton for what is called an introduction – of her
going into public under the auspices of a friend of Mrs. Elton's – probably
some vulgar dashing widow, who, with the help of a boarder just made shift
to live! The dignity of Miss Woodhouse of Hartfield was sunk indeed!

Mrs. Elton is indeed a vulgar and officious woman; her friends are
almost certainly awful and Emma is right to resent her offers. But
not quite on those grounds; the assumed poverty of Mrs. Elton's
friend is not relevant, by the standards of the objective narrator, and
the dignity of Miss Woodhouse of Hartfield, even if invoked with a
touch of self-irony, ought not to be invoked at all. Here it is the
uncontrolled colloquial impatience that is the stylistic danger signal.

Emma is not judging, she is merely reacting to a stimulus; and in Jane Austen's hierarchy of values spontaneous reaction is inferior to judgment. The effect of such passages is dual; in the first place they are spirited, amusing, revelatory of character, etc., in the second (or perhaps not second) they show an unremitting authorial vigilance over the slightest nuances of behaviour and expression.

At times the stylistic indications of insincerity are very slight. It is necessary that they should be slight, for the structure of the work depends on mysteries and tensions that must not be prematurely released. A state of affairs is suggested by the writing which later turns out not to be the true state. Yet the false state must be established, if only provisionally; and it is the business of the style to do this. A mere psychologism will not suffice as an explanation of these passages. It is a matter of formal discretion; the relative concealment of the true state of affairs is part of the formal structure of the work. It is also indeed part of what, following Ricardou, we may call the *fiction*, the antecedent structure of events out of which the work is made. In Jane Austen's narrative economy there are mysteries but not mystifications. False directions are always linked to psychological plausibilities. The reader must be allowed to go astray, but he must not be constrained to do so; and the data on which a correct judgment could have been based are always present, however inconspicuously. In the latter half of the book Emma is deceiving herself about her relation with Frank Churchill. She fancies he is in love with her, and half fancies that she is in love with him. On his return to Hartfield after an absence she thinks that his affection has declined and persuades herself that she is entirely relieved about this (chapter 37). Here we find no sudden and unconsidered reaction, no lapses into a near vulgar colloquialism. Emma in her own eyes is behaving with great prudence and correctness, and the language in which her thoughts and acts are presented is itself prudent and correct. All the same it is extremely conventional; the expressions are of a perceptible banality. 'Her own attachment had subsided into a mere nothing – it was not worth thinking of . . . If a separation of two months should not have cooled him, there were dangers and evils before her . . . She wished she might be able to keep him from an absolute declaration.' When they meet she has a self congratulatory phrase about exercising 'all her quick observation', and as a result decides 'it was a clear thing he was less in love than he had been'. This is the language in which the commonplace novels discuss commonplace love affairs. It is neither the language of the heart nor that of the head.[3]

Emma is capable of better, and there are passages of coloured narrative, decidedly coloured by her subjectivity, in which there is no misdirection and no stylistic signals to suggest it. Characteristically these occur in scenes of undeception, of anagnorisis, where things are at last recognised for what they are. Such a passage occurs at the end of chapter 48, when Emma is reflecting on her culpable misjudgment of Jane Fairfax:

Mrs. Weston's communications furnished Emma with more food for unpleasant reflection, by increasing her esteem and compassion, and her sense of past injustice towards Miss Fairfax. She bitterly regretted not having sought a closer acquaintance with her, and blushed for the envious feelings which had certainly been, in some measure, the cause. Had she followed Mr. Knightley's known wishes, in paying that attention to Miss Fairfax which was every way her due; had she tried to know her better; had she done her part towards intimacy; had she endeavoured to find a friend there, instead of in Harriet Smith, – she must, in all probability, have been spared from every pain which pressed on her now. Birth, abilities, and education had been equally marking one as an associate for her, to be received with gratitude; and the other – what was she? . . . Of all the sources of evil surrounding the former, since her coming to Highbury, she was persuaded that she must herself have been the worst. She must have been a perpetual enemy. They could never have been all three together, without her having stabbed Jane Fairfax's peace in a thousand instances; and on Box Hill, perhaps, it had been the agony of a mind that would bear no more.

The careful, responsible, evaluative abstractions that we noted in the objective narrative are here in action again: *esteem, compassion, the sense of past injustice; that attention to Miss Fairfax that was in every way her due; birth, abilities, and education had been equally marking one as an associate for her.* We have moved away from the language of the lady novelist, the ordinary cant about absolute declarations and lovers cooled by separation; and we are back with the language of the *Rambler* and *Idler*, which is also the language of the narrator herself.

These various shades of coloured narrative in their turn shade into the free indirect style – the actual quotation of the words of one of the characters, but in the syntactical forms of indirect speech. There is some dubiety in Jane Austen whether to put such fragments into quotation marks or not, and there is some variation between different editions.

Harriet listened submissively, and said, 'it was very true; it was just as Miss Woodhouse described – it was not worth while to think about them – and she would not think about them any longer'. But no change of subject would avail.

Here Harriet's words are in quotation marks; whilst Mr. Elton's love-making cited above was without them. These virtual quotations are in general less subtle and of less structural importance than the more vaguely defined sorts of coloured narrative. They enliven the surface texture and they give quick informal glimpses into character; and often they do no more.

6

We come now to the dialogue – direct speech in which there is no intervention by the narrator. With coloured narrative it is Jane Austen's principal fictional tool, but in one obvious sense there is less to be said about it. The style of an author is hardly exhibited in those parts of his work where he has formally abdicated and handed over to his characters; and any simple attempt to refer the handling of the dialogue to mere expressivity, to the author's convictions, attitudes and intentions is doomed to failure. In these parts of the work such links are necessarily indirect, mediated through the freewill of the characters. Yet dialogue is part of the total structure – in Jane Austen's case an extremely important part; and we must enquire into how it plays its part in the economy of the whole.

In thinking about dialogue in the novel we often make use of an implied comparison with some assumed norm of conversational discourse. We cannot help observing that in Henry James' later work the dialogue is highly stylised, and pretty uniformly stylised, so that all the characters, even the children, talk in much the same way. It is a commonplace that in Scott's novels the heroes and heroines tend to use a conventional literary language while the other characters use some sort of class or local dialect, usually much more idiosyncratic and vigorous in idiom and vocabulary. In both these observations the idea of a standard conversational language is tacitly invoked, and divergencies from it are registered. But this criterion is very rough and uncertain. We do not really know what the standard conversational language of past times was like. Our evidence of it is mostly derived from novels, and the argument becomes circular. We can compare Dickens' fictional version of the Cockney speech of his time with the supposedly authentic transcriptions of such speech in Mayhew. But the suspicion arises that Mayhew is possibly employing a convention imitated from Dickens. Manners and speech habits change fairly rapidly; what would be natural at one time might seem pompous and artificial twenty years later; and until the advent of the tape-recorder there is no certain check.

Yet the reader of novels almost unconsciously registers the speech of the characters as natural, affected, pompous or vulgar or what not, without any solid evidence about the standard speech of the day – without any evidence that a linguist could find acceptable. He can do this because it is a matter of internal relations. He is not in fact comparing the speech of the characters to a standard outside the work, but to a standard set or implied within the work itself. Novelists will be found to vary widely in the sort of scales they set up and the importance they attach to them. Some use a very wide range of speech patterns, some a very restricted one; some seem to make a large claim to mimetic accuracy, some seem to regard it with indifference. Jane Austen's scale is a narrow one. All her characters are such as could be met (though not necessarily approved) in the drawing-room of a gentleman's house. So the whole range of dialect and popular speech is excluded. None of her characters are intellectuals or religious geniuses – so learned and prophetic discourse is equally absent. Intimate or disturbing emotional experience is generally avoided or presented indirectly, or merely suggested. In every respect then her dialogue keeps to the middle range of moderately educated speech, and any discriminations that it makes are made within that closed series.

It is a general rule that the smaller the range of dialogue employed the finer will be the distinctions that it draws. In *The Rainbow* and *Women in Love* (if we may take these two novels together as the single enterprise that they originally were) Lawrence employs the whole range between the barely articulate rustic speech of Tom Brangwen and the extremely self-conscious utterance of Birkin, highly charged both emotionally and intellectually. In such a wide span the finer shades of polite conversation are not likely to count for much. In Jane Austen almost everything is polite conversation, and the relatively small variations of tone become all important. There is some external evidence that she realised this to be so and that these details of style were very much a matter of conscious reflection. We find her writing to her niece, who also wrote novels, under her aunt's guidance, 'Sir D. A. you always do well; I have only taken the liberty of expunging one phrase of his, which would not be allowable, "Bless my heart" – it is too familiar and inelegant.'

This exact care for appropriateness is the most obvious quality of Jane Austen's dialogue, and it is in their conversation that the characters are most openly revealed.

'You understand the force of influence pretty well Harriet; but I would have you so firmly established in good society as to be independent even of Hartfield and Miss Woodhouse. I want to see you permanently well-connected, and to that end it would be advisable to have as few odd acquaintances as may be; and therefore I say that if you should still be in this country when Mr. Martin marries, I wish you may not be drawn in by your intimacy with the sisters, to be acquainted with the wife, who will probably be some mere farmer's daughter without education.'

'To be sure. Yes. Not that I think Mr. Martin would ever marry anybody but what had had some education, and been very well brought up. However I do not mean to set up my opinion against yours – and I am sure I shall not wish for the acquaintance of his wife. I shall always have a great regard for the Miss Martins, especially Elizabeth, and should be very sorry to give them up for they are quite as well educated as me. But if he marries a very ignorant vulgar woman certainly I had better not visit her if I can help it.'
(Chap. 4)

This short extract exhibits almost in its entirety the contrasted natures of Emma and Harriet and the relations between them; and does it with the utmost economy of means. The three times repeated 'I would have you', 'I want to see you', 'I wish you may not', is enough to establish Emma's assumptions. One phrase 'I do not mean to set up my opinion against yours', and two bits of naive and dubious grammar, 'anybody but what had had some education', and 'as well educated as me', are enough to show Harriet's childishness and uncertainty. But it is to be noted that this adds nothing to the message we have already had. We have already been told by the narrator that Emma is rather too fond of her own way and that Harriet is a humble, grateful and submissive little girl. The conversation puts flesh on the bones, but it is not the vehicle of a new revelation; and this is regularly so. I cannot think of a single case in *Emma* (or in Jane Austen in general) where the dialogue does more than enlarge and illustrate, though with incomparable justice and vivacity, positions that the narrator has previously outlined. The dramatic propriety is perfect but it is the adjunct to a narrative judgment not a drama in itself.

Of course the dialogue has other functions. It is the principal means by which the action is carried on. The fragment of conversation above tells us nothing new about what Harriet is, what Emma is, or what the relation between them. But it initiates an important part of the plot. It shows us that Harriet is deeply attached to Robert Martin, that she feels at home in his world, that she is tied to it by gratitude and affection. It shows Emma attempting to detach her from this allegiance. It shows too that though Harriet can be overborne in argument her heart remains unconvinced. And this is the mainspring of the first action of the book – until Jane Fairfax and Frank Churchill come on the scene. The dialogue performs this function throughout. Jane Austen rarely presents an action that she cannot dramatise.

Indeed the dialogue is entirely functional. It rounds out and fulfils the characters, it advances the action; and it is limited pretty closely to those purposes. The mere exhibition of mimetic virtuosity which Jane Austen could easily have indulged, is kept well under control. It is allowed a little licence in the flat, mainly comic characters, Miss Bates, or Mr. Collins in *Pride and Prejudice*; and no-one could wish it away. But the exuberant garrulity of Dickens' Mr. Jingle or Sairey Gamp, going far beyond any function they perform in the plot, is hardly to be found in Jane Austen's work. There are other renunciations too. We do not get a verbatim report of Mr. Knightley's proposal and Emma's acceptance, for that is outside the ordained emotional limits. We never hear Robert Martin speak, for he is outside the ordained social limits. Servants, coachmen, etc. are mentioned, but as well as being invisible they are mute.

It is noticeable that material objects, physical details and practical arrangements appear very little in the speech of the most approved characters.

Mr. Weston ... walking briskly with long steps through the passage, was calling out –
'You talk a great deal of the length of this passage my dear. It is a mere nothing after all; and not the least draught from the stairs.'
'I wish' said Mrs. Weston 'one could know which arrangement our guests in general would like best. To do what would be most generally pleasing must be our object – if one could but tell what that would be.'

(Chap. 29)

Mr. Weston, a man of brisk not particularly perceptive common sense, talks of passages, draughts and stairs; Mrs. Weston, a person of altogether superior sensibility, talks in an abstract evaluative vocabulary – 'to do what would be most generally pleasing must be our object'. And in the closing sentences of the book describing the wedding of Emma and Mr. Knightley it is the vulgar and malicious Mrs. Elton who speaks of white satin and lace veils; when 'a small band of true friends who witnessed the ceremony' are referred to, we hear only of their wishes, their hopes and their confidence in the perfect happiness of the union.

Concern with clothes, objects and material details is always the sign of inferiority in the novels. Anyone in Jane Austen who talks about sprigged muslin or boiled eggs is either bad or in some degree ridiculous. If we need any demonstration that her novels are not mere transcripts of her daily experience; that the narrator in charge of her fiction is an ideal construct different from her daily self, we have only to compare her novel with her letters.

How do you like your flounce? We have only plain flounces. I hope you have not cut off the train of your bombasine. I cannot reconcile myself to giving them up as morning gowns; they are so very sweet by candlelight. I would rather sacrifice my blue one for that purpose . . .

These words from a letter to her sister Cassandra could never have been uttered by one of Jane Austen's heroines. She does not herself conform to the austere standard that she sets for them. The early letters are full of chatter about balls and young men; the later ones are full of apple pies, spruce beer, prices and servants, cloaks and pelisses, crepe and bombasine and things coming back from the wash. The rattle, the gossip and the housewife appear in page after page of the letters; but no character in the novels whom we are asked to approve is allowed to exhibit these qualities. Their language is much more severely restricted; it is the language of judgment. They may make errors of judgment, but judgment is their function, and everything else is subordinated to it. The trivia of domestic circumstance may surround them, but we only see them in a state of disengagement. We never hear Emma talking about the housekeeping.

As to the quality of the judgment, we have already noted, in discussing the coloured narrative, the slight shifts of tone by which error or deviation is registered. In general, vivacity is slightly suspect; the correct judgments are usually rather dry and negative in tone. This is not to make any unwarranted conjecture about the author's preferences or intentions; by correct judgments I mean simply those that are borne out by the course of events. The narrator is permitted to be sharp and lively and also right; but when the characters are sharp and lively they are most often slightly wrong. The pattern is set by the dialogue on match-making between Emma and Mr. Knightley at the end of chapter 1. Emma gives a high-spirited but harmless account of how she had helped on Mr. Weston's courtship of Miss Taylor, and congratulates herself on her success. Mr. Knightley's reply is coolly disparaging.

'I do not understand what you mean by success' said Mr. Knightley. 'Success supposes endeavour. Why do you talk of success? Where is your merit? What are you proud of? You made a lucky guess; and that is all that can be said.'
'And have you never known the pleasure and triumph of a lucky guess? I pity you. I thought you cleverer, for depend upon it a lucky guess is never merely luck; there is always some talent in it and as to my poor word success which you quarrel with I do not know that I am so entirely without any claim to it. . . . If I had not promoted Mr. Weston's visits here and given many little encouragements, and smoothed many little matters it might not have come to anything after all.'
'A straight-forward open-hearted man like Weston, and a rational un-affected woman like Miss Taylor may be safely left to manage their own concerns. You are more likely to have done harm to yourself than good to them by interference.'

   Mr. Knightley's vocabulary – *endeavour, merit, straightforward, rational, unaffected* – seems a little ponderous for the occasion, and Emma's coy vivacity excusable enough; but of course Mr. Knightley turns out to be right. Emma's attempts at match-making are her most serious mistakes. It is the style of the *Rambler*, the lexicon of sober moral evaluation that is justified by the event; and so it is to be throughout the book. Mr. Knightley, who is never wrong, maintains this style more consistently than anyone else. He is everywhere a pricker of bubbles, the foe of unregulated fancy. The acutest passages of moral and psychological analysis are accorded to him. In his presence conversation is always lifted from the familiar and the anecdotal to the level of general reflection; the characters become types; and the actual persons around him assume the air of personae in a moral apologue.

'Another thing must be taken into consideration too – Mrs. Elton does not talk to Miss Fairfax as she speaks of her. We all know the differences between the pronouns he or she and thou, the plainest spoken amongst us; we all feel the influence of a something beyond common civility in our personal intercourse with each other – a something more early implanted. We cannot give anybody the disagreeable hints that we may have been very full of the hour before. We feel things differently. And besides the operation of this as a general principle you may be sure that Miss Fairfax awes Mrs. Elton by her superiority both of mind and manner; and that face to face Mrs. Elton treats her with all the respect which she has a claim to. Such a woman as Jane Fairfax probably never fell in Mrs. Elton's way before – and no degree of vanity can prevent her acknowledging her own comparative littleness in action, if not in consciousness.'   (Chap. 33)

It is this kind of speech, thoughtful, well-ordered, analytical and generalising; carefully composed and yet not too formal for ordinary social intercourse, that is at the summit of Jane Austen's dialogue scale. This is the pattern from which all other types of conversation are a decline.

7

At this point we have come full circle; the kind of speech just described is identical in its qualities with the objective narrative with which we began. And here the stylistic pattern of the novel begins to become clear. Mr. Knightley, Mrs. Weston, Jane Fairfax, Emma in her best moments, Frank Churchill in his rather fewer best moments, all talk like the narrator. Emma when she is going wrong, Frank Churchill when he is going wrong, diverge from the narrator's standard. Other characters by one idiosyncrasy or another never attain it. The lesser deviations mark them merely as simpler or less perceptive than the central characters. Greater deviations mark them as in some way deficient or absurd, amiably like Miss Bates or Harriet; unamiably like Mr. Elton; in extreme cases vulgarly or maliciously like Mrs. Elton. The characters we are to approve assimilate their speech to the objective narrative, and do so most completely when we are most to approve of them. In proportion as the characters diverge from this norm they are ridiculous or bad. The objective narrative sets the standard by which all the rest is measured.

It is possible to imagine a novel in which the characters and actions are not subjected to value judgments of any kind. Naturalist fiction often claims to be value-free in this sense. These claims usually turn out on examination to be ill-founded, and the attempt to write in this way usually involves some measure of self-deception. But it is certainly true that the part played by value judgments in the structure of a novel can vary very widely. They may be unconscious or concealed or ambiguous or only implicit in the structure of events. They may be manifest, explicit, articulate; they may step out of the narrative altogether and form a set of virtually separate disquisitions. The judgments professed by the author may be contradicted by the narrative; 'Never trust the author, trust the tale.' We can pretty easily place Jane Austen in this series. Her value judgments are clear and explicit, but they do not separate themselves from the narrative; they are not contradicted by the narrative; they are not ambiguous. In fact her novels are a singularly complete example of a particular kind of value structure which we are now in the position to describe.

In a Jane Austen novel the action, the characters, the values and the language all work in complete unison. By saying that the language is in unison with the other elements I mean that there is an exact linguistic structure by which the other structures are realised, and that they correspond in a direct and simple way. By now this has been pretty fully illustrated. The objective narrative is unambiguously factual and true. Since it is also compact of value judgments, they are enforced upon the reader as equally unambiguous and true. By leaning on the moral vocabulary and tone of Dr. Johnson, the acknowledged stage of an earlier generation, they gain an air of established and indubitable authority. A norm of judgment is thus set up at the opening, and repeated and reinforced at intervals throughout the book. The approved characters (i.e. the heroine, the man she marries at the end of the book, and their trusted friends) all employ the same style as the objective narrator – abstract, evaluative, unconcerned with trivia or material circumstances. When they depart from this style they are always going wrong, making false judgments – judgments that will be disproved by the event. Characters who do not use this style are always in some way deficient, intellectually or morally. When the objective narrative is noticeably intruded upon by the subjectivity of the characters, it is always a sign that the characters are departing from the norm. If they were not their subjectivity would be identical with the narrator's, and so undetectable. Every shade of deviation is distinguished by often delicate but in the end unmistakable linguistic markers. There is no confusion of levels. Superior characters temporarily recede from the norm, but inferior characters never advance towards it. The only ambiguity permitted is that the follies, blindnesses and mistakes are extremely entertaining, and are presented as such; we are allowed to enjoy what we do not approve; but the enjoyment in the end derives from observing deviations from the norm.

By saying that the characters and the values are in unison I mean that values are chiefly established by the characters, and that they are related in a direct and simple way. Characters are more approved or less approved, or not approved at all, quite openly; and the values that the novel seeks to establish are embodied in approved characters rather than in relationships, states of mind, or ways of life. (I can make this clearer perhaps by a contrary example: in Lawrence's *Women in Love* we are not particularly asked to admire or like Birkin or Ursula; but we are asked to see that they achieve a right relationship, are on the right path.) By saying that the characters and values are in unison with the action I mean that things turn out as they should, everyone gets what he deserves, neither more nor less. If hopes are frustrated and expectations disappointed – then they were extravagant hopes or unreasonable expectations. If certain characters achieve only a moderate fulfilment – then their capacities were moderate too. Events are precisely weighed out in proportion to the values we have been persuaded to set upon the characters.

In other kinds of novel these relationships are ambiguous or contradictory or harmonised with difficulty. In Jane Austen they are direct and simple. It is obvious that such fiction as hers could only be written when there was an accepted law of social and moral behaviour to which allegiance was generally paid. Jane Austen evidently does not suspect for a moment that any serious person could dispute her standards; and in her own day it appears no serious person ever did. (They began to do it in the next generation.) This is not to attribute to her a philosophy of mere social conformity; her standard, though it is far from heroic virtue, is plainly a good deal higher than any that actual society actually attained. But it is within the moral reach of actual society, and is acceded to without difficulty or strain. The main characters do not set out on voyages of exploration; they are, with some difficulties and cross-purposes, making for known goals. The known goals are represented in the narration by the style and values of the objective narrator; and they are usually represented in the fiction by one or more characters. In *Emma*, Mr. Knightley is always right; he is the *beau idéal*, a personal embodiment of the moral and social norm. The entire pattern of values is clear, certain and in the open. In a limited circle and for a limited time such a state of affairs is possible. It is this limited but authentic possibility that Jane Austen proposes to assert: and those who object that she leaves out the Napoleonic Wars and the lower classes have no just cause for complaint.

8

Even so, the structure of *Emma* is not at all like the structure of the real world. In the real world events and values do not work in unison, social fulfilments are not exactly proportionate to personal deserts. And style of speech is not an unambiguous indicator of character and value. It is an indicator, of course, but a far more deceptive and uncertain one than novels like *Emma* would suggest. The very perfection with which Jane Austen controls her linguistic apparatus cuts out the element of indeterminacy, of working things out, that is present in later novels – in Charlotte Brontë and George Eliot, for example. By their time society had grown more complex, less certain of its premises; the position of women, the sanctity of the established economic system, the foundations of religious belief had all been called in question; and their exploratory procedure is the response to this situation. Looking back from this point at Jane Austen it can be suggested that her fictional structure mimics the structure of a small closed society, without awareness of social change. But this is not wholly true either. Even within her own small chosen group, this orderly correspondence between social fulfilment and personal desert cannot actually have prevailed. Even within a group so little open to outside ideological pressure as hers was it can never have been true that integrity, attentiveness and good sense were sufficient to place all persons and all actions in their right position on a predetermined scale.

   A view of society such as this, however, cannot have imposed itself as it has done unless it were the expression of a real social force. It is the ethos of a group that we are concerned with, not that of an idiosyncratic individual. What is the social group within which we must situate Jane Austen's fiction if we are to explain its survival and its strength? Modern terminology is not very closely appropriate, and the massive abstractions of Marxism are too general, too little adapted to specific historical conditions, to be of much value. We could speak of Jane Austen's novels as embodying the values of the upper middle class, or the bourgeoisie; but the first transfers us to the wrong historical setting, while the last is too blunt an instrument to have much explanatory value. The class to which her work really belongs is the gentry, a group which can be tolerably well defined in late eighteenth century and nineteenth century England. At the top end of the scale it excludes the aristocracy – territorial magnates, their interests national rather than local, oriented towards positions of power in the state. At the lower end it shades rather indistinctly into the commercial bourgeoisie, who having established their position in business, can buy estates in the country and be admitted to country society. The gentry includes everything between these two limits; substantial landowners, small landowners, members of selected professions – the church, the army and the navy; and it continues to include them and their dependents even when their economic position is very modest indeed – half-pay officers and the widows of country parsons. This will be recognised as representing the limits of Jane Austen's world. Its consciousness of an identity and a homogeneity is expressed in Elizabeth Bennet's remark about her relation to Darcy: 'He is a gentleman; I am a gentleman's daughter: so far we are equal.' The fact that Darcy is rich and rather grand, while Elizabeth is poor and hampered by a ramshackle family is not crucial to her compared with their common participation in gentility.

For a long time it was more crucial to him; and this remark comes more easily from a woman than from a man. It is important that the social roots of Jane Austen's fiction are in the woman's world. This constitutes a sub-variety of the outlook of the gentry as a whole. Since women of this class were not directly engaged in economic activity they had no real relation with any other class. They were not employees, and were only employers on a minor domestic scale. They were not members of a service, nor engaged in politics. They therefore tend to see society as consisting of one class only – their own. Those outside it exist for their consciousness only in the most shadowy fashion; all attention is concentrated on the world of the gentry itself, which comes to be regarded as a microcosm of humanity. Without experience of fundamental class-relations, the gentlewoman makes an elaborate simulacrum of them within her own class. But this is a status system, not a class system; its different ranks are distinguished by degrees of prestige, not by opposition of economic interests; and the gradations become numerous and refined. Economic interests do indeed play a part in this woman's world; thinking only of the non-functional economic position of women we are apt to forget that women were actually playing for very high stakes. There was no other profession for them but marriage, and failure in this endeavour was failure indeed. On the other hand, a few weeks of courtship, a season at Bath, the happy accidents of a ball might mean the acquisition of a fine establishment and a fortune of ten thousand a year. For this reason minor social intercourse, balls, card-parties and morning visits, small matters of deportment and the arts of pleasing, become enormously important. There is neither cynicism nor triviality in thinking them important, for this was the arena in which women's whole destiny was decided. With all its limitations and cruelties from the woman's point of view it was not yet conceivable to the gentry that this mode of life would ever change. Isolated individuals might break away; but they were anomalies: a whole world of fantasy compensations could be evolved, as in the romances that Jane Austen parodies. But no serious alternative had entered the consciousness of the social group as a whole. All that could be done was to humanise and moralise the actual social and economic situation as far as possible. Religion, until the Evangelical revival, was a mildly regulative rather than a constitutive force in this kind of society; and the effective agent is an agreed social morality (agreed because it is the product of a single class) working on the real social and economic basis. In this endeavour fiction such as Jane Austen's had an important part to play.

So we can say if we like that her novels reflect the social consciousness of the feminine half of the upper bourgeoisie of her time. There are obvious analogies between the linguistic structure of *Emma* as I have described it and the class-and-status system as it appeared in the consciousness of women of this group. Everyone in *Emma* belongs to the same class; they are gentry, on a grand or a small scale. The only character outside this class who affects the action of the story is Robert Martin; he remains entirely shadowy and is kept off-stage. Harriet's status is ambiguous; she appears at first as a dependent of the world of the gentry; Emma attempts to give her a secure status within it; this attempts fails; she is allowed to slip down into the ranks of the yeomanry – and therefore to disappear. Correspondingly the linguistic range of the novel is confined to a middle area of more or less educated discourse; it includes neither the language of emotional and intellectual exaltation, nor popular speech. Within this group of gentlefolk there are numerous gradations of status, which largely shape the social action of the book. Within the linguistic community are numerous fine distinctions of modes of speech; these shape its linguistic structure. The social summit of Highbury society is occupied by substantial though not aristocratic gentlefolk, aware of a position that not everyone can aspire to, but stopping short of opulence and with no aspirations to power. The socio-ethical code of the novel is their code; it is well defined, not wholly easy of attainment and certainly not open to everyone; but it stops well short of heroic virtue and has no aspirations to sanctity. This code is given a clear linguistic embodiment, situated in the speech of the narrator, and, among the characters, pre-eminently in the speech of Mr. Knightley. Mr. Knightley is of course the largest landowner in the district. And with fair regularity, those who diverge from this linguistically established norm correspondingly decrease in status. Mr. Elton, who even before he exposes himself completely, is linguistically inferior (over-anxious, too flowery) is spotted early on by Emma as not of a family that requires any particular consideration. Harriet, the only character in the book who uses positively bad grammar, is also of illegitimate birth.

The linguistic scale does not correspond entirely with the moral scale. Miss Bates is a good woman in spite of the absurdities of her speech; but she is of very modest status. The one remark that expresses a shattering scepticism about this whole order of things occurs in connection with Miss Bates: 'She had no intellectual superiority to ... frighten those who might hate her into outward respect.' Much has been made of this, but in fact it stands alone in *Emma*, unsupported by the rest of the book. Intelligence, moral weight, insight, consort naturally with birth and position; below that summit virtue may have a slightly flexible position in the social scale. There are other places in Jane Austen where social position fails to carry moral authority with it; but this is always noted as an anomaly. And the Cinderella theme would require a discussion to itself. This presents a character who accedes to status by dint of virtue and accomplishment alone. She always does, however, accede to status, and it is considered proper that she should do so. In *Emma* this theme is absent, and the status system is reflected pretty directly in the narrative and linguistic structure.

We can repeat therefore that Jane Austen's novels reflect the social attitudes of the feminine half of the upper bourgeoisie of her time. But one cannot be content with the word 'reflect'. It is important to take the element of intentionality into account, to consider not only what social milieu a novel comes from, but where it points. And Jane Austen is far too active a writer to be considered as merely 'reflecting' anything. If we ask where her novels point, the answer I think is plain – they point backwards. It is of great significance that her most considered moral judgments call to mind the world of Johnson, and that the stylistic echoes are so marked as to make it clear they were intended to do so. That is to say that novels written in the revolutionary age are socially and morally oriented to the mid-eighteenth century. Charlotte Corday, Mary Shelley and Bettina von Arnim were among her contemporaries; *Werther* had appeared the year before she was born; she was perfectly acquainted with the Gothic novel; the play that caused all the trouble in *Mansfield Park* was Kotzebue's *Das Kind der Liebe; Emma* appeared in the same year as the third canto of *Childe Harold*: but Jane Austen returns us to the ethos of the *Rambler* – not because she was unaware of any other, but because she chose to do so. The world of which her novels present a corner was a world in convulsion, filled with wars, revolutions, the struggle for political liberty, black repression, miserable poverty and savage penal laws. To be sure, little of this came her way; it would be foolish to complain that a quiet lady living in the country had no very comprehensive view of the political and social stresses of her time. But it would be equally foolish to suppose that the structure of her world is that of any actual segment of society in Regency England. That would be to suppose that pastorals are written by shepherds.

It is important to be clear about the nature and limits of Jane Austen's realism. Within these limits, whatever they turn out to be, her novels are firmly embedded in social reality. Money, position, marriage and personal relations are considered as facts, not elements in a fantasy. Manners, social relations in the superficial sense, shades of conduct and the speech that accompanies them, are observed and rendered with careful fidelity. In her work we never meet those occasions, almost endemic in nineteenth-century English fiction, where we feel that the development of a character or a situation has been given a twist in response to novelistic convention, the exigencies of romance, or an uncontrolled impulse of the author's heart. Pass from manners to morals, and the same is true. Actions have their consequences; no one is let off by an illicit authorial tenderness; no one (with the possible exception of the Crawfords in *Mansfield Park*) is pursued by an unconscious authorial vendetta; judgments are minute and they are scrupulous. All this is an absolutely necessary concomitant of the linguistic structure of the novels; since that is an ordered system, the persons, manners and activities must also be obedient to a system. Anything uncontrolled or capricious, the sort of anomaly that would pass without remark in a novel of the picaresque tradition, is structurally impermissible in Jane Austen. It would not be a mere anomaly; it would be a fatal defect. And since the norm on which the novels are based (the social and moral values established by the objective narrator) is indubitably a real one, deduced from the actual world, not the product of fantasy or an idealising imagination, so everything else must be on the same level of actuality. Given Mr. Knightley, we must have Frank Churchill, not Will Ladislaw; given Mrs. Weston, we must have Harriet Smith, not Hetty Sorrel. Mimetic realism – the lively representation of idiosyncratic speech, for example – does indeed play a part in Jane Austen's fiction, but a subordinate part. It is pretty much confined to the mimesis of speech, for there is little setting of scenes and only the scantiest material detail. And even in the mimesis of speech more depends on the orderly ranging of speech-patterns in a scale of value than on the mere vivid oddities like Mr. Collins and Miss Bates, however memorable and enjoyable they may be. Verisimilitude, close observation of actualities in the world outside, there surely is; but the truth-values of Jane Austen are more readily explained on a coherence theory of truth than on a correspondence theory.

Finally, it is this very coherence that we must put to the question. How is it conditioned, what is its radical imperative? One kind of coherence in a work of fiction is the coherence of a lived experience, as in the kind of *bildungsroman* that is transmuted autobiography. Here nothing seems constructed, but everything holds together because it is centred in an involuntary, unique, intensely felt point of view. This is often the case with George Eliot, Charlotte Brontë and D. H. Lawrence; but surely not with Jane Austen. Her coherence springs from the will and the intelligence rather than from the deep unconscious roots of personality. It is even called into being by an act of the will; the spontaneous unconsidered letters display little of the characteristic insights and determinations that we find in the novels. In short, I see the novels as strongly ideological constructions. They are recommendations to regard society and experience in a certain way; they are powerful reinforcements of a particular class structure and of a moral structure adapted to support it. The reinforcement is powerful because the moral structure is a strong and coherent one. It would not be a valid system outside the closed social consciousness from which it arises; but that is not for lack of good material in its composition. It has been fortified by elements from older and more world-embracing systems than its own – for it comprehends a secularised Christian ethics, a tinge of Johnsonian stoicism, all lightened by a gaiety that goes back to the heroines of Shakespearian comedy. These in themselves are expansive forces, each reaching out to its proper transcendence – to God, to the Universe, to Love. But before they can reach too far a firm social outline is drawn around them, their strength is contained, limited, employed to give coherence and durability to a social code. No social group at this period can ever have been as closed as that represented in Jane Austen's novels. In bourgeois society there is always a leakage of consciousness from one class to another, and where there is this leakage there is always the anxious, the uneasy and the problematic. It may be slow, and it may not be attended to: in Jane Austen it is almost entirely dammed up. Coherence is attained by a deliberate limitation of possibilities.

There is a paradox here. It is because her novels tell the truth they do tell with such fidelity and accuracy that we can become aware of their not telling more. If Jane Austen had written the kind of tales she parodies in *Northanger Abbey* it would be absurd to put them to the question. If she had written in another genre altogether the question would not arise. Essays and lyrical poems can be the expression of moods so subjective and so short-lived as to be virtually immune to influence from the outer world. But the novel – the novel that is neither a fantasy nor an apologue – has entered into an engagement with history. How far has this engagement been fulfilled in Jane Austen's fiction? The usual answer, I believe, once we get beyond the reading that sees her simply as an intelligent entertainer, tends to exalt her creative discernment as though it were something timeless and ahistoric and to neglect her historically conditioned strength. The class whose ethos she is enforcing was to be culturally dominant throughout the nineteenth century, becoming more professional and less territorial in its basis, but in manners and morals essentially little changed. The signs of good breeding and right thinking recognised in her novels would still have been recognised in actual society up to the time of the first world war – recognised particularly readily by her own group, the women of her class. Extensions were made to the code, women who were only on the fringe of the gentry or altogether outside it made contributions to the cultural stream, and the male consciousness, more closely involved with economic and political life, perforce expanded far beyond any range possible to Mr. Darcy or Mr. Knightley. But something like Jane Austen's ethos remained ensconced in the homes of the dominant class, in their daily social intercourse, in their publicly recognised behavioural pattern for a hundred years after her time. Survivals and pockets of resistance have endured much longer.

If we neglect her femininity and consider her as a representative of her class as a whole she can still be seen as contributing substantially to a powerful stream. The refusal to entertain the possibility of class ideologies, the acceptance of the values of the upper bourgeoisie as non-historical absolutes, have been a strong element in English cultural history from Jane Austen's time to the threshold of our own day. From many points of view this has been a strikingly successful procedure. To be sure, during the course of the nineteenth century England gradually became a cultural backwater, English thought assumed progressively less importance in the European context, until now it has none at all. But after the worst horrors of early industrialism became mitigated (say from the eighteen fifties on) England became a land of relative prosperity and stability, and almost absolute peace. The careful filtering and censorship of ultimate conflicts that so irritates continental critics of the English novel (Lukacs, Arnold Hauser) corresponds to something entirely real in English social development. England had its revolutionary period early – in 1640, with its orderly and constitutional aftermath in 1688. It had no revolution in 1830 – only a Reform Bill in 1832.

England was the only country in western Europe where nothing whatever happened in 1848 (except of course the publication in London of the *Communist Manifesto*; and nobody noticed that). Jane Austen's work is one manifestation of an ingrained English habit of mind and action. We are glad to be assured that there is really nothing more, or that what we find in her is a model for all the rest. Our history inclines us, with reason, to listen to her suasions; and English criticism has treated them with an understandable partiality. Her work has had little impact outside the English-speaking world, and even within that world probably not much outside England itself. She is a far more accomplished novelist than many who occupy a place in world literature; but she does not belong to world literature all the same.

Securus judicat orbis terrarum: or does it? No estimate could be too high for the finesse and delicacy with which she has fulfilled her chosen enterprise. But we should be clear about what we are enjoying and why. Her fictional world corresponds to something real and lasting in English life – the achievement within bourgeois society of a tolerable way of living, the acknowledgement within bourgeois society of an ideal of conduct that can be respected, yet an ideal of which actual society need not fall too desperately short. If the French novelists are to be trusted this has never been possible within French bourgeois society; no serious novelist in France has ever been able to contemplate the bourgeoisie without total, inveterate and programmatic detestation. We have only to set Balzac against Dickens, Flaubert against Henry James, Nathalie Sarraute against Virginia Woolf. The root of this contrast is that the English bourgeoisie more than any other has achieved the dubious success of insulating itself spiritually and morally from other classes and other cultures. It has managed to make itself for long periods almost immune to the internal strains that must follow from class confrontation and world conflict. The enclosed completeness of Jane Austen's fiction corresponds to a deeply cherished English image. The English believe that she is truer to life than she is because she is indeed true to life as many of them have made it – as some of the best of them have made it. Men have made worse things; but they have projected better. No one could form an image of the better from reading Jane Austen.

SOURCE: 'Narrative and Dialogue in Jane Austen', in *Critical Quarterly*, XII (1970) 201–29.

NOTES

1. See Stephen Ullmann, *Style in the French Novel*, 2nd edn, 1964, pp. 37–8.
2. See M. Lips, *Le style indirect libre,* Paris, 1926; or, more compendiously, Ullmann, op. cit., pp. 94–101.
3. In the letters Jane Austen comments on a similar phrase in one of her niece's novels: 'I do not object to the thing, but I cannot bear the expression; – it is such thorough novel slang.' (Letters, ed. Chapman, p. 404.)

Sandra M. Gilbert and Susan Gubar
Jane Austen's Cover Story   (1979)

Austen's propriety is most apparent in the overt lesson she sets out to teach in all of her mature novels. Aware that male superiority is far more than a fiction, she always defers to the economic, social, and political power of men as she dramatizes how and why female survival depends on gaining male approval and protection. All the heroines who reject inadequate fathers are engaged in a search for better, more sensitive men who are, nevertheless, still the representatives of authority. As in *Northanger Abbey*, the happy ending of an Austen novel occurs when the girl becomes a daughter to her husband, an older and wiser man who has been her teacher and her advisor, whose house can provide her with shelter and sustenance and at least derived status, reflected glory. Whether it be parsonage or ancestral mansion, the man's house is where the heroine can retreat from both her parents' inadequacies and the perils of the outside world: like Henry Tilney's Woodston, Delaford, Pemberley, Donwell, and Thornton Lacy are spacious, beautiful places almost always supplied with the loveliest fruit trees and the prettiest prospects. Whereas becoming a man means proving or testing oneself or earning a vocation, becoming a woman means relinquishing achievement and accommodating oneself to men and the spaces they provide.

Dramatizing the necessity of female submission for female survival, Austen's story is especially flattering to male readers because it describes the taming not just of any woman but specifically of a rebellious, imaginative girl who is amorously mastered by a sensible man. No less than the blotter literally held over the manuscript on her writing desk, Austen's cover story of the necessity for silence and submission reinforces women's subordinate position in patriarchal culture. Interestingly, what common law called 'coverture' at this time actually defined the married woman's status as suspended or 'covered': 'the very being or legal existence of the woman is suspended during the marriage,' wrote Sir William Blackstone, 'or at least is incorporated and consolidated into that of the husband: under whose wing, protection and cover, she performs everything.'[1] The happiest ending envisioned by Austen, at least until her very last novel, accepts the necessity of protection and cover for heroines who wish to perform anything at all.

At the same time, however, we shall see that Austen herself 'performs everything' under this cover story. As Virginia Woolf noted, for all her 'infallible discretion,' Austen always stimulates her readers 'to supply what is not there.'[2] A story as sexist as that of the taming of the shrew, for example, provides her with a 'blotter' or socially acceptable cover for expressing her own self-division. Undoubtedly a useful acknowledgement of her own ladylike submission and her acquiescence to masculine values, this plot also allows Austen to consider her own anxiety about female assertion and expression, to dramatize her doubts about the possibility of being both a woman and a writer. She describes both her own dilemma and, by extension, that of all women who experience themselves as divided, caught in the contradiction between their status as human beings and their vocation as females.

The impropriety of female creativity first emerges as a problem in *Lady Susan*, where Austen seems divided between her delight in the vitality of a talented libertine lady and her simultaneous rejection of the sexuality and selfishness of her heroine's plots. In this first version of the taming of the shrew, Austen exposes the wicked wilfulness of Lady Susan, who gets her own way because of her 'artful' (Letters 4, 13, and 17), 'bewitching powers' (Letter 4), powers intimately related to her 'clever' and 'happy command of language' (Letter 8). Using 'deep arts', Lady Susan always has a 'design' (Letter 4) or 'artifice' that testifies to her great 'talent' (Letters 16 and 36) as a 'Mistress of Deceit' (Letter 23) who knows how to play a number of parts quite convincingly. She is the first of a series of heroines, of varying degrees of attractiveness, whose lively wit and energetic imagination make them both fascinating and frightening to their creator.

Several critics have explored how Lady Susan's London ways are contrasted to her daughter's love of the country, how the mother's talkative liveliness and sexuality are balanced against the daughter's silence and chastity, how art is opposed to nature.[3] But, if Lady Susan is energetic in her pursuit of pleasure, her daughter is quite vapid and weak; indeed, she seems far more socialized into passivity than a fit representative of nature would be. Actually, she is only necessary to emphasize Lady Susan's unattractiveness – her cruelty to her daughter – which can best be viewed as Austen's reflex to suppress her interest in such wilful sorts of women. For the relationship between Lady Susan and Frederica is not unlike that between the crafty Queen and her angelic step daughter, Snow White: Lady Susan seems almost obsessed with hatred of her daughter, who represents an extension of her own self, a projection of her own inescapable femininity which she tries to destroy or transcend even at the risk of the social ostracism she must inevitably incur at the end of the novel. These two, mother and daughter, reappear transformed in the mature novels into sisters, sometimes because Austen wishes to consider how they embody available options that are in some ways equally attractive yet mutually exclusive, sometimes because she seeks to illustrate how these two divided aspects of the self can be integrated.

In *Sense and Sensibility* (1811), as most readers of the novel have noted, Marianne Dashwood's sensibility links her to the Romantic imagination. Repeatedly described as fanciful, imaginative, emotionally responsive, and receptive to the natural beauty of trees and the aesthetic beauties of Cowper, Marianne is extremely sensitive to language, repelled by clichés, and impatient with the polite lies of civility. Although quite different from Lady Susan, she too allows her lively affections to involve her in an improper amorous involvement, and her indiscreet behavior is contrasted with that of her sister Elinor, who is silent, reserved, and eminently proper. If the imagination is linked with Machiavellian evil in *Lady Susan*, it is closely associated with self-destruction in *Sense and Sensibility*: when Elinor and Marianne have to confront the same painful situation – betrayal by the men they deemed future husbands – Elinor's stoical self-restraint is the strength born of her good sense while Marianne's indulgence in sensibility almost causes her own death, the unfettered play of her imagination seeming to result in a terrible fever that represents how imaginative women are infected and sickened by their dreams.

206 SANDRA M. GILBERT AND SUSAN GUBAR

Marianne's youthful enthusiasm is very attractive, and the reader, like Colonel Brandon, is tempted to find 'something so amiable in the prejudices of a young mind, that one is sorry to see them give way to the reception of more general opinions' (I, chap. 11). But give way they apparently must and evidently do. Eagerness of fancy is a passion like any other, perhaps more imprudent because it is not recognized as such. As delightful as it might first seem, moreover, it is always shown to be a sign of immaturity, of a refusal to submit. Finally this is unbecoming and unproductive in women, who must exert their inner resources for pliancy, elasticity of spirit, and accommodation. *Sense and Sensibility* is an especially painful novel to read because Austen herself seems caught between her attraction to Marianne's sincerity and spontaneity, while at the same identifying with the civil falsehoods and the reserved, polite silences of Elinor, whose art is fittingly portrayed as the painting of screens.

Pride and Prejudice (1813) continues to associate the perils of the imagination with the pitfalls of selfhood, sexuality, and assertion. Elizabeth Bennet is her father's favorite daughter because she has inherited his wit. She is talkative, satirical, quick at interpreting appearances and articulating her judgments, and so she too is contrasted to a sensible silent sister, Jane, who is quiet, unwilling to express her needs or desires, supportive of all and critical of none. While moral Jane remains an invalid, captive at the Bingleys, her satirical sister Elizabeth walks two miles along muddy roads to help nurse her. While Jane visits the Gardiners only to remain inside their house waiting hopelessly for the visitors she wishes to receive, Elizabeth travels to the Collins' establishment where she visits Lady Catherine. While Jane remains at home, lovesick but uncomplaining, Elizabeth accompanies the Gardiners on a walking tour of Derbyshire. Jane's docility, gentleness, and benevolence are remarkable, for she suffers silently throughout the entire plot, until she is finally set free by her Prince Charming. In these respects, she adumbrates Jane Fairfax of Austen's *Emma* (1816), another Jane who is totally passive and quiet, despite the fact that she is repeatedly humiliated by her lover. Indeed, although Jane Fairfax is eventually driven to a gesture of revolt – the pathetic decision to endure the 'slave-trade' of becoming a governess rather than wait for Frank Churchill to become her husband – she is a paragon of submissive politeness and patience throughout her ordeal, so much so that, 'wrapped up in a cloak of politeness,' she was to Emma and even to Mr. Knightley 'disgustingly . . . suspiciously, reserved' (II, chap. 2).

Just as Jane Bennet forecasts the role and character of Jane Fairfax, Elizabeth Bennet shares much with Emma who, perhaps more than all the others, demonstrates Austen's ambivalence about her imaginative powers, since she created in Emma a heroine whom she suspected no one but herself would like.[4] A player of word games, a painter of portraits and a spinner of tales, Emma is clearly an avatar of Austen the artist. And more than all the other playful, lively girls, Emma reminds us that the witty woman is responding to her own confining situation with words that become her weapon, a defense against banality, a way of at least *seeming* to control her life. Like Austen, Emma has at her disposal worn-out, hackneyed stories of romance that she is smart enough to resist in her own life. If Emma is an artist who manipulates people as if they were characters in her own stories, Austen emphasizes not only the immorality of this activity, but its cause or motivation: except for placating her father, Emma has nothing to do. Given her intelligence and imagination, her impatient attempts to transform a mundane reality are completely understandable.

Emma and her friends believe her capable of answering questions which puzzle less quick and assured girls, an ability shown to be necessary in a world of professions and falsehoods, puzzles, charades, and riddles. But word games deceive especially those players who think they have discovered the hidden meanings, and Emma misinterprets every riddle. Most of the letters in the novel contain 'nothing but truth, though there might be some truths not told' (II, chap. 2). Because readiness to talk frequently masks reticence to communicate, the vast majority of conversations involve characters who not only remain unaffected by dialogue, but barely hear each other talking: Isabella, Miss Bates and Mr. Woodhouse, Mrs. Elton and Mr. Weston are participating in simultaneous soliloquies. The civil falsehoods that keep society running make each character a riddle to the others, a polite puzzle. With professions of openness Frank Churchill has been keeping a secret that threatens to embarrass and pain both Emma and Jane Fairfax. Emma discovers the ambiguous nature of discourse that mystifies, withholds, coerces, and lies as much as it reveals.

Yet Austen could not punish her more thoroughly than she does, and in this respect too Emma resembles the other imaginative girls.

For all these heroines are mortified, humiliated, even bullied into sense. Austen's heavy attack on Emma, for instance, depends on the abject failure of the girl's wit. The very brilliant and assertive playfulness that initially marks her as a heroine is finally criticized on the grounds that it is self-deluding. Unable to imagine her visions into reality, she finds that she has all along been manipulated as a character in someone else's fiction. Through Emma, Austen is confronting the inadequacy of fiction and the pain of the 'imaginist' who encounters the relentless recalcitrance of the world in which she lives, but she is also exposing the vulnerable delusions that Emma shares with Catherine Morland before the latter learns that she has no story to tell. Not only does the female artist fail, then, her efforts are condemned as tyrannical and coercive. Emma feels great self-loathing when she discovers how blind she has been: she is 'ashamed of every sensation but the one revealed to her – her affection for Mr. Knightley – Every other part of her mind was disgusting' (III, chap. 2).

Although Emma is the center of Austen's fiction, what she has to learn is her commonality with Jane Fairfax, her vulnerability as a female. Like the antithetical sisters we have discussed, Jane Fairfax and Emma are doubles. Since they are the most accomplished girls in Highbury, exactly the same age, suitable companions, the fact that they are not friends is in itself quite significant. Emma even believes at times that her dislike for Jane is caused by her seeing in Jane 'the really accomplished young woman which she wanted to be thought herself' (II, chap. 2). In fact, she has to succumb to Jane's fate, to *become* her double through the realization that she too has been manipulated as a pawn in Frank Churchill's game. The seriousness of Emma's assertive playfulness is made clear when she behaves rudely, making uncivil remarks at Box Hill, when she talks indiscreetly, unwittingly encouraging the advances of Mr. Elton, and when she allows her imagination to indulge in rather lewd suppositions about the possible sexual intrigues of Jane Fairfax and a married man. In other words, Emma's imagination has led her to the sin of being unladylike, and her complete mortification is a prelude to submission as she becomes a friend of Jane Fairfax, at one with her too in her realization of her own powerlessness. In this respect, Mr. Elton's recitation of a well-known riddle seems ominous:

> My first doth affliction denote,
>   Which my second is destin'd to feel
> And my whole is the best antidote
>   That affliction to soften and heal. –   [I, chap. 9]

For if the answer is woe/man, then in the process of growing up female Emma must be initiated into a secondary role of service and silence.

Similarly, in *Northanger Abbey* Catherine Morland experiences 'the liberty which her imagination had dared to take' as a folly which makes her feel that 'She hated herself more than she could express' (II, chap. 10) so that she too is reduced to 'silence and sadness' (II, chap. 15). Although Marianne Dashwood's sister had admitted that 'thirty-five and seventeen had better not have anything to do with matrimony together' (I, chap. 8), Marianne allows herself at the end to be given away to Colonel Brandon as a 'reward' (III, chap. 14) for his virtuous constancy. At nineteen she finds herself 'submitting to new attachments, entering on new duties' (III, chap. 14). 'With such a confederacy against her,' the narrator asks, 'what else could she do?' Even Elizabeth Bennet, who had 'prided' herself on her 'discernment,' finds that she had never known even herself (II, chap. 13). When 'her anger was turned against herself' (II, chap. 14), Elizabeth realizes that 'she had been blind, partial, prejudiced, absurd' (II, chap. 13). Significantly, 'she was humbled, she was grieved; she repented, though *she hardly knew of what*' (III, chap. 8; italics ours).

All of these girls learn the necessity of curbing their tongues: Marianne is silent when she learns submission and even when 'a thousand inquiries sprung up from her heart . . . she dared not urge one' (III, chap. 10). When she finds that 'For herself she was humbled; but she was proud of him' (III, chap. 10), Elizabeth Bennet displays her maturity by her modest reticence: not only does she refrain from telling both her parents about her feelings for Mr. Darcy, she never tells Jane about Mrs. Gardiner's letter or about her lover's role in persuading Mr. Bingley not to propose. Whereas before she had scorned Mr. Collins's imputation that ladies never say what they mean, at the end of *Pride and Prejudice* Elizabeth refuses to answer Lady Catherine and lies to her mother about the motives for that lady's visit. Furthermore, Elizabeth checks herself with Mr. Darcy, remembering 'that he had yet to learn to be laughed at, and it was rather too early to begin' (III, chap. 16).

Emma also refrains from communicating with both Mrs. Elton and Jane Fairfax when she learns to behave discreetly. She manages to keep Harriet's secret even when Mr. Knightley proposes to her. 'What did she say?' the narrator coyly asks. 'Just what she ought, of course. A lady always does' (III, chap. 13). And at this point the novelist indicates her own ladylike discretion as she too refrains from detailing the personal scene explicitly. The polite talk of ladies, as Robin Lakoff has shown, is devised 'to prevent the expression of strong statements,'[5] but such politeness commits both author and heroine alike to their resolve 'of being humble and discreet and repressing imagination' (I, chap. 17). The novelist who has been fascinated with double-talk from the very beginning of her writing career sees the silences, evasions, and lies of women as an inescapable sign of their requisite sense of doubleness.

Austen's self-division – her fascination with the imagination and her anxiety that it is unfeminine – is part of her consciousness of the unique dilemma of all women, who must acquiesce in their status as objects after an adolescence in which they experience themselves as free agents. Simone de Beauvoir expresses the question asked by all Austen's heroines: 'if I can accomplish my destiny only as the *Other*, how shall I give up my Ego?'[6] Like Emma, Austen's heroines are made to view their adolescent eroticism, their imaginative and physical activity, as an outgrown vitality incompatible with womanly restraint and survival: 'how improperly had she been acting. . . . How inconsiderate, how indelicate, how irrational, how unfeeling, had been her conduct! What blindness, what madness, had led her on!' (III, chap. 11). The initiation into conscious acceptance of powerlessness is always mortifying, for it involves the fall from authority into the acceptance of one's status as a mere character, as well as the humiliating acknowledgement on the part of the witty sister that she must become her self-denying, quiet double. Assertion, imagination, and wit are tempting forms of self-definition which encourage each of the lively heroines to think that she can master or has mastered the world, but this is proven a dangerous illusion for women who must accept the fate of being mastered, and so the heroine learns the benefits of modesty, reticence, and patience.

If we recall Sophia's dying advice to Laura in *Love and Freindship* – 'Run mad as often as you chuse; but do not faint' – it becomes clear that Austen is haunted by both these options and that she seems to feel that fainting, even if it only means playing at being dead, is a more viable solution for women who are acceptable to men only when they inhabit the glass coffin of silence, stillness, secondariness. At the same time, however, Austen never renounces the subjectivity of what her heroines term their own 'madness' until the end of each of their stories. The complementarity of the lively and the quiet sisters, moreover, suggests that these two inadequate responses to the female situation are inseparable. We have already seen that Marianne Dashwood's situation when she is betrayed by the man she considers her fiancé is quite similar to her sister's, and many critics have shown that Elinor has a great deal of sensibility, while Marianne has some sense.[7] Certainly Elizabeth and Jane Bennet, like Emma Woodhouse and Jane Fairfax, are confronted with similar dilemmas even as they eventually reach similar strategies for survival. In consistently drawing our attention to the friendship and reciprocity between sisters, Austen holds out the hope that maturity can bring women consciousness of self as subject and object.

Although all women may be, as she is, split between the conflicting desire for assertion in the world and retreat into the security of the home – speech and silence, independence and dependency – Austen implies that this psychic conflict can be resolved. Because the relationship between personal identity and social role is so problematic for women, the emerging self can only survive with a sustained double vision. As Austen's admirers have always appreciated, she does write out accommodations, even when admitting their cost: since the polarities of fainting and going mad are extremes that tempt but destroy women, Austen described how it is possible for a kind of dialectic of self-consciousness to emerge. While this aspect of female consciousness has driven many women to schizophrenia, Austen's heroines live and flourish *because* of their contradictory projections. When the heroines are able to live Christian lives, doing unto others as they would be done, the daughters are ready to become wives. Self-consciousness liberates them from the self, enabling them to be exquisitely sensitive to the needs and responses of others. This is what distinguishes them from the comic victims of Austen's wit, who are either imprisoned in officious egoism or incapacitated by lethargic indolence: for Austen selfishness and selflessness are virtually interchangeable.

Only the mature heroines can sympathize and identify with the self-important meddlers and the somnambulant valetudinarians who abound in Austen's novels. But their maturity implies a fallen world and the continual possibility, indeed the necessity of self-division, duplicity, and double-talk. As the narrator of *Emma* explains, 'Seldom, very seldom, does complete truth belong to any human disclosure; seldom can it happen that something is not a little disguised or a little mistaken' (III, chap. 13). Using silence as a means of manipulation, passivity as a tactic to gain power, submission as a means of attaining the only control available to them, the heroines *seem* to submit as they get what they both want and need. On the one hand, this process and its accompanying sense of doubleness is psychologically and ethically beneficial, even a boon to women who are raised by it to real heroism. On the other hand, it is a painful degradation for heroines immersed or immured in what de Beauvoir would call their own 'alterity'.

SOURCE: Extract from *The Madwoman in the Attic: the woman writer and the nineteenth-century literary imagination* (Yale University Press, 1979) pp. 154–63.

NOTES

1. Sir William Blackstone, *Commentaries of the Laws of England, Book The First* (Oxford, 1765), p. 442.
2. Virginia Woolf, *The Common Reader* (New York, 1925) pp. 142, 146.
3. A. Walton Litz, *Jane Austen: a study of her artistic development* (New York, 1966), p. 43, and Margaret Drabble, "Introduction," *Lady Susan/The Watsons/Sanditon* (London: Penguin, 1974), pp. 13–14.
4. James Edward Austen-Leigh, *Memoir of Jane Austen*, p. 157.
5. Robin Lakoff, *Language and Woman's Place* (New York: Harper Colophon, 1975), p. 19.
6. Simone de Beauvoir, *The Second Sex*, p. 315.
7. See, for example, the most recent presentation of this argument by Everett Zimmerman, "Admiring Pope no more than is Proper: *Sense and Sensibility*," in *Jane Austen: Bicentenary Essays*, ed. Halperin, pp. 112–22.

Adena Rosmarin 'Misreading' *Emma*: the Powers and Perfidies of Interpretive History (1984)

> I do not write for such dull elves
> As have not a great deal of ingenuity themselves.
> —Jane Austen, *Letters*

The most intriguing characteristic of twentieth-century Austen studies is its consensual blandness. While the sustained marvels of her language and the ineffable nuances of her irony and affirmation insure continued discussion, Austen's stature has itself long since transcended inquiry, immune to both peril and reward.[1] In her own century debate was lively and her reputation an open question answered both by those who, like Macaulay, Lewes, and Tennyson, would compare her to Shakespeare and by those who found circumscription her most striking attribute.[2] But twentieth-century criticism has resolved this debate with a compromise: repeatedly praised for her faultless execution, for the accuracy with which she represents her subject, Austen is simultaneously faulted for her choice of that subject or, to be precise, for its psychological shallowness and social narrowness. Like Ben Jonson she is the victim of what Eliot called 'the perfect conspiracy of approval': 'To be universally accepted; to be damned by the praise that quenches all desire to read the book; to be afflicted by the imputation of the virtues which excite the least pleasure.'[3]

Such consensus and approval yield the curious phenomenon of diminutive greatness, what Ian Watt has called 'the enduring problem of Austen criticism: scale versus stature; the slightness of the matter and the authority of the manner.'[4] Solutions to this problem are manifold, but they invariably reduce to the argument that Austen's perfection is made possible by a refusal of risk, by a reach that does not exceed her grasp. Her significance is said to depend not on breadth or depth but on proportion.[5] We cannot fault this solution for being, like all solutions, shaped by the terms of the problem posed. But we can fault the choice of terms, the ongoing attempt to justify her art in terms of a mimetic poetics. Valuing form for its transparency to content and content for its real-life value, mimesis insures that Austen will rise on the one count and fall on the other and, moreover, that both evaluations will eventually occur together – as in fact they now do. It insures, in other words, that not only will there be an 'enduring problem' in Austen studies, one that opposes her stature to her scale, but that the very terms in which it is posed will preclude a satisfying solution.

Of all Austen's novels, *Emma* most forcefully challenges the explanatory powers of mimesis. It is her longest, has the next to fewest characters, and is the most spatially and socially circumscribed. Confined to the immediate vicinity of Highbury, *Emma* alone approaches Austen's own proffered if dubious ideal of '3 or 4 Families in a Country Village.'[6] Its truncated proposal scene seems conclusive evidence of Austen's emotional shallowness. Compared to the other novels, little 'happens' in *Emma* – Cardinal Newman complained of 'a want of *body* to the story' – and such action as there is, he continued, 'is frittered away in over-little things.'[7] Judged in terms of its subject matter, as Austen's interpretive history judges all her novels, *Emma* emerges as the most attenuated and, thus, one might expect, the least valued. The situation, of course, is just the reverse: *Emma* is repeatedly deemed Austen's masterpiece and, by many, the greatest English novel of the early nineteenth century.[8] The contradiction between scale and stature could hardly be more blatant, the 'enduring problem' more strongly phrased. While the interpretive history treats this contradiction as yet another instance of Austen's 'sedate and cloistered artistic virtue' – *Emma*, George Saintsbury tells us, is 'the absolute triumph of ... the strictly ordinary' – such glaring discrepancies between the value we place on a text and our success in justifying that value are more fruitfully treated as signs of stress in our interpretive model.[9]

Emma has always been read as a novel that tells the story of its title character: *Emma* is 'about' Emma.[10] The definition of that content, however, has itself been a matter for interpretation, the nineteenth century defining it socially, the twentieth psychologically. That *Emma* represents its heroine's growth is by now so accepted as to seem obvious, while further defining that growth and the relative transparencies of its formal embodiment has become yet another matter for interpretation, the agreed-upon disagreement required by a proliferating criticism.[11] Thus we find one critic arguing that *Emma* represents its heroine's moral awakening, another that it represents her sexual awakening, and yet another that it represents her perceptual purification, her passage from quixotic illusion to seeing self and world as they 'really' are.[12] The interpretive history has understandably approved such mimetic readings. The near coincidence of Emma's story with *Emma*, the straightforward chronology, the lack of narratorial complication and verbal self-consciousness – all help the novel approximate the mimetic ideal of accurate representation, of a transparently envisioned content. But this approval is also secured because like all schemata the mimetic model is self-supporting and exclusive, eager to constitute some textual 'facts' but blind to others. It is precisely this combination of constitutive power and blindness that renders interpretive models self-confirming or, what is the same, unable to 'correct' themselves or, what is again the same, immune to 'correction' by the text they have constituted. Austen's remarkable immunity to the vicissitudes of critical fashion and the remarkable blandness of contemporary Austen studies result from just such a schematic self-confirmation: mimesis must again and again give us essentially the 'same' Austen, esentially the 'same' *Emma*.

But if this is so, and I am arguing that it is, then how do readings ever change? How do we discover inadequacies if the model being used cannot 'see' them? By way of answer I suggest that we pay increased and systematic attention to the interpretive history, positing that its record of agreed-upon deficiencies in a text deemed otherwise 'perfect' is a probable if disguised record of the *model*'s deficiencies and that its record of what I call 'dangling insights,' observations repeatedly made and just as repeatedly abandoned, is an unwitting record of what that model cannot 'see'. We would then find that mimesis, like all models, reads both aggressively, displaying textual 'facts' that constitute support, and defensively, converting its own deficiencies into 'flaws' in the text and suppressing 'facts' that would weaken its case.

Thus does the canonical reading discover in its every version the same flaws in *Emma*. Despite increasing emphasis in the interpretive history on Emma's psychological development, the 'content' of the novel remains deficient, remarkable for its emotional shallowness and social narrowness. (The quotidian and provincial lives of the '3 or 4 Families' – their picnics, dances, visits, dinner parties, devotion to talk, and lack of explicit passion – 'prove' both deficiencies.) Mr. Woodhouse emerges as initially amusing but finally tiresome, Jane

Fairfax as too good and too distant to be a good character, and Emma herself, the heroine Austen predicted 'no one but myself will much like,' as not good enough to be a good heroine.[13] The happy ending fails to satisfy because it is too protracted, or because Emma's reform is suspect, or because the events that enable it – the death of Mrs. Churchill, the robbing of the chicken-house – seem contrived.[14]

Austen's great problem in constructing *Emma* is said to be the control of our response to its 'flawed' subject, and the critic's greatest problem in defending *Emma* to be explaining that control. Emma is flawed as a person but not as a character, the defense goes, because her pride, snobbery, gullibility, and self-deception are what enable the comedy and, indeed, the plot – such as it is. But because comedy, or at least this comedy, also requires our sympathy, our desire for the heroine's reform and reward, Austen must simultaneously shield us from those very flaws: by immersing us in Emma's mind, by distorting and distancing the superior Jane, by telling rather than showing the consequences for others of Emma's blunders, by showing rather than telling their consequences for Emma herself. Too much shielding, however, destroys the comedy, and so, as a corrective to Emma's vision, we pay a few carefully scheduled visits to the mind of the man who both sees Emma clearly and loves her. The resulting balance of sympathy and judgment is Jamesian in its precision, and Wayne Booth's unfolding of that balance, as W. J. Harvey observes, 'cannot be bettered and need not be repeated.'[15] *Emma*, thus explained, is at its mimetic best.

Best, however, falls strikingly short of perfect. The Churchill–Fairfax engagement presented Austen with a choice: she could either withhold knowledge of the engagement from the reader, thereby creating our 'mystification,' or not, thereby creating our 'pleasure in observing Emma's innumerable misreadings of his behavior.'[16] Keeping the reader guessing or, worse yet, in the dark is always deemed a mistake by a mimetic model: it signifies faulty representation. And so it is not surprising that Austen's choice of mystification has been attacked as 'perhaps the weakest aspect of this novel.'[17] Worse yet, as Booth continues, 'her efforts at mystification seem second-rate.'[18] In short, a poor choice, poorly executed.

There is no glossing over the seriousness of the supposed mistake. Since Austen's choice, as Harvey points out, 'becomes the main structural agent and narrative strategy of the novel,' attacking it must be 'radically damaging.'[19] While Harvey goes on to defend the choice, arguing that it keeps our attitude towards Emma from becoming *too* ironic, what is most interesting about his argument is, first, a question that mimesis refuses to answer:

What I am sure of is that were the reader fully aware from the outset of the true facts then the irony would become ponderous and schematic. Why this should not be so at a subsequent reading when the reader has such foreknowledge is a mystery that I can't pretend to explain.[20]

And second, an insight it leaves dangling:

we, too, share the frailty of the characters, not merely by being human, but also, in a special sense, by being readers. In other words, *Emma* is a novel which constantly tempts us into surmise, speculation, judgment: the process of reading runs parallel to the life read about. Hence the need for mystification and hence the delayed revelation which shows us how we, too, are liable to mistake appearances for realities and to arrive at premature conclusions. The novel betrays us to ourselves.[21]

Both question and insight vanish as suddenly as they appear, strikingly unconnected to the argument in which they are embedded. Writing after Harvey, Alistair Duckworth agrees that 'the opacity of the plot is quite deliberate.'[22] But because he also reads *Emma* as 'about' Emma – Duckworth explores Emma's choice of 'inherited order' over spontaneity – he must, like Harvey, abandon the point. Mimesis can make sense of the Churchill–Fairfax mystery only insofar as it enables our sympathetic response to Emma, which is a kind of mirroring, or insofar as it doesn't, in which case it becomes a flaw. Inquiry into our reading of the novel – as distinguished from our reading of its heroine – must remain out of schematic bounds precisely because, like all schemata, mimesis tolerates no creations but its own.

Only Graham Hough, in his essentially formalist analysis of *Emma*'s discourse, more than mentions the insight: 'Half the energy of the book would be gone if the reader did not share in her mistakes . . . the structure of the work depends on mysteries and tensions that must not be prematurely released.'[23] While Hough goes no further – one is left wondering *why* the structure is thus dependent and *how* prematurity is decided – that 'mysteries' and 'mistakes' can be valued at all is owing to his explicit rejection of a mimetic schema: 'the truth-values of Jane Austen are more readily explained on a

coherence theory of truth than on a correspondence theory.'[24]
Granted – a coherence theory can admire what mimesis condemns.
But because each theory is similarly uninterested in affective
dynamics, simple admiration of *Emma*'s 'mysteries' and 'mistakes'
explains no more than does condemnation: each assumes an Austen
of diminutive greatness. Both Hough's conclusion and its condescension follow inevitably from his poetics and, more particularly,
from this assumption: 'men have made worse things; but they have
projected better. No one could form an image of the better from
reading Jane Austen.'[25]

In a mimetic poetics, the ideal reader is passive. His only act, if it
can be called that, is to view the represented content of the text. To
read *Emma* mimetically is to watch Emma's education with dis-
passionate sympathy, any excess involvement or doubt signaling a
fault either in our reading or in Austen's art.[26] Particularly un-
welcome is irony's deliberate invocation of such a fault: by inviting
us to doubt the text, it upholds this act as inherently interesting and
valuable; by depending on the interpretive skill of the reader, it
implies a reality that needs interpreting and a reader actively
involved in that interpretation. More directly than any other way of
meaning, irony flouts the fundamental commitments of mimesis, to
a reality independent of text and reader; to a medium transparent to
that reality.

Austen's penchant for irony has not gone unrecognized. But the
Augustan clarity of her most remarked-upon ironies ameliorates
their philosophical sin, making them unimpeachable, even virtuous.
The irony of her most famous sentence ('It is a truth universally
acknowledged that a single man in possession of a fortune must be in
want of a wife.') has proven mimetically admirable for just this
reason: surface meaning seems so transparently deceptive and 'real'
meaning so perfectly envisioned that truth appears less abused than
served, less obscure than 'light, and bright, and sparkling.'[27] But the
ironies of *Emma are* obscure. Frequently only suspected in our
reading and yet more frequently overlooked, they are often recognized only retrospectively:

In short, she sat, during the first visit, looking at Jane Fairfax with twofold
complacency; the sense of pleasure and the sense of rendering justice, and
was determining that she would dislike her no longer. When she took in her
history, indeed, her situation, as well as her beauty; when she considered

what all this elegance was destined to, what she was going to sink from, how she was going to live, it seemed impossible to feel any thing but compassion and respect; especially, if to every well-known particular entitling her to interest, were added the highly probable circumstance of an attachment to Mr. Dixon, which she had so naturally started to herself. In that case, nothing could be more pitiable or more honourable than the sacrifices she had resolved on. Emma was very willing now to acquit her of having seduced Mr. Dixon's affections from his wife, or of any thing mischievous which her imagination had suggested at first. If it were love, it might be simple, single, successless love on her side alone.[28]

Made possible by Emma's misimagining, this irony is realized only when we recognize that misimagining as such. True, we are warned – notice the string of 'mights,' the allusion to her 'imagination' – but the warnings as well as her supposition of unrequited love are disarmed by their insertion into a meditation on forgiveness. By contrast with Emma's previous imaginings, these appear so meritorious that their credibility seems assured. Only later do we learn that this assurance is as false as the lines are mimetically misshapen. They are faithful to Emma's thought, but this immediate fidelity only creates the radical infidelity of that thought – and ours – to her world.

And yet such lines occur throughout *Emma*. In particular they pervade the blended narrative, an admixture variously conflating and juxtaposing the disinterested voice of the narrator and the interested voice of an individual character, usually Emma.[29] The reliability of this narrative ranges from total to nil, and signs of this wavering reliability range from conspicuous to absent. In *Emma* Austen regularly and with virtuosity explores the whole of both ranges:

Emma wished he would be less pointed, yet could not help being amused; and when on glancing her eye towards Jane Fairfax she caught the remains of a smile, when she saw that with all the deep blush of consciousness, there had been a smile of secret delight, she had less scruple in the amusement, and much less compunction with respect to her. – This amiable, upright, perfect Jane Fairfax was apparently cherishing very reprehensible feelings.
(243)

The text here demands that we step deftly from what is admirable ('Emma wished he would be less pointed') to what is not ('yet could not help being amused'), from what seems to be reliably reported ('she caught the remains of a smile') to what is possibly reliable (it 'had been a smile of secret delight') to what is an obvious but not unconvincing supposition ('Jane Fairfax was apparently cherishing very reprehensible feelings'). While the increasing dominance of Emma's voice over the narrator's signals decreasing reliability, the smoothness of the blend invites us not to notice: we see as Emma sees and take her vision as true. But were we to notice, we would yet be misled, for we later learn that Jane Fairfax was indeed cherishing such feelings – only not for Mr. Dixon. The doubleness of the passage is such that we must be wrong even if we aren't.

Dialogue in *Emma* is often similarly misleading, as in this passage, which follows closely on the above:

He brought all the music to her, and they looked it over together. – Emma took the opportunity of whispering,
'You speak too plain. She must understand you.'
'I hope she does. I would have her understand me. I am not in the least ashamed of my meaning.'   (243)

Along with Emma we are here led to infer that it is Jane's illicit love for Mr. Dixon that justifies Churchill's immediately preceding attempt to shame her: 'True affection only could have prompted it [the gift of the pianoforte]' (242). We later learn that the affection to which he alludes is his and that we have inferred wrongly. But even had we not, which is unlikely, we would yet be wrong, for we also learn that his doubleness is itself shameful – as is his attempt to shame. Once again, the text tempts us to err.

To subsume so many choices under the rubric of 'flaw' and such complex and extensive interpretive activity under the guise of passive watching makes little explanatory sense. The novel makes better sense if we begin with these choices and that activity, unfolding the value of the novel in their terms. We would begin, that is, by assuming that Austen meant the reader to be mystified, to make many of the same interpretive errors or, as Booth aptly puts it, many of the same misreadings that Emma makes. No longer would the reader have the luxury of condescension, of always seeing more clearly than Emma. In an explanatory model that concentrates not on what *Emma* represents but on what the experience of reading *Emma* is like, the reader not only watches Emma's education, he reenacts it, learning from his misreading and the subsequent re-reading it makes possible. The novel becomes our tutor, the very act of reading our lesson.

But before we can be tutored, we must become needy of tutoring. If we are to feel responsible for our misreading, to feel not that we are tripped but that we stumble, we must acquire the hubris already possessed by Emma as the novel opens. The main business of Volume I is to engineer this acquisition, to inflate our confidence both in the text and in our ability to read. Our moral and perceptual superiority to Emma is immediately and repeatedly emphasized – 'The real evils of Emma's situation were the power of having rather too much her own way, and a disposition to think a little too well of herself' (5) – and we, the narrator's confidants, settle back to watch the heroine's fall. We are not disappointed. Even Emma recognizes her moral abuse of Robert Martin and Harriet. But our earlier and more complete recognition seems to confirm our superiority, which is then inflated to complacence by the obvious display of Elton's interest in Emma and her blindness to it. His compliments are as excessive as her reading of them is erroneous: ' "it is his gratitude on Harriet's account" ' (49). And, as if her error were not explicit enough, the narrator makes it more so: 'Emma, too eager and busy in her own previous conceptions and views to hear him impartially, or see him with clear vision ... walked on' (110). Emma refuses John Knightley's hint of Elton's interest – ' "Mr. Elton in love with me! – What an idea!" ' (112) – but the refusal only plants the thought more firmly in the reader's mind, where it is further nourished by yet another narratorial announcement of Emma's blindness: 'she walked on, amusing herself in the consideration of the blunders which often arise from a partial knowledge of circumstances, of the mistakes which people of high pretensions to judgment are for ever falling into' (112). We are instructed to convert Emma's judgment of her brother-in-law into her unwitting and therefore ironic self-judgment. But the very act of doing so generates a further irony that here eludes us: by complacently assigning 'high pretensions' to Emma and refusing to recognize them in ourselves, we repeat her complacence. Only much later do we become capable of such self-recognition.

The Elton episode ends with his proposal, an event that confirms our suspicions of both Elton and Emma and thus our faith in ourselves as readers. It also ends with Emma's elaborately displayed and penitent rereading of his past actions, an event that invites our faith in her moral and perceptual reform. But both confirmation and invitation are temptations: our superiority to Emma as a reader is unearned, and her reform turns out to be false. Explained thus, the heavy-handed irony of the episode makes a new and better sense: it at once enables the tutoring of the last two volumes and complicates that tutoring, making it more arduous and thus more effective. Having learned both hubris and complacency, we forge ahead, doubly handicapped by interpretive sin. The combination proves our undoing.

As we leave Volume I the novel broadens and deepens. We need more information and less distraction to continue making sense of Emma's world, but, not incidentally, we get precisely the reverse. Miss Bates, Jane Fairfax, Frank Churchill, and Mrs. Elton are introduced. The helpful narrator of Volume I appears less frequently and more enigmatically, intimating that more is known than is written – Jane Fairfax's 'account to her aunt contained nothing but truth, though there might be some truths not told' (166) – or less – 'Mr. Knightley, who, for some reason best known to himself, had certainly taken an early dislike to Frank Churchill' (343). Thrown back on our own overconfident and desensitized resources, we are tempted to trust Emma. But because the Elton episode has left her not less unreliable but only more subtly so, the temptation is as dangerous as it is irresistible. Moreover, our very mode of making sense, the passive reading sufficient to the cloistered world of Volume I, becomes suddenly and unexpectedly outmoded, replaced by a hermeneutic dance of bewildering complexity.

We spend the rest of the novel learning the steps of this performance, but our first extended lesson takes place as Volume I closes. Emma is telling Mr. Knightley that Frank Churchill has once again postponed his long overdue visit and 'to her great amusement, perceived that she was taking the other side of the question from her real opinion, and making use of Mrs. Weston's arguments against herself' (145). Our competence as readers is here challenged. Warned that Emma only pretends disagreement with Mr. Knightley's condemnation of Churchill, that the dialogue is in actuality a joint monologue, we must remember throughout its four pages to replace apparent meaning with inferred intent. We must, that is, perform the characteristic dance of irony.[30] In the next two volumes our moves will be hesitant or delayed, but here they are not only sure-footed but foreseen.

Or are they? Emma begins as announced, arguing pro forma, but as the 'argument' ends her pretense seems to have become the reality:[31] ' "I will say no more about him," cried Emma, "you turn every thing to evil. We are both prejudiced; you against, I for him, and we have no chance of agreeing till he is really here" ' (150). At what point Emma begins to argue in earnest is significantly difficult to determine. But if we do not begin as instructed we err, and if we end as instructed we likewise err. Inclining away from its announced path and obscuring its inclination, the scene presages the hermeneutic obliquity of the lást two volumes. It also initiates that obliquity, camouflaging Mr. Knightley's jealousy and love with moral indignation even as it makes them available for our later recollection, warning us of Churchill's duplicity even as it begets our interest and thus our blindness. Like Emma we are ready for some excitement, and ' "We must not be nice and ask for all the virtues into the bargain" ' (149). The trap, in short, is nicely laid.

The end of Volume I, then, marks our hermeneutic nadir: hubris and complacency are at their height, our faith in the novel's conventional design at its most naive. From here on the growing subtlety of Emma's misreadings increasingly challenges and thus develops our reading competence, our misreadings and Emma's becoming increasingly alike, both in kind and degree, till our reading of Churchill's letter shows them to be one. This convergence is the novel's major affective strategy. It is not, however, its only one. While most of our readings are prompted by and repeat Emma's, not all do so – nor are all mistaken. At times our reading of Emma's world is superior to hers (as in the Elton episode and later in the Churchill–Fairfax mystery), at times congruent and justly so (as in her assessments of Mrs. Elton and Mr. Knightley), and at times disturbingly inferior (as in her impeccable regard for her father). Mapping our interpretive progress and Emma's reveals a correspondence that is striking but nevertheless approximate. This approximation suggests the working of a more complex strategy, an intent to tempt us to more than a simple repetition of Emma's experience.

Supporting this suggestion are others, which lead to yet more radical complexities. First of all, we read a book whereas Emma reads her world. This difference should warn us that the two readings are not only here and there divergent but always epistemologically distinct: Emma interprets a 'real' world whereas the reader interprets interpretations of her world. Our attempts to make sense of that world are accordingly efforts to gauge the correspondent accuracies of the minds that most immediately read it: a central consciousness usually beclouded but intermittently pellucid, a narrator seemingly artless but occasionally devious and always artful, a loquacious spinster whose 'nonsense' unexpectedly turns out to be the least 'interpreted' and thus the most strictly lucid sense of all. But further complicating our attempts is the distinctly bookish cast of Emma's mind: not only is her world already fictional, but the mind primarily responsible for reading that world is itself noticeably informed by fictional categories.

Reading *Emma* is thus a doubly bookish enterprise, its doubleness difficult to unwind, its difficulty part of the novel's heuristic design. As Lionel Trilling observes, Emma is 'like Don Quixote and Emma Bovary' in that 'her mind is shaped and deceived by fiction.'[32] Trilling's observation inserts *Emma* into that long tradition of fiction whose power derives from the display of its own fictionality. But the novel also belongs in the 'female Quixote' tradition, which, taking its name from Charlotte Lennox's popular *The Female Quixote* (1752), satirizes heroic romance.[33] We know from Austen's letters that she read Lennox's book at least twice and, while writing *Emma*, was reading a similar satire, Eaton Barrett's *The Heroine* (1813).[34] Aware of both romance and anti-romance, Austen wrote for readers similarly aware. But her revisions and diffractions of genre and anti-genre are so radically recombinant that no degree of awareness enables a safe negotiation of the novel. We find 'heroines' where least expected, Jane Fairfax and, to a lesser extent, Harriet Smith assuming the generic role of victorious orphan while Emma plays fairy godmother – even to her surrogate mother. Churchill, so obviously 'heroic' in his rescue of Harriet and his flirtation with Emma, is just as obviously 'unheroic' in his treatment of Jane Fairfax. Still, he does end as a hero, if only to his betrothed, and Emma, while only half an orphan, nevertheless does what all romantic heroines do: she marries the hero.

Emma's generic invitation thus proves deviously difficult to accept. The varying and variously emergent symptoms of romance and its satiric double are, taken individually, obvious enough. But taken together and in turn, each genre reveals the other as inadequate to make sense of the novel as a whole, and each revelation casts our reading competence yet more deeply in doubt. But even more radically strategic than this generic uncertainty is the novel's manipulation of its own fictionality. The very exigencies of plot work as temptations, and we find ourselves trapped by our readerly desires, helplessly running in the grooves of Emma's tritely romanticizing imagination: Will Frank Churchill come? Will he and Emma fall in love? Emma's quixotic drama here and throughout unites with our performance as readers, a union that confounds the conventionally appropriate maneuvers for a reader of fiction with what are shown to be inappropriate maneuvers for a person in the world. Thus does the very act of reading the novel *as* a novel implicate us in Emma's faulty imagination. Thus does our very competence as readers prove our undoing.

Such sweeping strategies are particularized in a myriad of distinctive warpings, the most extensive of which, as its disrepute in the interpretive history implies, is the Churchill–Fairfax mystification. While we assign greater moral guilt to Churchill than to Fairfax, deception being for him a delight and for her a humiliation, from a hermeneutic point of view each is equally deceptive, from a heuristic point of view each an equally potent tutor. Explained thus, Austen's choice of mystery over irony is transformed from 'perhaps the weakest aspect of the novel' to, perhaps, the strongest.

But however central the strategic role of this mystification, it remains but one among the many deceptions that weave *Emma*'s heuristic design. The narrator, initially so helpful, increasingly handicaps us by withholding information that Emma does not have – such as the fact that Harriet loves Mr. Knightley rather than Frank Churchill – as well as information Emma does have – such as the history of Miss Bates's social status. We are asked to entertain an increasing number of alternative interpretations. Hence the triple camouflage of the Churchill–Fairfax engagement: Emma, with Churchill's overly enthusiastic collaboration, conjures an attachment between Jane and the never-seen Mr. Dixon; Mrs. Weston conjures an attachment between Mr. Knightley and Jane; Emma conjures her own romance with Churchill. The last two of these hermeneutic decoys also camouflage the eventual connection between Emma and Mr. Knightley, making us feel that we, like Emma, are again blind to the obvious.

The text's ample support of these more or less incompatible alternatives compounds our difficulty. Jane's reticence, illnesses, fetchings of mail, reluctance to leave Highbury, and smiles of 'secret delight' are until late in the novel all convincingly explained by Emma's hypothesis. Mr. Knightley's 'love' for Jane is rendered plausible if not probable by his repeated praise and defense, by his offering his carriage to Jane, and by passages such as this:

'I know how highly you think of Jane Fairfax,' said Emma.
'Yes,' he replied, 'any body may know how highly I think of her.'
'And yet,' said Emma ... 'perhaps, you may hardly be aware yourself how highly it is. The extent of your admiration may take you by surprize some day or other.'
Mr. Knightley was hard at work upon the lower buttons of his thick leather gaiters, and either the exertion of getting them together, or some other cause, brought the colour into his face, as he answered,
'Oh! are you there? – But you are miserably behindhand. Mr Cole gave me a hint of it six weeks ago.'   (287)

Despite his immediate and, as we later learn, genuine denial of interest in Jane – 'I never had a thought of her in that way, I assure you' (288) – the narrator's coy allusion to 'some other cause' than 'exertion' makes us suspect that denial, and the remarks that close the scene seem to confirm our suspicion:

'Well, Mrs. Weston,' said Emma triumphantly when he left them, 'what do you say now to Mr. Knightley's marrying Jane Fairfax?'
'Why really, dear Emma, I say that he is so very much occupied by the idea of *not* being in love with her, that I should not wonder if it were to end in his being so at last.'   (289)

Mr. Knightley's genuine admiration of Jane additionally substantiates the possibility of his love, just as the genuine friendship between Emma and Churchill, which does not end with their respective attachments, substantiates her romantic fantasy. Because both relationships are as true as they are sham, we are tutored not only in reading but in the ineffable complexity of male-female relationships – a complexity that has been considered beyond Austen's power to notice, let alone articulate.

Many scenes are meticulously ambivalent, lending themselves first to one interpretation, then to its revision, and then, frequently, to a revision of that revision. At Donwell Abbey, for instance, Emma comes upon Mr. Knightley and Harriet:

She joined them at the wall, and found them more engaged in talking than in looking around. He was giving Harriet information as to modes of agriculture, &c. and Emma received a smile which seemed to say, 'These are my own concerns. I have a right to talk on such subjects, without being suspected of introducing Robert Martin.' – She did not suspect him. It was too old a story. – Robert Martin had probably ceased to think of Harriet.   (360–1)

The scene, as here presented, foregrounds two possible interpretations: either Mr. Knightley is 'introducing Robert Martin,' an interpretation Emma rejects, or he is talking about 'modes of agriculture,' an interpretation Emma – and probably the reader – accepts. The former runs interference for the latter, blocking the interpretation Harriet later uses to 'prove' his love for her:

they had been walking some time before Emma came, and he had taken pains (as she was convinced) to draw her from the rest to himself – and at first, he had talked to her in a more particular way than he had ever done before, in a very particular way indeed! – (Harriet could not recall it without a blush.) He seemed to be almost asking her, whether her affections were engaged. – But as soon as she (Miss Woodhouse) appeared likely to join them, he changed the subject, and began talking about farming.

Emma's version suddenly seems to support Harriet's, and, if we recall them, the carefully planted words of that scene ('She did not suspect him. It was too old a story.') lend further if ironic support. But Harriet's version is itself soon supplanted:

'I am now very willing to grant you all Harriet's good qualities. I have taken some pains for your sake, and for Robert Martin's sake, (whom I have always had reason to believe as much in love with her as ever,) to get acquainted with her. I have often talked to her a good deal. You must have seen that I did. Sometimes, indeed, I have thought you were half suspecting me of pleading poor Martin's cause, which was never the case.'   (474)

Emma's early reading of the incident – that Mr. Knightley was 'pleading poor Martin's cause' – here resurfaces, bringing the misinterpretive process full circle but not to its close. We take Mr. Knightley's reading as 'true' – partly because it comes last, partly because it is his – but even here the suspect early reading lingers, doubly rejected but also doubly discussed, a shadow reading with, it seems, a life of its own. The point is not that the text has difficulty arriving at the 'truth' but that it strives to make *our* arrival belated, difficult, and never quite certain.

The novel is dense with such meticulously ambivalent incident, and if we broaden our notion of 'incident' to include more strictly verbal happenings, it becomes yet more densely misleading. Words, whether alone or grouped, assume the status of events. Hence the word game played by Churchill, hence his 'blunder.' Like Austen, he has designs on his reader – to Emma, he says, 'I want to puzzle you again' (347) – and, like Austen's, his design is achieved, albeit darkly. But this darkness is justified if we recall her famous complaint about *Pride and Prejudice* – 'The work is rather too light, and bright, and sparkling; it wants shade.' – and observe that *Emma*, owing largely to Churchill and the manifold if ultimately heuristic repetitions of his design in that of the novel, has no such deficiency.[35] Even individual sentences manifest devious design, as when we read of Donwell Abbey's avenue of limes: 'It led to nothing; nothing but a view at the end over a low stone wall with high pillars, which seemed intended, in their erection, to give the appearance of an approach to the house, which never had been there' (360). This cadenced sentence flatly asserts that the walk led to 'nothing,' only to qualify that nothing into something, a 'view' left in abeyance and 'pillars' made doubly moot: they only *seem* an *appearance* of an approach to the house. But even this much certainty crumbles as we connect 'which had never been there' to its immediate antecedent, a 'house' that is patently 'there.' Our retreat to the penultimate antecedent, the 'approach,' reveals *it* as now not 'there,' a revelation that recalls our initial and by now much revised sense that the walk led to 'nothing.'

But of all such verbal events in the novel, two stand out as being of particular significance, both for our reading and for our criticism: the monologues of Miss Bates and Churchill's remarkably long and remarkably placed epistolary apologia near the end of the novel. The monologues have been mimetically and not unjustly explained as amusing, as characterizing their speaker, and, by some critics, as a kaleidoscopic mirror of Highbury.[36] Indeed, their almost tactile impression of life as it is lived very nearly justifies their extensive presence. But for all their lucidity, the monologues conceal as much as they reveal. Their extravagant length, their absorption with trivia, their radically associative structure – all conspire to provide the reader with rich and repeated occasions for careless reading. We are tempted to think, 'here she goes again,' to pay inattention, to miss, as Emma misses, the clues that lie in full view on the monotonous monologic surface:

'It was before tea – stay – no, it could not be before tea, because we were just going to cards – and yet it was before tea, because I remember thinking – Oh! no, now I recollect, now I have it; something happened before tea, but not that. Mr. Elton was called out of the room before tea, old John Abdy's son wanted to speak with him. Poor old John, I have a great regard for him; he was clerk to my poor father twenty-seven years; and now, poor old man, he is bed-ridden, and very poorly with the rheumatic gout in his joints – I must go and see him to-day; and so will Jane, I am sure, if she gets out at all. And poor John's son came to talk to Mr. Elton about relief from the parish; he is very well to do himself, you know, being head man at the Crown, ostler, and every thing of that sort, but still he cannot keep his father without some help; and so, when Mr. Elton came back, he told us what John ostler had been telling him, and then it came out about the chaise having been sent to Randall's to take Mr. Frank Churchill to Richmond. That was what happened before tea. It was after tea that Jane spoke to Mrs. Elton.'   (382–83)

We later learn that Frank Churchill's going *caused* Jane Fairfax to speak to Mrs. Elton, with all that that entailed, but this dazzling display blinds all but the most attentive of readers to the connection. Reading Emma's response further deepens our inattention – 'There was nothing in all this to astonish or interest' (384) – and virtually insures that only in retrospect will we realize, in the full sense of the word, our hermeneutic laziness.

But these monologues are also strategically devious in a more active sense. However amusing, they irritate Emma, and partly because we tend to feel as she feels, partly because they are as they are, they also irritate us – so much so, in fact, that we are maneuvered into subscribing to Emma's insult on Box Hill. Recall that Frank Churchill has been trying to enliven the party by demanding from each person present 'either one thing very clever . . . or two things moderately clever – or three things very dull indeed' (370):

'Oh! very well,' exclaimed Miss Bates, 'then I need not be uneasy. "Three things very dull indeed." That will just do for me, you know. I shall be sure to say three dull things as soon as ever I open my mouth, shan't I? – (looking round with the most good-humoured dependence on every body's assent) – Do not you all think I shall?'
   Emma could not resist.
   'Ah! ma'am, but there may be a difficulty. Pardon me – but you will be limited as to number – only three at once.'   (370)

The interpretive history of *Emma* repeatedly records this moment as 'the emotional climax of the novel.'[37] But it is only some three pages later, when Mr. Knightley takes Emma's arm on their return to the carriage, that the climactic significance of the insult is revealed:

'I wish you could have heard how she talked of it – with what candour and generosity. I wish you could have heard her honouring your forbearance, in being able to pay her such attentions, as she was for ever receiving from yourself and your father, when her society must be so irksome.'

'Oh!' cried Emma, 'I know there is not a better creature in the world: but you must allow, that what is good and what is ridiculous are more unfortunately blended in her.'

'They are blended,' said he, 'I acknowledge; and were she . . . a woman of fortune, I would leave every harmless absurdity to take its chance, I would not quarrel with you for any liberties of manner. Were she your equal in situation — but, Emma, consider how far this is from being the case. She is poor; she has sunk from the comforts she was born to; and, if she live to old age, must probably sink more. Her situation should secure your compassion. It was badly done, indeed! — You, whom she had known from an infant, whom she had seen grow up from a period when her notice was an honour, to have you now, in thoughtless spirits, and the pride of the moment, laugh at her, humble her. . . . This is not pleasant to you, Emma.'   (375)

Nor, might we add, is it pleasant to us. Because our need to recollect and be tutored has become as great as Emma's, her guilt becomes ours, and in the page upon page of elaborately detailed remorse that follows we are denied the luxury of distance. It is a stunning scene, but it is *our* experience as much as Emma's that makes it so. The insult is so well prepared by our growing irritation, so irresistibly invited by Miss Bates's own remark, and so well camouflaged by its brevity and the surrounding pages of verbal play that we are distracted from both Miss Bates's pain and the implications of our distraction. All but the most meritorious of readers become Emma's ready accomplices and, thus, her fellow penitents. Here, as always in *Emma*, guilt is developed after the act, its belatedness being in part what makes it guilt: we could and should have known better but didn't. Our sense is not that insignificant events suddenly become significant — although, strictly speaking, this is what happens — but that we suddenly if retrospectively see the significance they have always had. Recessing the climax from our immediate recognition is, then, precisely what lends it such climactic force. It is also what places that force beyond the explanatory reach of a mimetic poetics: the design of the scene must remain as mimetically unaccountable as the guilt its reader incurs.

After Box Hill, Miss Bates immediately becomes less present in the text and, when present, less irritating. Immediate also is her acquisition of social status and emotional sensibility. A mimetic model can explain these changes only as occurring *in* Miss Bates — an explanation that musters little textual support — or as randomly occurring revelations of her character — an explanation that denies Austen's Jamesian control. An effective model, however, would find significance in the event of our recognizing those changes, which do not affectively exist independent of such recognition and which, as they come into existence, confirm and extend our guilt. It would note that the revelation of her social decline is displaced from its 'natural' site, the narrator's introductory history (21), to where it can most effectively awaken this guilt. With our sympathy repressed and her personality quite literally reduced to its verbal element, caricature became possible, but precisely insofar as it did we were tempted to read Miss Bates as less than the person she suddenly and disturbingly becomes on Box Hill. The changes 'in' Miss Bates, I am suggesting, are less adequately explained realistically than strategically: they are yet another instance of fictional convention turned to a heuristic end.[38]

Following the Box Hill climax, the hermeneutic momentum of the novel accelerates. Revelation follows close upon revelation, rereading upon rereading. Chief among these is Churchill's letter, an epistolary tour de force that removes the puzzlement from many puzzles, correcting Emma's and our misreadings of his 'proposal' to her, his odd humors at Donwell Abbey and Box Hill, his comings and goings, Jane's illnesses, and, in general, all 'strange things' (439). The letter thus occasions an intense retrospective tutoring. But it also tempts us to make a new and quite literal misreading. Armed with the starts and stops that conventionally betoken sincerity, packed with intense self-recrimination and equally intense praise of our favorites, the letter subtly but all the more thoroughly defuses our every attempted judgment of its writer. We should, as is usual in *Emma*, know better. Not only has the text repeatedly upheld brevity as *the* epistolary virtue, but Mr. Knightley himself has already passed judgment on Churchill's letters: 'He can sit down and write a fine flourishing letter, full of profession and falsehoods. . . . His letters disgust me' (148–9). But such warnings occurred some three hundred pages earlier, and we have been allowed to grow forgetful. Our guard is down, and any residual resistance to Churchill's blandishments is cancelled by the letter's length, as seductive as it is incriminating, by the immediacy and fullness of its presentation, by the curiosity it not only piques but satisfies. Emma, in spite of herself, is fully taken in:

This letter must make its way to Emma's feelings. She was obliged, in spite of her previous determination to the contrary, to do it all the justice that

Mrs. Weston foretold. As soon as she came to her own name, it was irresistible; every line relating to herself was interesting, and almost every line agreeable; and when this charm ceased, the subject could still maintain itself, by the natural return of her former regard for the writer, and the very strong attraction which any picture of love must have for her at that moment. She never stopt till she had gone through the whole; and though it was impossible not to feel that he had been wrong, yet he had been less wrong than she had supposed – and he had suffered, and was very sorry – and he was so grateful to Mrs. Weston, and so much in love with Miss Fairfax, and she was so happy herself, that there was no being severe; and could he have entered the room, she must have shaken hands with him as heartily as ever.   (444)

It is either a very cantankerous or a very cagey reader who refuses to share this mood of comic forgiveness and hymeneal celebration. Once again, the blended narrative does its heuristic work, moving us from the narrator's reliable reporting and moral endorsement to Emma's voice, marked by the string of adolescent 'so's,' back to the narrator and what we take as true and approved: 'could he have entered the room, she must have shaken hands with him as heartily as ever.' But Emma's reading, which confirms our own, is yet another trap laid for the reader. Only when Mr. Knightley enters do we and Emma learn just how wildly we have misread. For some three pages he unfolds our joint and quite literal misreading, both revealing and by his revelation exorcising the hermeneutic and moral complacencies we have learned to share with Emma.

   That the novel emphasizes this letter has been duly noted in the interpretive history, but the emphasis is explained as, at best, one of those 'virtues which excite the least pleasure.' Thus U. C. Knoepflmacher:

Jane Austen's willingness to reproduce this letter in its entirety is in marked contravention of the indirect method with which she so skillfully treated Frank's earlier messages. Her willingness to devote two full chapters to the letter and to its impression on Emma and Mr. Knightley give a deliberate explicitness to her earlier moral judgments. By freezing the motions of her plot at its most delightful juncture, by converting Emma's overjoyed bridegroom into a frowning moralist who didactically expounds upon the 'beauty of truth,' Jane Austen reminds us that her own function as author is to instruct, as well as to amuse.[39]

The price of this reminder is indeed high – too high, I would suggest, for the novel to negotiate without serious loss. But such a loss is an artifact of a model that locates our response in what is represented: the epistolary Frank Churchill, the preaching Mr. Knightley. Explained in affective terms, however, terms that define instruction less as what we see than as what we do in order to see, the emphasis emerges as perfectly placed, an enabling virtue rather than an inexplicable flaw.

But what about the sacrificed love scene, the plot frozen at its 'most delightful juncture'? To answer this question is to answer similar questioning of the proposal scene, a scene typically read in the interpretive history as an evasion, proof that in the presence of passion Austen was either uneasy or inept.[40] An affective model, however, finds these denials perfectly in keeping with the novel's strategic arousal and deflation of our fictional expectations: once again, it implicates us in the tritely romantic so as to cleanse us of quixotic fault. To read the famous or, if you will, infamous lines – 'What did she say? – Just what she ought, of course. A lady always does' (431) – is to be reminded suddenly and again that we are not viewing but reading, to exchange illusioned reality for the power of the illusion.

As *Emma* draws to its close, our reading grows dense with such reminders and exchanges. Like Emma we are denied access to Jane, and our frustration at this denial dramatizes how far even pity is tainted with the voyeuristic curiosity so natural to readers of fiction. The revelation of Harriet's true and quite ordinary parentage explodes yet another presumption of conventional fiction. The much-criticized chance happenings that enable the 'happy' ending instruct us in the futility of plotting in a contingent world, teaching us to accept that which, like grace, arrives unsought and unexpected. The text continually presents us with self-portraits, which by our failure to see them as such become self-fulfilling. 'With insufferable vanity had she believed herself in the secret of everybody's feelings; with unpardonable arrogance proposed to arrange everybody's destiny. She was proven to have been universally mistaken . . .' (412–13). Tempted to see these lines as descriptive of Emma alone, we again incur the 'insufferable vanity' and 'unpardonable arrogance' endemic to readers of fiction. Even in the concluding paragraph, the text continues its honing of our hermeneutic skill: reading that 'The wedding was very much like other weddings,' we cannot but conjure white finery; reading further – 'where the parties have no taste for finery or parade' (484) – we cannot but be chastened, reprimanded one last time for imagining what we have been invited to imagine.

This fusion of formal means and affective end is ingenious to the point of brilliance: the design of the text *is* its design on the reader; our repeated discovery of its fictionality a repeated discovery of self. But the fusion also, if paradoxically, enables *Emma*'s look of unillusioned reality, the sense it gives us of being in contact with life itself. As Chaim Perelman has noted, 'everything that prompts perception of a device ... will prompt the search for a reality that is dissociated from it.'[41] So it is in *Emma*, where repeated quixotic unveilings not only develop our interpretive skill and discover us to ourselves but also give us the impression of reaching ever deeper towards an underlying reality. Like all such approaches, this one is illusory. But the illusion is powerful, fully capable of motivating and then justifying our hermeneutic struggle.

And, as the interpretive history frequently notes, reading Austen's masterpiece is just such a struggle: '*Emma* is a very difficult novel,' writes Trilling, 'more difficult than any of the hard books we admire.'[42] While the difficulties of Proust, Joyce, and Kafka lessen with repetition, 'the difficulty of *Emma* is never overcome.'[43] No number of repeated readings will 'permit us to flatter ourselves that we have fully understood what the novel is doing. The effect is extraordinary, perhaps unique.'[44] If this is so, and I think that it is, then *why* is it so? Trilling, not unexpectedly, locates the source of difficulty in the ' "heroine whom no one will like." ' But such dislike is not only inadequate to explain 'unique' effects; it cannot begin to account for the intensity of our response as Trilling himself articulates it:

In *Emma* the heroine is made to stand at bay to our adverse judgment through virtually the whole novel, but we are never permitted to close in for the kill – some unnamed quality in the girl, some trait of vivacity or will, erects itself into a moral principle, or at least a vital principle, and frustrates our moral blood-lust.[45]

This is the boldest dangling insight in the novel's interpretive history. While Trilling goes on to attribute 'this interference with our moral and intellectual comfort' to Austen's 'malice,'[46] an attribution that leaves unexplained the sources and shape of that discomfort, the present essay has sought to make our interpretive difficulty signify, taking it to be the source of both the novel's power and the tendency of that power to evade explanation. What Trilling calls Emma's 'vitality,' a vitality that is also the text's, is not at odds with our 'moral blood-lust' but, rather, is its consequence. As always, in reading as in life, difficulty and enigma quicken the attention, and in *Emma* this quickening of our hermeneutic and moral attention defines our experience. Continually invited to infer, to enact what E. H. Gombrich calls the 'beholder's share,' we repeatedly learn that we have inferred incorrectly.[47] Both processes – inference and correction – intensify our experience and, with repetition, make it anxious and even, as Trilling notes, vengeful.

Wolfgang Iser has observed that 'during the process of reading, there is an active interweaving of anticipation and retrospection, which on a second reading may turn into a kind of advance retrospection.'[48] Just so. But *Emma* is peculiar in that this 'advance retrospection' is built in, so that even on first reading our performance is anxious and on subsequent readings is no less so. In short, *Emma* generates suspense, not surprise. The failure to make this distinction has led the interpretive history of *Emma* to worry uncommonly the problem of repeated readings, to puzzle, as Harvey does, an effect that not only does not lessen with repetition but is, as a much earlier critic noted, 'squared and squared again.'[49] *Emma*'s advance retrospection coils and uncoils our hermeneutic suspicion – in reading after reading.

A direct consequence of this accumulated suspicion is the suspect ending of the novel. While the interpretive history not unexpectedly considers this suspicion a 'flaw' and seeks its cause in our distrust of Emma's represented reformation, an affective model finds its cause in the sheer momentum of our interpretive activity, in our doubt not of Emma but of ourselves. That the novel's last sentence is its most *autho*ritative is hardly accidental, and I will venture that its authority signals Austen's attempt to cancel this doubt and bring our reading to a halt: 'But, in spite of these deficiencies, the wishes, the hopes, the confidence, the predictions of the small band of true friends who witnessed the ceremony, were fully answered in the perfect happiness of the union' (484). The novel slams shut. But the interpretive momentum is such that some readers continue through the closed door and go into the interpretive history, putting on record an open-ended *Emma*.

An affective model claims that the value of *Emma* is best justified not in terms of mirroring Emma – the novel, as Booth notes, 'scarcely skims the surface' of *her* experience – but in terms of our struggling attempts to negotiate its hermeneutic difficulty.[50] It also claims that the pleasure of the text, to borrow Barthes's phrase, is a matter of negotiating this same difficulty, for we, like Mr. Knightley, come to love what we dwell on: 'I could not think about you so much without doating on you, faults and all; and by dint of fancying so many errors, have been in love with you since you were thirteen at least' (462). By unfolding this power and pleasure, an affective model argues its case: that it explains *Emma* better than a mimetic model or, what is the same, that it gives us a better *Emma* – a novel cleared of inexplicable deadwood, exempt from diminution on the basis of content, and possessed of emotional force as well as formal perfection. An explanation persuades, however, not only by unfolding a 'better' literary text but also by explaining previous attempts to explain.[51] The affective model of *Emma* thus doubly argues its superiority: by giving us a more fully explicable text *and* by explaining the mimetic reading, by making a better sense of both the literary text *and* its interpretive history. This second making of sense is conventionally recessed. But by treating the interpretive history as itself a text inviting explanation, we have found that explaining *Emma* and explaining *Emma*'s interpretive history are not two separate activities but one.

SOURCE: 'Misreading *Emma*: the powers and perfidies of narrative history', in *English Literary History*, 51 (1984) 315–42.

NOTES

The research for this study was made possible by an Andrew W. Mellon Faculty Fellowship at Harvard University. I am deeply grateful to the Andrew W. Mellon Foundation and Harvard University for this support.

1. Even Austen's bicentennial could find little pretext for the customary 'reevaluation'. Among the many volumes or issues devoted specifically to the bicentennial, see *Nineteenth-Century Fiction* 30.3 (1975); *Studies in the Novel* 7.1 (1975); John Halperin, ed., *Jane Austen: Bicentenary Essays* (Cambridge: Cambridge Univ. Press, 1975); Joel Weinsheimer, ed., *Jane Austen Today* (Athens: Univ. of Georgia Press, 1975); Juliet McMaster, ed., *Jane Austen's Achievement: Papers Written for the Jane Austen Bicentennial Conference at the University of Alberta* (London: Macmillan, 1976).

Exceptions to this immunity do occur. See E. N. Hayes, '*Emma*: A Dissenting Opinion', *Nineteenth-Century Fiction*, 4 (1949) 1–20. Hayes announces his exceptional stance in his first sentence: 'To write other than a sympathetic and admiring essay on Jane Austen is to face the danger of being attacked and even reviled by both readers and critics of her works.'

See also J. Donald Crowley, who, in his 'Jane Austen Studies: a Portrait of the Lady and Her Critics' (*Studies in the Novel*, 7 [1975]), points out 'Since 1952 . . . depreciations have become almost endangered species' (139). But in a larger sense most Austen criticism is, as Avrom Fleishman remarks of Marilyn Butler's *Jane Austen and the War of Ideas* (Oxford: Clarendon, 1975), 'a subtle and disturbing exercise in denigration' ('The State of the Art: Recent Jane Austen Criticism,' *Modern Language Quarterly*, 37 [1976], 288). Indeed, her virtual immunity to outright attack in effect depends upon the subtlety and persistence of such denigration, upon what I call the notion of diminutive greatness. Fleishman is among the few who rebut the 'limitationist' theory of Austen's art – see *A Reading of Mansfield Park: An Essay in Critical Synthesis* (Minneapolis: Univ. of Minnesota Press, 1967).

2. Much nineteenth-century criticism of Austen is collected in B. C. Southam, ed., *Jane Austen: The Critical Heritage* (New York: Barnes and Noble, 1968); and Judith O'Neill, ed. *Critics on Jane Austen* (Coral Gables, FL: Univ. of Miami Press, 1970).

3. T. S. Eliot, 'Ben Jonson,' in *Selected Essays* (New York: Harcourt, Brace & World, 1964) 127.

4. Ian Watt, Introduction, in *Jane Austen: A Collection of Critical Essays*, ed. Ian Watt (Englewood Cliffs, NJ: Prentice-Hall, 1963) 12.

5. For examples of this 'solution,' which is a kind of depreciation, see Graham Hough, 'Narrative and Dialogue in Jane Austen,' *Critical Quarterly*, 12 (1970): 'Coherence is attained by a deliberate limitation of possibilities' (227); Barbara Hardy, *A Reading of Jane Austen* (New York: New York Univ. Press, 1976): 'On her sensitive scales, little things weigh heavy' (21); Mark Schorer, 'The Humiliation of Emma Woodhouse,' in *Jane Austen*, ed. Watt: 'Morality in the novel lies not in spread but in scale' (98).

6. Jane Austen, 'To Anna Austen,' 9 Sept. 1814, Letter 100, *Jane Austen's Letters to her Sister Cassandra and Others*, ed. R. W. Chapman (New York: Oxford Univ. Press, 1979) 401.

7. John Newman, 'To Mrs. John Mozley,' 10 Jn. 1837; rpt. in Southam, 117. See also Sir Walter Scott's review of *Emma* in *The Quarterly Review* (March 1816); rpt. in Southam, 65: '*Emma* has even less story than either of the preceding novels.' A recent instance of this repeated complaint is found in Susan Morgan, *In the Meantime, Character and Perception in Jane Austen's Fiction* (Chicago: Univ. of Chicago Press, 1980) 41: '*Emma* is an extreme case. Less happens in this novel than in any of the others.' In addition to readings such as those preserved in collections like Southam's, the interpretive history also records a multitude of obscure and virtually anonymous readings that are nevertheless intriguing and perhaps more accurately reflective of what was assumed to be true by everyone. For example, see Joseph Jacobs' introduction to his edition of *Emma* (London: George Allen, 1898), which perfectly states the 'limitationist' case against *Emma*: 'That she has her limitations is obvious. The life she portrays with such fidelity is in itself not a very exciting or interesting division of the human comedy. The stream is clear and smooth, but it is by no means deep . . . She avoids, as if by instinct, the torrents and depths of human passion' (viii).

8. For example, see Butler, 250.

9. The comment on Austen's 'sedate and cloistered artistic virtue' is Hardy's, 13. Saintsbury's comment is from *The English Novel* (New York: Dutton, 1913), 198. Such comments often function as commonplaces in the interpretive history, taking on a life and force of their own through frequent quotation. See, for example, Marvin Mudrick's use of Saintsbury's comment in his *Jane Austen: Irony as Defense and Discovery* (Berkeley: Univ. of California Press, 1968) 183.

10. Among the major studies that read *Emma* as 'about' Emma's development are Morgan; Mudrick; Butler; Schorer, 'The Humiliation of Emma Woodhouse'; D. W. Harding, 'Regulated Hatred: An Aspect of the Work of Jane Austen,' in *Jane Austen*, ed. Watt, 166–79; Alistair M. Duckworth, *The Improvement of the Estate: A Study of Jane Austen's Novels* (Baltimore: Johns Hopkins Press, 1971); Jane Nardin, *Those Elegant Decorums: The Concept of Propriety* (Albany: State Univ. of N.Y. Press, 1973; A. Walton Litz, *Jane Austen: A Study of Her Artistic Development* (London: Chatto & Windus, 1965); Andrew W. Wright, *Jane Austen's Novels: A Study in Structure* (New York: Oxford Univ. Press, 1953); Stuart Tave, *Some Words of Jane Austen* (Chicago: Univ. of Chicago Press, 1973).

11. Analyses of Austen's style and form characteristically emphasize how they body forth either the novel's subject or the author's 'moral' attitude towards that subject. Thus Schorer argues that Austen's dead metaphors (analyzed more fully in 'Fiction and the "Analogical Matrix," ' in *The World We Imagine* [New York: Farrar, Strauss and Giroux, 1968], 24–45) enable us to gauge Emma's moral progress. See also Hough; Norman Page, for whom 'the moral basis of the author's judgments' resides 'in her language' (*The Language of Jane Austen* [New York: Barnes & Noble, 1972], 48); and Edgar F. Shannon, Jr., '*Emma*: Character and Construction,' *PMLA*, 71 (1956), 637–50.

12. The arguments are those of Schorer, 'The Humiliation of Emma Woodhouse'; Joseph M. Duffy, Jr., '*Emma*: The Awakening from Innocence,' *ELH*, 21 (1954), 39–53; Kenneth Moler, *Jane Austen's Art of Allusion* (Lincoln: Univ. of Nebraska Press, 1968).

13. Austen's remark is quoted by James Edward Austen-Leigh, *Memoir of His Aunt* (Oxford: Clarendon, 1926), 157. Examples of these attitudes may be found, among other places, in Scott; Morgan; and Mudrick.

14. See Mudrick; Duffy; Litz; and Schorer, 'The Humiliation of Emma Woodhouse'. Sheldon Sacks, in *Fiction and the Shape of Belief* (Chicago: Univ. of Chicago Press, 1964), tackles the 'problem' of the ending most directly (see 16–19), arguing that the protraction is necessary to the working out of the subsidiary relationships among the characters.

15. W. J. Harvey, 'The Plot of *Emma*,' *Essays in Criticism* 17 (1967), 48. See also Wayne Booth's analysis in *The Rhetoric of Fiction* (Chicago: Univ. of Chicago Press, 1961), chap. 9.

16. Booth, *Rhetoric of Fiction*, 255.

17. Booth, *Rhetoric of Fiction*, 255.

18. Booth, *Rhetoric of Fiction*, 255.

19. Harvey, 48.

20. Harvey, 54.

21. Harvey, 57.

22. Duckworth, 161.

23. Hough, 211–12.

24. Hough, 227. Because a correspondence or mimetic theory deemphasizes the medium in favor of the represented object, formalist analyses such as Hough's typically invoke a coherence theory of art. But Hough's analysis is atypical for Austen studies, which prefer to discuss her style in terms of correspondence, insofar as it defers to her subject. Hence Schorer's praise of her *dead* metaphors.

25. Hough, 229.

26. See Plato, *Republic*, X, trans. Benjamin Jowett, in *The Dialogues of Plato* (Oxford: Clarendon, 1953). See also Mudrick, for whom irony is not part of Austen's conscious artistry; and Litz, who argues that 'Jane Austen does not intend that our vision should be in any way affected by Emma's blindness' (147).

27. The phrase is Austen's, in 'To Cassandra Austen,' 4 February 1813, Letter 77, *Letters*, 299. She is referring to *Pride and Prejudice*: 'The work is rather too light, and bright, and sparkling; it wants shade.' Reuben Brower gave the phrase critical currency in his 'Light and Bright and Sparkling: Irony and Fiction in "Pride and Prejudice," ' in *The Fields of Light: An Experiment in Critical Reading* (New York: Oxford Univ. Press, 1962).

28. Jane Austen, *Emma*, ed. R. W. Chapman (Oxford: Clarendon, 1946), 167–68. Subsequent citations will be included in the text. My reading adapts and expands the methodology of 'affective stylistics,' defined by Stanley Fish in 'Literature in the Reader: Affective Stylistics,' *New Literary History* (1970); rpt. in Stanley Fish, *Is There a Text in This Class? The Authority of Intepretive Communities* (Cambridge: Harvard Univ. Press, 1980), 21–67. To my knowledge the only use of this interpretive model in Austen studies is Carole Berger's 'The Rake and the Reader in Jane Austen's Novels,' *Studies in English Literature: 1500–1900*, 15 (1975), 531–44. Berger concentrates on the Churchill–Fairfax affair, rebutting Booth by arguing that it makes us aware, insofar as we are also victims, of the moral consequences of secrecy and accordingly brings us closer to Emma.

29. Hough distinguishes five kinds of discourse in *Emma*: 'the authorial voice'; 'objective narrative'; 'coloured narrative'; 'free indirect style'; 'direct speech and dialogue.' Hough rightly regards the third and fourth kinds as different in degree rather than kind, and I combine them in my notion of 'blended narrative.' This form of discourse hovers between narratorial voice and direct speech, the grammatical forms being those of reported speech, the idiom being the character's. The French call this area *le style indirect libre*, the Germans *erlebte Rede*.

30. See Booth, *A Rhetoric of Irony* (Chicago: Univ. of Chicago Press, 1974).

31. Austen may be invoking a pedagogical practice in rhetorical training: arguing *in utrumque partem*, on both sides of the question.

32. Lionel Trilling, Introduction, *Emma* (Boston: Houghton Mifflin, 1957), xvi.

33. The fullest exploration of Austen's use of the tradition is Moler's. See

also Henrietta ten Harmsel, *Jane Austen: A Study in Fictional Conventions* (The Hague: Mouton, 1964).

34. See 'To Cassandra Austen,' 7 January 1807, Letter 48, *Letters*, 173: 'To Cassandra Austen,' 2 March 1814, Letter 92, *Letters*, 377.

35. Austen, 'To Cassandra Austen,' 4 Feb. 1813. See note 27.

36. See Trilling, Introduction, xvii–xviii.

37. See Shannon and Duckworth for examples.

38. Discussing Austen's characters nonrealistically is a recent and intriguing development in Austen studies. The strongest challenge to the 'characters are people' approach is Joel Weinsheimer's 'Theory of Character: *Emma*,' *Poetics Today* 1.1–2 (1979), 185–212. Sacks develops an elaborate system of nonrealistic character analysis but prefers not to 'mix' the modes of action-model fiction and satire – a point on which he is faulted, with specific reference to Miss Bates, by James R. Kincaird, '*Fiction and the Shape of Belief*: Fifteen Years Later,' *Critical Inquiry*, 6 (1979), 211–12. Harriet and Mr. Elton also change in ways that are more fruitfully discussed in strategic rather than realistic terms.

39. U. C. Knoepflmacher, 'The Importance of Being Frank: Character and Writing in *Emma*,' *Studies in English Literature: 1500–1900*, 7 (1967), 654.

40. See Edd Winfield Parks, 'Exegesis in Austen's Novels,' *South Atlantic Quarterly* 111 (1952), 117, who comments that the scene is a 'typical evasion . . . quite possibly she felt that this matter was too intimate for public display; more probably, she distrusted her ability to handle sentimental dialogue in a natural, convincing manner.' Anthony Trollope calls this 'evasion' 'a cowardice which robs the reader of much of the charm which he has promised himself' (Bradford A. Booth, 'Trollope on *Emma*: an Unpublished Note,' *Nineteenth-Century Fiction*, 4 [1949], 247). Trollope's response confirms my point.

41. Chaim Perelman and L. Olbrechts-Tyteca, *The New Rhetoric: A Treatise on Argumentation* (Notre Dame: Univ. of Notre Dame Press, 1969), 457.

42. Trilling, Introduction, viii.

43. Trilling, Introduction, viii.

44. Trilling, Introduction, ix.

45. Trilling, 'Mansfield Park,' in *Jane Austen*, ed. Watt, 125.

46. Trilling, 'Mansfield Park,' 125.

47. E. H. Gombrich, *Art and Illusion: A Study in the Psychology of Pictorial Representation* (Princeton: Princeton Univ. Press, 1960).

48. Wolfgang Iser, *The Implied Reader: Patterns of Communication in Prose Fiction from Bunyan to Beckett* (Baltimore: Johns Hopkins Univ. Press, 1974), 282.

49. Reginald Farrer, 'Jane Austen, *ob*. July 18, 1817,' in *The Quarterly Review*, 228 (July 1917); rpt. in O'Neill, 22.

50. Booth, *Rhetoric of Fiction*, 163. The comment is made about Austen's general practice, not just Emma specifically.

51. The fact that criticism of Austen, whether the informal 'readings' of her own time or the formal analyses of our own, has been increasingly

collected, annotated, and analyzed is a significant sign and cause of the growing importance of interpretive history in criticism. A 'Norton Critical Edition' (see *Emma: An Authoritative Text: Backgrounds, Reviews, and Criticism*, ed. Stephen M. Parrish [New York: Norton, 1972]) both implies and creates the interdependence of text and interpretive history (which includes, of course, Austen's own 'readings'). 'Casebooks' (see *Emma: A Casebook*, ed. David Lodge [London: Macmillan, 1968]) similarly imply and create this interdependence, as do volumes such as Southam's, which are devoted to tracing the interpretive history *as* history, and the criticism on the criticism, which, aside from the introductions to such volumes, includes such separate studies as Fleishman's. The lengthy bibliographies that invariably accompany all the foregoing not only assist further criticism but, again, imply and create the importance of *this* criticism. The self-consciousness or maturation of the interpretive history, as evinced by such increasing codification, self-reference, and accessibility, comes into being simultaneously with the critic's increasing attention to this history.

SELECT BIBLIOGRAPHY

The following books and articles are, in the editor's opinion, of particular interest as contributions to the criticism of *Emma*; though, for various reasons (such as limitations of space), it was not possible to represent them in the main body of this book.

Booth, Wayne C., 'Emma, *Emma*, and the Question of Feminism', *Persuasions (Journal of the Jane Austen Society of North America)* (Dec. 1983) 29–40. See the Introduction, p. 25, for an account of this conference address.

Bradbrook, Frank, *Emma* (Arnold, London, 1961). This careful and sensitive short study, designed primarily for students, is particularly informative about the relationship of *Emma* to earlier English literature.

Butler, Marilyn, *Jane Austen and the War of Ideas* (Clarendon Press, Oxford, 1975). See the Introduction, pp. 23–4, for an account of the chapter on *Emma* in this book.

Duckworth, Alistair M., *The Improvement of the Estate: a study of Jane Austen's novels* (Johns Hopkins Press, Baltimore & London, 1971). The chapter entitled '*Emma* and the Dangers of Individualism' compares the novel interestingly with earlier and later literary treatments of this theme, and with Jane Austen's own *Mansfield Park*.

Duffy, Joseph M., 'Emma: the Awakening from Innocence', *Journal of English Literary History*, XXI (1954) 39–53. This lively and provocative essay minimises the social texture of the novel and treats it as a fairy-tale-like story of the heroine's passage from innocence to experience.

Honan, Park, *Jane Austen: her life* (Weidenfeld & Nicolson, London, 1987). This, the most recent and thorough biography of Jane Austen, usefully places her novels in the context of her life and times. See especially chapter 18, 'A Progress to Carlton House', for discussion of *Emma*.

Hughes, R. E., 'The Education of Emma Woodhouse', *Nineteenth-Century Fiction*, XVI (1961) 69–74. Emma progresses from an immature conception of love divorced from material values, *via* an equally immature concern with material values divorced from love, to a mature reconciliation of the two in her final self-awareness and marriage to Knightley. Hughes discriminates usefully between 'microscopic' and 'microcosmic' readings of Jane Austen (see Introduction, p. 22.)

Harvey, W. J., 'The Plot of *Emma*', *Essays in Criticism*, XVII (1967) 48–63. See the Introduction, p. 21, for an account of this article.

Johnson, Claudia L., *Jane Austen (Women, Politics and the Novel)* (Chicago U.P., Chicago, 1988). See the Introduction, pp. 24–5, for an account of the chapter on *Emma* in this book.

Litvak, Joseph, 'Reading Characters: Self, Society and Text in *Emma*',

PMLA, 100 (1985) 763–73. See the Introduction, p. 26, for an account of this article.

Litz, Arthur Walton, *Jane Austen: a study of her artistic development* (Oxford U.P., London, 1965). 'By allowing us to share Emma's inner life without being limited by it, Jane Austen has avoided the dichotomy between sympathetic imagination and critical judgment which runs through the earlier novels.'

Olsen, Stein H., 'Do You Like Emma Woodhouse?' *Critical Quarterly*, XIX (1977) 3–19. A shrewd but somewhat chilly essay, arguing that the proper interpretation of the novel depends on our completely accepting the value-system of Highbury society, totally alien as this is to most modern readers.

Schorer, Mark, 'The Humiliation of Emma Woodhouse', *Literary Review*, (Summer 1959) 547–63. Although Jane Austen is not given to overtly figurative expressions, Schorer demonstrates that the language of *Emma* is saturated with dead or buried metaphors drawn from commerce and property, the counting house and the inherited estate, creating the sense of a world of insistently *material* values against which the action, concerned with refinement of sensibility and moral discrimination, is ironically juxtaposed. The novel is concerned with the mutual adjustment of these two scales of value in the fate of the heroine.

Shannon, Edgar J., '*Emma*: Character and Construction', *PMLA*, LXXI (1956) 637–50. A riposte to Marvin Mudrick's reading of *Emma* (see above, pp. 96–118). Shannon's argument that Emma's reformation is genuine, and is meant to be interpreted as such, gains considerable weight from his sensitive demonstration of the pattern of counterpointed motifs that invite us to contrast the mature with the immature Emma.

Smith, LeRoy, *Jane Austen and the Drama of Woman* (Macmillan, London, 1983). See the Introduction, pp. 24–5, for an account of the chapter on *Emma* in this book.

Tanner, Tony, *Jane Austen* (Macmillan, London, 1986). The chapter on *Emma* is an acute and well-written re-examination of the paradox of the unlikeable heroine who is nevertheless liked.

Tave, Stuart Malcolm, *Some Words of Jane Austen* (Chicago University Press, Chicago, 1974). Tave examines some key-words in *Emma*, such as 'imaginist', 'elegance', 'delicacy' and 'ease', and points to the fine distinctions that are made in the novel between true and false versions of these qualities.

Weinsheimer, Joel C., '*Emma* and its critics: the value of tact', *Women and Literature*, 3 (1983) 257–72. An interesting and thoughtful discussion of why critics have been slow to apply recent developments in literary theory to the novels of Jane Austen, and whether it is appropriate to do so.

NOTES ON CONTRIBUTORS

WAYNE C. BOOTH has taught at the University of Chicago for most of his professional life, and is the author of, among other works, *The Rhetoric of Fiction* and *A Rhetoric of Irony*.

MALCOLM BRADBURY is Professor of American Studies at the University of East Anglia, and a well-known novelist and critic. His most recent work of criticism was a collection of essays entitled *No, Not Bloomsbury*.

SANDRA M. GILBERT and SUSAN GUBAR taught at the University of Indiana when they began their collaboration on the monumental *The Madwoman in the Attic: the woman writer and the nineteenth-century imagination*, which was nominated for the 1979 National Book Critics Circle Award.

GRAHAM HOUGH was Professor of English at Cambridge University, now retired. He is a poet, and the author of several works of literary criticism, including *An Essay on Criticism*.

ARNOLD KETTLE was Professor of English at the Open University, and the author of *An Introduction to the English Novel*.

MARVIN MUDRICK teaches at the University of California, Santa Barbara, and is the author of *Jane Austen: Irony as Defense and Discovery*.

ADELA ROSMARIN teaches at the University of Miami.

LIONEL TRILLING taught at Columbia University, and was the author of many distinguished works of criticism, including *The Liberal Imagination* and *Beyond Culture*.

INDEX

Note: for obvious reasons, references to Jane Austen, *Emma* and Emma Woodhouse are not included; neither are references of any kind within quotations from the novel.